Sach Kahun Toh

PRAISE FOR THE BOOK

'*Sach Kahun Toh* is a fascinating window into the sensibilities and influences of one of our finest actors.'—*The Hindu*

'Much of *Sach Kahun Toh's* easy charm resides in Neena Gupta's wisdom while looking back, in excavating lessons in failing, and resistance to be a stereotype—even as a rebel. Celebrities write about life to restore their public persona, storify their legacy. Neena Gupta uses life to dismantle her persona, rewrite her legacy . . . an immensely readable book.'—*Indian Express*

'Her honesty is endearing and it is what makes *Sach Kahun Toh* worth reading . . . what keeps you hooked is Neena's straightforward, sometimes melancholic, wise-with-age-and-experience voice. This is a woman looking back at her tumultuous life with grace and forgiveness.'—Film Companion

'*Sach Kahun Toh* is a lovely piece of nostalgia . . . a real take into Bollywood, stripped off the glam, and focused on the hard work, the struggle and the heartbreaks. With four decades of experience in the industry, an unconventional personal journey, and a will to continue doing good work, when Neena sat to write her autobiographical novel, *Sach Kahun Toh*, the same charm and honesty flowed through the pages. A perfect read for the weekend, the book is a deep dive into the good old days where Bollywood actors were more like close-knit families, the theatre was the mark of good acting, and moong dal pakodas sold by street vendors were a treat. It's a dive into simpler times; the life of Neena without any of the drama. While Bollywood is a huge part of the book, your takeaway is the simple charm of a woman who is brave, resilient and refuses to back down.'—*Elle*

'The title of Neena Gupta's new memoir, *Sach Kahun Toh,* translates to "If I may speak the truth". The expression holds myriad interpretations. It could be an innocent admission, a brutal confession, or a trigger to utter the truth. While Neena may come across as the one with brutal confessions and the power to damage you with her frank demeanour thanks to her media-fed perception, her book firmly suggests that the woman behind the words is an innocently introspective individual trying to assess life so far in her 60s. If there is any sign of brutality, it is directed towards herself. She does not skim over but deeps dive into her regrets. But that comes inseparably attached with the pride she harbours for how far she has come, as an actor, a mother, and a woman . . . With *Sach Kahun Toh*, Neena Gupta turns her refreshingly forthright, candid gaze on her own life and journey.'—Firstpost

'As she [Neena] makes you privy to her journey—right from her childhood to her National School of Drama days, from a struggling artiste to an actor of immense calibre who found her real groove at ripe 60—you meet a real woman.

One of substance, yes, but, above all, a woman who is as humane as we all are, with her fair share of fears, insecurities, doubts, ambition, dreams and desires. Now diffident, now confident, she emerges as a person and actor who has risen to great heights despite odds and insurmountable obstacles. Cinephiles might today acknowledge the tremendous talent of the *Badhaai Ho* actor, but Gupta tells you with unconcealed candour and honesty, how it has not been a smooth ride. Rejections, humiliations, slights, slurs—both at the personal and professional level—define her engaging story, told sans artifice.'—*Tribune*

'Over the years, we have all known and appreciated Neena Gupta's candidness. The actress-filmmaker is not known for mincing words, and that's exactly what she has done in her autobiography *Sach Kahun Toh* . . . her candour makes this autobiography engaging & relatable.' —Pinkvilla

Sach Kahun Toh

AN AUTOBIOGRAPHY

NEENA GUPTA

EBURY
PRESS

An imprint of Penguin Random House

EBURY PRESS

USA | Canada | UK | Ireland | Australia
New Zealand | India | South Africa | China

Ebury Press is part of the Penguin Random House group of companies
whose addresses can be found at global.penguinrandomhouse.com

Published by Penguin Random House India Pvt. Ltd
4th Floor, Capital Tower 1, MG Road,
Gurugram 122 002, Haryana, India

First published in Ebury Press by Penguin Random House India 2021

ISBN 9780670095278

Typeset in Adobe Garamond Pro by Manipal Technologies Limited, Manipal
Printed at Replika Press Pvt. Ltd, India

www.penguin.co.in

Contents

Preface

'When will you write a book about your life?' I would often be asked by friends, family and the media.

'Maybe soon,' I'd respond while actually thinking, 'Maybe never.'

For the longest time I didn't think I had anything to say that deserved its own book. The few times I did sit down to write, I gave up for several reasons.

I didn't want to hurt the children or grandchildren of the people I would probably mention in my book.

I didn't want the world to know my family's dark secrets.

I didn't want anyone to speculate even further about my motivations or the decisions I have taken in my life.

And, deep down, I honestly didn't think my life story was good enough to deserve its own book.

Sometimes, I get very angry when I read about myself in the papers. The image the media and my fans have of me is very different from who I am.

Neena Gupta, the actor, director, producer and public personality is described as strong, honest (to a fault) and unbothered by societal pressures.

The original rebel, they still say, because I brought a child into this world out of wedlock. *Unapologetic*, they write, because I have made no attempts to hide my relationships. *Self-confident*, they reason, because I always hold my head high.

The media doesn't know me. Nobody knows the real me.

But writing a book would mean opening up and revealing my deepest, darkest secrets to the world. It would mean publishing all the mistakes I have made in my life. Revealing that I let men walk all over me. Confessing on paper that the strong, confident and self-assured Neena Gupta actually suffers from a severe lack of self-esteem. She's flawed. Chipped. Broken.

'But you know, your story could inspire people who have also suffered and are still suffering,' my friends would tell me.

An inspiration? Me? What could I say that could inspire someone? Again, you see, I didn't have a high opinion of myself.

But in the first half of 2020, when the country went into a lockdown to battle the COVID-19 crisis, I found myself in Mukteshwar, a beautiful, scenic village in Uttarakhand. It was peaceful, serene and absolutely breathtaking. It was here I realized I had nothing to do other than battle my own thoughts. I started to reflect on and relive my life's journey.

Taking long, leisurely walks every day, appreciating the sounds of the birds and basking in the chill of the mountain air, I would ask myself, 'Why should I write a book? What do I have to say that could help and inspire someone?'

And I realized two things that made me feel immensely hopeful.

Why should I write a book?

Because, sometimes, it's very therapeutic to read about someone else's ups and downs. About their falls and failures and how they picked themselves back up and moved on. When *saas-bahu* serials hit television screens in the early 2000s, there were lots of people who said, 'Gosh. What rubbish is this.' But they were a minority because the majority loved these shows. Their lives and financial circumstances may have been different, but they identified with the characters. The dutiful bahu, the conniving *bua*, the evil saas and the dedicated husband, who was caught in the middle of it all. People would watch them because they wanted to see what the characters would do next, how they would get out of bad situations, and felt inspired that perhaps they too could overcome the problems that plagued their lives.

The other reason was that I could not keep things bottled up any more. The many incidents in my life have either made me stronger or broken me, and I honestly needed to purge myself by getting it out. I knew reflecting about my life, journey and the things I've had to overcome would make me feel better and lighter.

For the longest time, I told myself that I was not good enough. But that ends here and now with this book, because I am good enough and I want people, especially women, to know that if, despite my flaws, my broken relationships and circumstances, I could get up, get going and look really good while doing it, so can you!

So why would anyone want to read about me? Because I have something to say and for the first time in my life, I'm going to share it with the world.

My life's journey, not narrated by the media, but by Neena Gupta, herself.

Part 1

Delhi Girl

1

Rishtey Hi Rishtey, Mil Toh Lein

Galli No 1, Karol Bagh, New Delhi

When I was a child, I lived next door to Professor Arora, a lecturer in a local college as well as a matchmaker. Every summer, when we would travel further up north to stay in Nainital, we'd look out of the train or bus windows to catch a glimpse of his hand-painted advertisement: *Rishtey hi rishtey, mil toh lein, Galli No 1, Regar Pura, Karol Bagh, New Delhi.*

His house in Karol Bagh always had a lot of visitors. We'd see potential grooms and brides, along with their families, lining up. When a match was approved by both sides, we'd all get sweets as a treat. We prayed for these '*rishta pakka hua*' moments every day, us children most of all.

Delhi in the 1960s was a wonderful place. Growing up, I lived in many houses—one in the Western Extension Area and another in Dev Nagar—but my fondest memories are from our time in Galli No 1, Regar Pura, Karol Bagh.

Built on a fifty-yard plot, the house was modest but comfortable. The ground floor had one room which had a sofa, and at night we'd add a cot for my brother, Pankaj, and I. The first floor had another room that served as my parents' bedroom. Above that was our *chhat*, a terrace under the open, starlit skies, where we slept during the sweltering months of summer. It was my job to go up after dinner to sprinkle water on the floor to release some of the heat that got trapped during the day. We would then plug in a few table fans using electricity from the small storage room that was up there. The bedding would be spread out on the floor, and we'd enjoy a gentle, cool breeze that was circulated by the fans as the water started to evaporate. On the nights it happened to rain, well, we would quickly get up, carry our bedding on our backs and run towards the room on the terrace to wait it out.

They don't make houses like that any more. Even my daughter, Masaba, is often surprised when I tell her about our kitchen, which wasn't indoors, but in the covered veranda behind the house. It didn't have a counter for my mother to stand and cook. Instead, we had a gas stove on the floor where all our food was prepared. Our spices and other ingredients were kept on a shelf above this, but it was at least a meter or so above because my mother, if she didn't have everything together next to her while cooking, would stand up multiple times to get a jar of salt or turmeric.

When top chefs today insist on mise en place before cooking, I find myself laughing because back in the day the importance of keeping all the ingredients ready and at arm's length wasn't about organization, but a matter of convenience if you didn't want to strain your back. After we had finished our homework and had nothing better to do—who had televisions in those days?—Pankaj, who was two and a half years younger, and I would sit on either side of our mother in the kitchen and watch her work. She wasn't the best cook, but she was competent, and the cooking process was absolutely fascinating to a child's eye.

We didn't have a dining table around which we all sat as a family and discussed our day. Pankaj and I would just grab our brass plates and sit on either side of my mother to be served.

We didn't have servants. Just one lady who came twice a day to clean the house. So, we learnt to pick up after ourselves at an early age.

Thinking back on my childhood, I'm struck by a myriad of emotions that involve smells, sounds and tastes.

We didn't have air conditioners back in those days. But we didn't need them because in the summer, we'd bring out a mat made of *khus* (vetiver grass) which was sprinkled with water. The khus would then emit a beautiful smell that I associate with afternoon naps and also cool down the room quite a bit. We did eventually, many, many years later, get an air cooler and retire this age-old contraption.

Summer also meant that jamuns would be in season, so we'd wait for the evening when the jamun wallah would come around singing, '*Jamun kale kale aah; jamun bade raseele aah.*' The minute we'd hear this melodious call, we'd run out into the street to buy them. On days he didn't come around, we'd collect jamuns that had fallen from the trees lining our street, as long as they weren't too bruised. We'd then toss them in salt to soften them up and gorge on them before gleefully displaying our tongues, stained purple, to our mother to see whose was darker. Whoever had the darker tongue won this game. We were fierce competitors.

It wasn't just the jamun wallah who had a song. There were numerous vendors who visited Galli No 1 to sell a variety of treats to the residents. There was a man who sold moong dal pakodas on a cart that he served with mooli kas and red chutney. The dal moth vendor also sold moong sprouts dyed yellow with turmeric and tossed with lemon, onion, tomato, coriander and a very special masala. Then there was the man who sold sugarcane juice which was an absolute favourite with the kids because it was fascinating to watch him extract the juice by turning a lever on —a tedious job— on his hand-operated machine.

These were rare treats though because we weren't allowed to eat them every day. The reasons being that our parents didn't want our appetites for dinner ruined and also, we had to be frugal so as to live within our means.

I didn't grow up wealthy, but I wasn't in want of anything either. Our middle-class lifestyle taught me to eat and drink in moderation and the fact that all our favourite foods were seasonal meant that we didn't have the option of gorging on them whenever we pleased.

I loved those days because they taught me how to appreciate the things we take for granted today. I can tell you that the cauliflower of my childhood tasted so much better than the stuff that is available in our markets all year round. The same goes for carrots, the long, red ones, which were a winter special and came with the promise of gajar halwa. Oh, and the corn we ate—not the golden variety we have today but the desi, white corn—was a short-term visitor, but among the foods we missed most when they went out of season. The lady who brought the corn cart around used to boil them in water flavoured with salt and the peels and then serve them to us, broken in half, with a delicious red chutney I crave to this day.

We weren't spoiled with sweets or ice cream. Instead, a promise of good behaviour meant that my father would come home with ganderi—sugarcane that was peeled and chopped into bite-sized pieces—wrapped up in his handkerchief. Those were among the best evenings I remember as a child.

My father and brother

There was also a tandoor at the end of the lane, which I remember clearly. It was manned— rather, 'womanned'—by a big-boned woman who was constantly sweating because of the heat it emitted. The tandoor was dug right into the ground and was a hub for children who would be sent by their parents with ghee-covered pedas—round balls of dough—for cooking. We'd sit around chatting and watch as she would use two long iron rods to cook the rotis. Sometimes she also sold kali dal or kadi which we would take home in utensils from our own homes. My mother would add her own chaunk to the curry and serve it to us for dinner.

Those were simpler times and we learnt to make a little go a long way. If our mattresses got lumpy, or our pillows wore out, we would hail down the man who came around a few times a month. He had a long implement that resembled a harp, and we always heard the strums of that single string long before we caught sight of him. We used to call him mattress wallah and he would come in and fluff out the cotton in our mattresses, smoothing out the lumps, making it as good as new again. Worn pillows were fluffed too and the linings replaced with new ones by the local tailor.

When our brass plates looked worn or had accumulated a trace of minerals that were present in the water, the polish wallah was invited to give them a good shining.

We didn't have to leave the comfort of our home for anything because all these wallahs, who have slowly disappeared over the decades, would roam around, singing their songs, strumming their implements or clanging their plates.

Delhi, Karol Bagh especially, was a very different place back then. It was simple, rustic, and our memories are filled with love, laughter and a very warm, close-knit community. Our area was home to many families that were much like mine—comfortable, but not outwardly wealthy. We had very simple, middle-class values and everyone always looked out for each other.

The area was filled with lots of children who were around our age, and we spent our evenings playing games right outside on the street. We played Posham Pa; Chupan Chupaee, hide and seek; Pitthu, which involved throwing a rubber ball at seven stones stacked on top of each other; and Kho Kho. It was a hoot, and I imagine our parents were reassured of our presence by the sound of our shouts as we all competed to talk over one another in a bid to be heard.

Some days, us children would take off to a garden nearby with pockets filled with atta for the ants. Our elders used to tell us that this was a very good thing to do because it brought good karma. But we mostly just loved to sit around and stare at the ants carrying the tiny grains of atta to their anthill.

We didn't have gadgets to distract us or mobile phones to text each other, but we had transistors that brought us news, songs and plays. When I was a child, I was glued to the transistor and called it my brother. I took it with me all over the house. The kitchen, the terrace, and even put it next to my pillow at night.

We had books—I was a dedicated member of the Gharelu VPP Library Yojna—that we read voraciously. This wasn't a physical library. It was a mail-order library which sent out a catalogue of books in stock. I would scan the catalogue and place an order for seven books every month, which would be returned and replaced the following month. I used to finish my books within ten days and then wait for the next month's books to come around.

We had friends with whom we laughed, fought and played. We had our parents, and the time we all got to spend with each other now feels like a privilege.

My mother was a woman of firm principles and strong, Gandhian ideals. She was also very well educated given the times—she had two master's degrees, one in Sanskrit and the other in political science. I always knew she wasn't like the other women on our street because while my friends' mothers were simple and homely, my mother was strong, independent and smart. She was highly regarded in the community and women often sought her help or advice in personal matters. She was the first person they came to when their husbands weren't around and a cheque needed to be written or some legal or bank process to be understood. She had a reputation for being very honest, which meant that many women often left their expensive jewellery or money in her care.

While my mother never made any distinctions between how she treated me and my brother, she was still a product of the patriarchy that plagued society. I realized quite young that while my mother was equally strict with us, the utensils in the house still had my brother's name etched on them. This was a normal practice during those days among families because they wanted to ensure they got their utensils back in case they sent food or sweets in them over to their neighbours' homes.

My mother was also never called by her name, Shakuntala. Instead, as was the tradition in those times, she was called Pankaj ki Mummy. If someone's name was Kala, their mother was called Kale ki Mummy, and Tillu's mother was Tillu ki Mummy. This was the case even if the daughters, like me, were older than their brothers. Daughters were regarded as *paraya dhan* who would one day get married and leave the house while the sons would stay back.

With Ma and my brother Pankaj

This didn't bother me though because my parents never made us feel different. We were both loved and scolded equally. My mother was very strict and pushed us to do our best in our studies. She would sit down with us while we studied for our exams and made it a point to help us with the subjects in which we were weak. Pankaj, who would grow up to become a chartered accountant, was a good student.

As for me, I did well in everything except maths. It was just not my subject, and I could barely get my head around the concepts of addition and multiplication leave alone algebra and geometry. I remember this one time, while I was still a student at Bal Bharti School, a primary school that only had up to class 5, a teacher flung

School picture (standing third from left, top row)

a test paper in which I had scored three out of ten in my face, and I was petrified of showing it to my mother.

In class 6, I started going to Vidya Bhawan, an all-girls' secondary school. Much like my primary school, Bal Bharati, Vidya Bhawan was also a Bengali school which meant that over half of the girls were Bengali. We still had our subjects in English, but we had Bengali as one of our language subjects. To this day, I can read and write a bit of Bengali and speak enough to get by.

I made lots of good friends here though we lost touch over the years. I remember how we all would sit around the table at lunchtime and swap our tiffin boxes. The Bengali girls, I noticed, would always sit together and eat from their tiffin boxes with the lids still on. I always wondered why this was. Maybe they were shy when someone watched them eat. In fact, a lot of us felt shy if someone was watching us while we opened our dabbas. But it's something I remember distinctly and wonder about even today.

Looking back on my childhood and reflecting on the simplicity of my life has left me with a deep appreciation for everything I have earned today. My beautiful, spacious apartment in Mumbai, the holiday home my husband, Vivek, and I have in Mukteshwar, my full-time helper who takes such good care of me that I don't have to worry about anything . . . It's been a beautiful journey from where I came from to where I have arrived today.

I know many of my readers are waiting for me to get to the juicy bits of my life. Don't lie. I know there's a part of you that only picked up this book to read about my relationships and the controversies that have been part of my media image for decades now.

But I hope you will also appreciate these stories from my childhood because without them, I don't know who I would be today. We all come from somewhere. We all have our own stories. Some of you might read mine and remember your own humble childhoods, making you realize that I'm no different from you. Others might read about how we managed to stay happy and healthy within our means and on tight budgets and realize that I'm not the person they think I am.

It's important for me to talk about my early years because it is the foundation of who I would become one day. I really want to paint you a picture of where I came from because without it, the juicy bits are just that—quick gratification with no substance, forgotten the minute the next big story comes out.

Did I know then that I would one day become a National Award–winning actor, director and writer? I don't know. My dreams those days were very simple.

For example, every summer, we would take a bus to Nainital with our mother to escape the Delhi heat. My father would join us for a week or two if he could, but for the most part it was just us three. We'd rent a small flat in the main market and bring along our own stove and utensils. We'd go shopping for groceries and eat all of our meals at home. We didn't go sightseeing because having visited so many summers in a row, we'd pretty much seen everything there was to see.

But there was always one place I wished so dearly to visit but it was off limits to me. The Boat House Club in Mallital, Nainital, looked beautiful from the outside. I'd often stop and stare at it and wonder what went on in there. I'd see couples, families and children going in and out and tug at my mother's hand to take me in as well.

'We can't go inside,' she'd snap.

'Why not? Those people are all going in.'

'They're all members of the club. We aren't members so we aren't allowed inside.'

'So, let's become members, no?'

'They don't give memberships to people like us . . . '

People like us, she said, did not aim to be members of such a place. We were different. Our family wasn't the sort to go out for dinner or stay late at parties. In fact, we didn't go out much at all. We liked to eat early and sleep early. Go about our work the next day. The club culture was just not part of our aims or ambitions. But I was very curious. I just wanted to go and see what was going on inside.

'Don't we know any members?' I asked. 'What goes on in there?'

'Who knows?' she said. 'We don't have any friends who are rich or connected enough to be members of such clubs.'

All those summers, I'd gaze at the club wistfully, dreaming of the day when I would finally get to go and see what lay within.

But can you believe that this dream finally came true only a few years ago? My husband Vivek's cousins are members of the Boat House Club and while we were staying at our Mukteshwar house, very close to Nainital, we were invited to spend an evening there.

I remember feeling like a child who had finally got the treat she had been waiting for all these years. It was just as beautiful as I had imagined. But instead of walking around, giddy with excitement, and hobnobbing with the crowd, I sat by myself in a corner and just reflected on my journey. I marvelled at how much my life had changed from the time I was a little girl.

In that moment, I also missed my mother and brother, both of whom are no more, because I know for a fact that they too would have absolutely loved to be in there with me.

2

Bhenji

As I got older, my first real set of issues hit me; prime among them was puberty. Talk among my friends quickly shifted from 'childish' things like dolls and games to periods and boys. My body was also changing by this time and it all started to become a bit too confusing.

My school didn't have sex education. At home, my mother told me the very basics of what a period was and what needed to be done at that time. But she didn't go beyond that either. Romance with boys was forbidden—that was made clear to me—and I never had the guts to ask her about sex.

If you think that the subject of periods is awkward in this century, despite all the awareness around

Me in my school uniform

it, you won't believe how much worse it was when I hit puberty. Young girls never dared to step up to a chemist and ask for sanitary pads. It was up to our mothers to purchase them or our fathers if they weren't too squeamish. And even then, they would be wrapped up in a dark plastic bag or a newspaper to ensure nobody saw them.

As for sex and romance, all our knowledge was based on what we understood from the songs and scenes in Hindi cinema. There was

13

a film in 1966 called *Pyar Kiye Ja* and the girls at school, including me, couldn't even say the name out loud without blushing and giggling.

Pyar according to us was intriguing, elusive and, not to mention, forbidden. So, it's no wonder it's all we thought or talked about.

I'm not proud to admit this, but thanks to the society I grew up in and the Hindi films I watched, which skirted the issue of sex and romance by using flowers and whatnot, I actually thought that a simple kiss could impregnate a girl. I didn't find out the real workings of sex until I finished my BA course. That's how clueless I was! That's how clueless we all were.

When I was in secondary school, my family decided to leave our wonderful neighbourhood and community in Regar Pura and shift to a bigger house. My father had his eye on a beautiful property at 7A/38, Western Extension Area. It belonged to a renowned dancer called Shambhu Maharaj ji.

When we went for a viewing, however, my father wasn't allowed inside. His wife was in purdah, kept her head and face covered, but Maharaj ji still didn't want another man in the house. I found this strange given how worldly he seemed and the fact that he performed for huge, cheering crowds for a living.

Only my mother and I were allowed into the house. When we saw it, we knew that this would make for a perfect home. So we told our impressions to my father who then went ahead with the purchase. We didn't get to move in immediately because Shambhu Maharaj ji wanted a period of six months to move out. He offered to pay us rent in the interim, and we shifted to a smaller, temporary house until we got possession.

Shambhu Maharaj ji was a nice man though. He came to drop off the rent money on time every month and even developed a friendship with my father. They would sit and drink tea together and discuss culture and politics. We lost touch with him when he finally vacated the house and moved away.

7A/38 WEA is where I lived all through school and college until I left for the National School of Drama (NSD) in 1978. It was a beautiful neighbourhood with wonderful people, most of them Bengalis and south Indians. But there were families from other communities too.

Our area in WEA was very close to a *shamshan* ghat, a crematorium ground, and there were often mourners walking by our house carrying dead bodies. If the wind shifted its direction at the wrong time during a cremation, we'd have to shut our windows to keep the smell of burning flesh away. It was a very surreal feeling, living so close to a place where people's last rites were completed. But it was also humbling, a reminder of how short and fleeting life could be.

My mother soon made new friends in the area and once again established herself as a strong, honest and educated lady. She made many friends who would often come visit her for chai and a chat.

One of them was Mrs Bhalla. She and her husband, Mr Bhalla, owned a house which was diagonally opposite ours. They lived on the ground floor and rented out the top floor. They had no children of their own but seemed to be perfectly happy with each other.

Ma with a friend

Mr Bhalla was a huge man who towered over everyone, but in contrast, Mrs Bhalla, who was five feet tall, looked almost childlike and petite. My mother and I would often try to pull her leg, saying, 'He's a mountain. How did he end up with you?'

Mrs Bhalla had a good sense of humour. She'd sniff and say, 'My husband says that he always wanted to marry a short woman because he believes they stay younger for longer.'

I used to find this funny and would tell her so. But she never took it the wrong way because she sincerely felt he was right. I cannot deny that they were a very cute couple.

Another lady my mother befriended was Mrs Singh, who lived down the road. She and her husband seemed very normal from the periphery. But Mrs Singh often complained about how unhappy she was with her husband. I was often around when she and my mother would have tea and chat. They never referred to their husbands by name or even as 'my husband'. In those days, most women would just refer to their husbands as 'yeh' and depending on who was speaking, we knew which 'yeh' they were referring to.

Mrs Singh, a well-dressed woman, who liked to take care of herself and go out at times, was upset that her husband didn't want the same things as her. Instead, he kept himself locked up in a shrine in his house and would just pray, chant and listen to bhajans all day.

It was very strange for me to see that the couple who had grown-up children, all married and settled abroad, were having compatibility issues at such a late stage in their life. It also didn't help that they were constantly disagreeing on everything. Mrs Singh found solace in travelling to Canada or America where her children were settled and spending months at a time. On the other hand, Mr Singh didn't want to leave the comfort of his house.

I think things finally got really bad when their tenants, a very nice south Indian family, came to my mother and said that they were conflicted. Apparently, Mr Singh had insisted they pay him the rent while Mrs Singh had said it should be paid to her. They didn't want to offend either of them or take sides.

Eventually Mrs Singh left WEA and Mr Singh for good and went and settled with her children abroad.

WEA holds so many memories for me. Prime among them being my first romance. I was around fifteen at the time, and it was with a boy named Babu (name changed) who lived in the house right behind mine.

He was sweet and not too bad to look at. What we had was innocent because we barely ever spoke!

It happened one summer when Delhi's heat was beating down on us, and we all decided to sleep on the roof.

We started just seeking each other out from the corner of our eyes on the streets while hanging out with friends. Then at night, when I would go up to set up the bedding and sprinkle water on the floor to release the trapped heat, he would miraculously be on his roof at the same time. So, we started staring at each other and, soon, got a little bolder and exchanged smiles.

Nobody knew about us because as much as we liked to discuss love and romance, none of us dared confide in friends about a real-life romance. You never knew when someone would get too virtuous or jealous and expose your secret to your parents.

Babu and I never went on a date or even talked much. Our romance only consisted of eyeing each other from afar and if it was a really good day, we'd run into each other while picking up bread or eggs at the nearby shop.

But eventually, we started getting bolder and that is perhaps why we finally got caught. It happened one evening when we were both on the terrace. Gone were our shy smiles and we didn't sneak glances any more. We were openly staring at each other and communicating something through gestures. My mother walked in just when we were laughing about something and realized what was going on. She was livid and dragged me into the house. I got a verbal lashing that night and that was the end of our affair.

I was still young, and my mother was an intimidating authority figure. I didn't have the guts to cross her again, so from then on, I kept my head down and my nose clean. I still giggled and fantasized about the perfect romance with my friends, but my cryptic interactions with Babu eventually lost their charm (for me at least) and fizzled out.

Looking back, I wish our parents hadn't treated the subjects of sex and romance as taboo. That they hadn't forced us to repress our basic instincts and keep us in the dark about how things worked. I know now that they were only trying to protect us from making mistakes, but how would we know any better if just having the basic knowledge of these things was forbidden?

Around the same time, a young girl ran away with the son of a dhobi, and tongues were wagging in the whole neighbourhood. It was the biggest scandal around and the poor dhobi not only lost his business in our area, but was also blamed for the actions of his son. The girl too was slandered. They said that she was too forward, too bold, too desperate . . . her parents felt more ashamed than heartbroken.

'See, this is what happens when you misuse your freedom,' my mother told us. 'No matter what, Neena, please don't do anything like this to us.'

A few years later, in an even bigger scandal, the girl returned home with a baby. The father of the child, the son of the dhobi, had apparently fled after the child was born.

'No girl from a respectable family should run away and get married,' my mother said. 'See how that poor girl was used and thrown by that boy?'

The girl's parents, to their credit, took her back in but felt that they couldn't hold their heads up in our community any more. So they packed up, sold their house and shifted to an area where nobody knew them and they could start afresh.

This is honestly one of the more heartening ends to such a story. There were also cases where women were promised marriage by men if they slept with them and then dumped when they got pregnant. There were girls who were lured away by sweet-talking men who then turned on them and raped them.

I know that these things happen even today. That parents are automatically more protective of their daughters than their sons because they don't want their *ghar ki izzat* defiled. But the difference is that back then, if something happened to us, we couldn't tell our parents for fear of suffering their ire. This was the case even if we weren't at fault.

One time I visited a doctor for an eye infection. My brother, who was accompanying me, was asked to sit in the waiting room. The doctor started with examining my eye and then went down to check out other areas that were unconnected with my eye. I was scared stiff while it was happening and felt disgusted all the way home. I sat in a corner in the house and cried my eyes out when nobody was looking. But I didn't dare tell my mother about this because I was so scared that she would say that it was my fault. That I had probably said or done something to provoke him.

This happened to me many times at the doctor's. There was also a tailor who got too handsy when he was taking my measurements. But I couldn't say anything about it. I had to keep going back to them. Why? Because I felt like I had no choice. If I told my mother that I didn't want to go to them, she would ask me why and I would have to tell her. I didn't want this because I felt very scared and ashamed of what had been done to me. I wasn't the only one. Many girls in those days who suffered abuse chose to keep quiet rather than tell their parents about it. They were scared of being blamed. They were ashamed that they had unknowingly done something to bring it upon themselves. It wasn't until many years later, when I started having open conversations with my girlfriends, that I realized that these incidents were actually quite common. '*Arre yeh toh hota hai*, yaar.' We used to talk about it like it was so normal. But we didn't dare complain to our parents because that would mean that the little freedom we had would be taken away. Or worse—that we would be blamed for bringing it upon ourselves.

Children, who are as young as three years old, are now being taught the difference between a 'good touch' and a 'bad touch'. I cannot believe that we as teenagers were not taught about either and what we should do if such a thing happened. Maybe this knowledge would not have stopped me from being molested. But knowing that my parents would stand by my side and fight for me would have made those attacks much more bearable.

But nobody wanted to discuss these matters because they were awkward topics? They thought that too much knowledge would lead us astray? That we would think we were equal to men?

To my knowledge, boys weren't told about these things either, but they didn't have their freedom curbed. They were allowed to run amok and do as they pleased while the burden of upholding our morals was placed on our shoulders.

When I was sixteen years old, a friend's brother propositioned me. I was shocked. He was a bit older and had just got married to a very nice, beautiful girl. My brother and I were over at their house for lunch. It was awkward to say the least because everyone realized that his eye was following me around and that he was being overfriendly with me. I took it in my stride though because I was afraid of being blamed. I somehow managed to shrug off his advances politely and without offending him or his family. I hated that I was the one who needed to be careful and afraid when it was him who was being a sleaze—in front of his whole family, no less.

And once again, I couldn't say anything about this to my friends or my mother because I was afraid that they would blame me and take away more of my freedom.

But whatever said and done, my mother went above and beyond what was expected of women in those days.

She pushed me to do better in school and drilled

Ma getting a certificate for completing a
Russian course

into me the importance of a career when other girls were being groomed to be future housewives.

'You have to get the highest degree there is,' she used to tell me. 'You must become an IAS officer.'

She herself had been a schoolteacher before she married my father. She used to love working and earning her own money, but once my brother and I were born, she decided to quit her career to raise us. I don't know if that brought her personal fulfilment. But I think she used to push me to have a career because she wanted me to have more options than she did.

For my part, I listened to my mother and did well in school. I was still terrible at maths but I excelled in everything else.

In class 9, I also got to take on optional subjects in addition to our regular curriculum. I took up home science and learnt how to cook, keep a spotless kitchen and even sew. To many it seemed like a soft subject that was perfect for women who wouldn't be pursuing a career. But I learnt a lot of useful skills that I use to this day. I love to cook, I manage my kitchen to make it function seamlessly and while I'm not a seamstress, I do know how to sew on a button and darn a tear in a dress.

Those were conflicting times to grow up in because on the one hand we, as girls, were told that our ultimate destination was marriage. The way we were brought up and the curbs on our lives because of our gender often made us believe that marriage was our ticket to freedom.

I had many friends for whom marriage meant getting really nice clothes, expensive jewellery and the chance of finally experiencing romance like they did in the movies. They thought that having a husband would get them more freedom to go out and watch movies and that their husbands would indulge them and protect them from everything. Like I said, we learnt everything we knew about love and romance from movies. Therefore, so many of my friends learnt the hard way that if life with their strict parents was like standing in a frying pan, marriage was like jumping into fire.

With my school friends

For many of my friends, marriage was even worse than living with their strict and overprotective parents. Marriage, they realized, meant that life as they knew it was over because now they were living under someone else's roof and having to follow someone else's rules. You didn't just get a husband in a marriage, you also got a mother-in-law, a father-in-law, new *bhaiyas* and *bhabhis*. At home, if we disagreed with our parents, we'd quarrel but also make up quickly. In a new house, once married, you couldn't do that because there were very clear expectations from a good *bahu*.

We thought marriage meant freedom. But, in reality, it was a cage. A *pinjra* where a girl just didn't leave her parents behind, but, in many cases, also her identity. My friend Nilima's (name changed) in-laws, as part of their customs and traditions, changed her name to Sunita (name changed) because they believed that a girl must leave her entire self and identity behind to acclimate to her new life as a wife and bahu.

It was a very difficult time to be a woman because our hopes and dreams meant very little in the grand scheme of things. We didn't know any other way of life either. So naive, inexperienced girls, including me, who were tired of their parents limiting their freedom, made some very questionable choices.

* * *

When I passed out of class 11, I got really good marks and hoped to go to one of the top colleges at the time. Back then, school, known as higher secondary, was up to class 11. After that, we did three years of bachelor's, followed by two years of master's and so on.

Once I finished school, I dreamed of an education in one of the 'posh' colleges like Miranda House, Lady Shri Ram or Jesus and Mary. I had the marks for it but, unfortunately, not my parents' permission.

For my mother, Miranda and Lady Shri Ram represented a kind of 'poshness' that she associated with immorality. The girls here were seen to be 'modern' because they wore stylish Western clothes and didn't speak Hindi. They were also perceived as more forward, the kind who had boyfriends and went out openly on dates.

'*Ladki bigad jayegi*,' my mother told my father when I tried to rope him in to make a case for these colleges.

Another concern was that I would have to go outside my area— my schools till then had been at walking distance or a very short bus ride from home. Going to Miranda meant that I would have to board the U-Special (University Special) bus and travel for over an hour in God knows what conditions. In short, my mother was afraid of losing control of me, but she also feared for my safety. Buses in Delhi weren't safe even in those days.

That is how I found myself in Janki Devi Mahavidyalaya doing a BA Pass course. My subjects were political science, Hindi, Sanskrit and English.

Janki Devi was everything that Miranda House and Lady Shri Ram were not. It wasn't considered posh and the crowd there was anything but 'hoity toity' as we used to say.

Janki Devi, in short, was called a *bhenji* college, and I was destined to be one of them. But looking back at these times and reflecting on the term 'bhenji', I believe it was a very unfair word which was used to typecast my all-girls college.

Bhenji is a Hindi word which is used to refer to girls and women who are older than us out of respect when we don't know their names. Sometimes, even the sabji wallahs call women much younger than them 'bhenji' out of sheer respect.

I don't understand how this word came to be associated with women who:

Don't speak English as their first language.
Dress only in Indian clothes like a salwar kameez or sari.
Read only Hindi literature.
Are traditional and don't subscribe to modern ideologies.

When I think about it, yes, this would describe most of the women in my college. But it was prejudicial and narrow-minded because it didn't leave much room to look at how intelligent we were. How talented we were. How witty we could be.

In Janki Devi, I met a lot of women who were very intelligent, articulate (in a language that wasn't English, yes) and very modern in their own right. Many would go on to marry traditionally, but so would the girls from the so-called modern colleges. But there were girls, even among the married ones, who would petition for women's rights, organize morchas to protest atrocities committed against women and for equal pay and opportunities.

Also, just because we didn't communicate in English all the time didn't mean we couldn't. In fact, in many careers like journalism, social work, even acting, our 'vernacular' languages, our multilingualism helped many of us reach great heights.

I will always stand up for my fellow bhenjis because I know now how rich, vast and varied our influences are. Today, if someone tries to make fun of the way I speak English or correct my pronunciation, I turn around and ask them what their mother tongue is. Is it Hindi? Tamil? Punjabi? Do they know how to read their native language? Do they know who the most profound poets or authors are in their native literary texts? No? Then it's time to get over this colonial hangover and respect those who do. We're just as articulate and intelligent. But just because we speak and think in a different language doesn't make us less intelligent than the rest.

At the time, however, I was still young and cared about how I was perceived, so I was, at first, a bit miffed at having to go to a bhenji college. But, in retrospect, I am glad I did because I got to meet so many amazing people, found confidence to explore things I was truly interested in without being judged and, in general, to shine.

Eventually I learnt to embrace my inner bhenji but that's probably because I had more freedom to morph between modern and traditional.

The crowd at Janki Devi was very simple and, like many women of my generation, extremely repressed. We weren't allowed to talk to a boy who wasn't our brother, father or husband (yes, many of my classmates were forced into marriage very young).

Being an all-girls' college, we were heavily deprived of male interaction. We'd fantasize about having boyfriends. We'd sit around the periphery of our campus and gaze longingly as boys rode on their bikes to pick up their girlfriends after college.

I'd sigh wistfully and ask myself why I was still single. 'I'm so much better looking than these girls,' I'd tell myself. 'Even I should have a boyfriend who comes and picks me up on a bike.'

There were two boys in particular whom all the girls would wait to see every day. They were well dressed, good looking, and one of them had eyes that were a unique shade of grey. It wasn't until decades later when I was talking to Shakti Kapoor about my college days that he revealed that he too used to live in WEA and had a girlfriend who went to Janki Devi.

'I used to come and pick her up on my bike,' he said.

I laughed so heartily when he said this because it's such a small world, isn't it? We had grown up pretty much all our lives in the same area but had never crossed paths. I also couldn't believe that he was one of the two boys whom all the girls knew, and whose girlfriend we all envied.

Jealousy was rampant in Janki Devi. There was also a lot of judgement between groups. The more modern girls judged the 'bhenjis' because they thought they made the college seem backward. The more traditional girls judged the ones who wore fashionable clothes because they thought they had loose morals. Bra straps sticking out (even by mistake) was treated like it was something to be very shameful about.

'Your bra strap is showing,' a girl would whisper to another when such an occasion arrived, tucking the strap back into her blouse. It was a kind gesture. But it was pointless, I thought, because who was looking at us in our all-girls' college? It was hilarious.

My college had its complications—don't all colleges?—but it offered a wide range of extracurricular activities, which I found myself delving into with great enthusiasm.

I played hockey—centre forward and right out. I won numerous awards in debate competitions. I also took interest in the union and stood for college elections. But that didn't pan out because a few goons who wanted their own candidate to win caught hold of me and threatened me. When you look at me now and consider my media image, you wouldn't believe how scared I was back then when I was threatened. I was timid and easily rattled. You might even say I was a pushover. As a child, when my mother would send me out to the street behind our house with a bucket to get buffalo milk, I would freeze every time someone pushed past me. We would all put our buckets in a line, waiting our turn, and if somebody came and kicked my bucket out of the way or shoved me out of the queue, I would run home crying. Luckily, the self-confidence I lost because of college politics was reinstated in other areas and activities.

My mother was strict, yes. But she loved to buy me trendy clothes which is what made me one of the best-dressed girls in college. My mother herself was very stylish and had great taste in clothes. She only wore saris, but they were elegant and tasteful. They were very expensive, but they didn't have the sparkles and shine that is often associated with expensive clothes. She never put 'fall' on her saris because she liked the way they flowed and the fact that she could wear them both ways if one side got dirty when she was travelling by bus.

Fashion show in college, with me on the left

She was a regular at the American Embassy auctions and would come home laden with really nice and fashionable clothes for me. There would be sleeveless dresses and some outfits were outright sexy for the times.

'I'm the one who is spoiling you,' she would laugh as she watched me jump at her shopping bags. The outfits she bought me were nothing less than the ones famous actresses

Another modelling shot, with me on the right

at the time wore. There were bellbottoms—the hottest trend— beautiful dresses, tops with spaghetti straps and short sleeveless kurtas.

Thanks to my mother
and all the clothes she bought
me, my sense of style didn't
go unnoticed and the
organizers of events at college
always ensured that I
participated in every fashion
show.

I started doing some
theatre, but I was too shy
to ask for the good roles. I
would attend the auditions,
and while I initially didn't

Playing a servant in a college play

get any parts, eventually I started getting bits and pieces. One of my
first roles was of a servant in a play. I still have that picture.

Eventually, my parts got bigger, but they were all male parts
because I was taller than the other girls.

I knew I deserved better. I would stand in front of the mirror
and recite the lines of all the female actresses. I always felt I was
better than them. But I didn't have the courage to say this to

In a college play, with me in the hat

anybody during rehearsals. Because I was severely lacking in self-confidence too.

But these small parts and male roles would eventually take me to the university specials where I would meet my first boyfriend who would soon (a bit too soon) become my first husband.

3

Ladki Bigad Gayi

His name was Amlan Kusum Ghose. A Bengali studying at IIT-Delhi. He lived on campus and also participated in university theatre specials. We met at an inter-college event and hit it off immediately.

My area in WEA was filled with Bengalis. Besides attending a Bengali school, we also lived very close to a Bengali club, attended Saraswati Pooja and Durga Pooja. Oh, and I was also born in Calcutta and eventually moved to Delhi sometime during my childhood.

One can say, Bengali culture, along with Punjabi, was among my most defining influences while growing up.

So it felt natural then to date a Bengali boy. I would sneak into his hostel to spend time with him. I got along with all of his friends too.

Amlan and I would meet in secret on campus, his hostel or near my house. His parents lived in another city but his grandfather lived in my lane so he would spend festivals and holidays in WEA.

There was a bit of a gang culture around WEA. A Bengali gang and a Punjabi gang were constantly locking horns over who 'owned' the area.

My old flame, Babu, was part of the Punjabi gang while Amlan, who didn't officially belong to the Bengali gang, was still associated with them.

The Punjabi gang, I heard one day, didn't like the fact that I, a half-Punjabi girl, was going around with a Bengali boy. They took offence. Babu especially felt he had some ownership over me because of our brief flirtation.

There was a lot of drama because Amlan and I couldn't be seen in the areas they frequented or called their *ilaka*. But we managed to go on dates in his car instead of a taxi. We'd spend more time near IIT-Delhi, whenever I could get enough time away from home, so that we wouldn't be recognized.

But the gang wouldn't let up. I heard one night that there had been a huge fight behind my street where a Bengali boy had been thrashed with metal chains and pipes. I was afraid for a moment that it was Amlan, but it wasn't. It was a very sweet and innocent boy who had been mistaken for Amlan. I felt really bad for him, but I didn't know how to stop this from happening either. All I could do to keep from getting into trouble at home as well—because, above all, I was afraid of my mother finding out—was feign ignorance.

Having a boyfriend was strictly forbidden, but I got a thrill out of it. In my close circle, nobody knew about my relationship except a few friends, two of whom lived in my area. While sneaking around and going on dates was fun for those of us who had boyfriends, I knew it wasn't easy for the rest of the girls because their lives were either more controlled by orthodox parents or they simply didn't have the courage to speak to boys.

I know this because there was a lot of jealousy around my relationship. I know this because I too was one of these girls before I met Amlan. But as our relationship got more serious, I found myself really happy and getting bolder and more confident by the day.

While my friends, Nilima (name changed) and Kavita (name changed), weren't allowed out of their homes in anything but salwar kameez, I would wear bell bottoms—the hottest trend back then— with a long kurta that I would tuck into my pants once I was out of my mother's line of sight.

Make no mistake, my mother still put a lot of restrictions on me. I wasn't even allowed to go watch a movie in theatres with girlfriends because she found Hindi films to be completely distasteful (she herself preferred world cinema and often attended film festivals with my father that I didn't have any interest in at the time).

But once I exited the house and went to college, I did as I pleased. I was good at studies and my marks were always high. There were no complaints against me. It was only a matter of time before the penny dropped.

It happened on a day I was really looking forward to. I was going to skip a few lectures and go watch a movie with Amlan. I left the house with a smile that held a secret shared by only a few. I sat through class in a jolly mood, barely able to concentrate. But I got a sudden jolt when I looked up and spotted my brother standing right outside. He was gesturing to me to come out immediately.

I excused myself and went over to speak to him.

'Come home now,' he said, looking very serious. 'Mom wants to talk to you.'

'Now? What could be so important that it couldn't wait?'

'I don't know,' he replied. 'But she thinks you're bunking college.'

I froze. How could she have found out?

At home, my mother was livid. She asked me directly why I was planning to bunk classes. Where was I planning to go? And with whom . . .

I feigned confusion and lied. 'Nothing, I wasn't planning on going anywhere . . . '

'Okay good,' she said, not looking satisfied at all. 'Now sit at home.'

I was shocked and confused. I was also feeling anxious because Amlan would be waiting for me outside the cinema hall. How was I going to get word to him that I wouldn't be able to make it?

As the evening progressed and the film started and ended, I kept thinking who could have told my mother that I had planned to miss classes? And then it struck me. It had to be my friends Kavita and Nilima. They were the only ones I had told. They must have sold me out. But why? I fumed over this for days. Thinking back, I realize it must have been their envy of my freedom, the clothes I wore and the fact that I wasn't primed for marriage like they were.

It's very important for me to take a moment here to reflect as best as I can on the differences in our upbringings. My mother, whom I always thought was standing between me and my freedom, wasn't doing so because she was orthodox. She was just being protective in the way she knew best. She always spoke to me about my marriage as something that would happen some day. She dreamed of me getting the highest degree and eventually becoming an IAS officer.

Ma taking me out in a stroller

But my friends Kavita and Nilima were told time and again that the only expectation from them was that they became good housewives.

I always thought that my mother was orthodox. But, in reality, she was anything but. She didn't follow the same practices that my other friends' parents did. For example, at Kavita and Nilima's house, women weren't allowed to step into the kitchen if they were on their period. Nilima's bhabhi always had to wear a chunni (even if she was in her nightgown) and keep her head covered in the presence of her father-in-law. In contrast to their parents (and I include their fathers in this too), my mother was extremely well educated with two MAs, and the fact that she not only let me wear halter tops on occasion, but also bought me stylish 'modern' clothes, made them believe that I had a really easy life.

So, I don't blame them for being jealous of me for having the guts to date a boy. Tattling on me probably made them feel better, morally superior, for doing something that was a taboo for them.

As young girls, we were all suppressed and repressed in our own ways. Some of us more than others. I couldn't entirely blame them for begrudging me for having what they weren't even allowed to dream of. This is probably why I never bothered to ask them why they did what they did.

I somehow managed to keep my relationship a secret for a little longer. But as we got more serious, I decided to tell my mother myself. She wasn't happy obviously and tried to control my freedom even more. In turn, I started getting very creative about what I said at home without resorting to too many lies. I used my extracurricular activities as an excuse. (Do you think this is why secret relationships are often referred to as 'extracurricular activities' in pop culture?)

One day, Amlan and his friends made a plan to go to Srinagar on a holiday, and I couldn't imagine missing the experience. But when I asked my mother, who was already very exasperated, she said something that led me to make a very rash and stupid decision.

'Unless you get married, you cannot go anywhere with him,' she stated.

'Accha?' I said. 'So if I get married to him then I can go?'

And just like that, we found ourselves in a marriage hall, being wed in an Arya Samaj ceremony. The only people who attended from my side were my parents and my brother. His parents didn't approve of him having a relationship with a non-Bengali girl. So we decided to not inform them because they didn't live in Delhi anyway. From his side, only three of his closest friends—whom I was very close to as well and considered my family—attended.

How young and naïve was I that I made such an important life decision solely so I could go on a trip with my boyfriend?

In retrospect, though, this was the mindset back then.

'Do whatever you want once you get married,' we were told over and over again.

At my wedding to Amlan, with my brother Pankaj

When I think about this statement now, I realize the logic behind it is so archaic and flawed, not to mention dangerous and counterproductive.

'*Ladki bigad jayegi*,' my mother would always tell my father about everything I was allowed to do. It had been one of her main motivations for keeping me close to her in WEA instead of letting me go to a university for my BA.

Years later, though, we would laugh about this life choice she made on my behalf and my rebellion that followed.

'*Kya faida hua?*' I would ask. '*Ladki bigad gayi na*, even though you put me in an all-girls' college?'

* * *

Once Amlan and I got married, I could finally stop hiding and meeting him. I didn't have to make up any excuses for why I was going to stay late in college. I didn't have to hide my relationship from the world. We went to Srinagar with his friends and came back very, very happy.

Another good thing that came out of this marriage was that the Punjabi gang finally stopped bothering us. Amlan and I could now walk down the street hand in hand if we wanted, and we could eat at all my favourite places in WEA.

The two of us shifted to a small rented flat in Rajender Nagar. Amlan had just graduated from IIT and was still looking for a job. We didn't have much, but I was still quite tickled because I was finally on my own.

My relationship with my mother wasn't pleasant during that time, because she felt I should stay home for a few more years and move in with Amlan only when he got a good job and settled down. I was often very rude to my mother and said some very hurtful things. But I didn't dwell on my guilt for too long because marriage, I thought, was my ticket to a new life and unlimited freedom.

I graduated with flying colours, thoroughly and completely in love with Sanskrit. I was finally free to apply to Delhi University for MA.

Every morning, I took the U-Special bus that dropped me off right outside D-School (Delhi School of Economics). My MA Sanskrit classmates weren't very fond of me initially because I was what they considered 'modern'—a girl who wore fashionable clothes, including backless blouses, and watched English films. I also didn't get along with them because we didn't have much in common. The Sanskrit students were called 'Bodiwallas'—a traditional pundit with a shaved head except for a small patch at the back.

So instead of hanging around our department's canteen, I spent more time in the D-School canteen where I found more like-minded people. Initially, they too had preconceived notions about me for being a Sanskrit student and would joke about my accent or my clothes (on days I decided to wear a sari, imagine the irony!) But nobody was cruel or discriminatory. In time, when they realized that we all had much in common and were on the same intellectual wavelength, they took me into their fold.

This didn't go down well with my Sanskrit classmates, who called me 'shameless' because I had male friends and sometimes, not often, I skipped class to sit in the economics department canteen, having debates or playing Matchbox—a game where players were challenged to flip a matchbox into an empty glass.

But once my classmates realized that I wasn't a 'floozy' but a very passionate student who loved Sanskrit, they stopped judging me too much. When I received top marks in the first year, they dropped all their inhibitions and started trying to befriend me so they could ask for my notes.

The passion I felt for Sanskrit is something that still surprises people because I could have picked any subject—politics, Hindi, English—but there was something about this language that brought me immense joy.

I especially loved the texts of Kalidasa. My favourite text was a poem called *Megh Dhoot*, a deep, romantic poem about a demon who is banished by a king into exile. From his hidden abode in the mountains, he calls upon a cloud to send messages of love and longing to his beloved. A part of this poem has stayed with me. It's where the cloud asks the demon, 'How will I recognize your beloved?' And the demon replies, 'Look for the woman who has tears in her eyes. She won't see you because her eyes would be blurry with tears and her wrists would be so thin from starving that her bangles would be dangling from them.' The route that Kalidasa has chalked up in this poem, quite fascinatingly, still exists in the world today, our teacher professed, and we sighed as we heard these words. It doesn't sound like much when you read this in English. It sounds beautiful in Sanskrit.

My professor was a bit of a rock star among the Sanskrit crowd because he could recite *Megh Dhoot* from memory. He had a really good voice, and his eyes would glaze over as he stared out the window. As young, giddy girls, how we wished it were us he was thinking about when he recited the poem.

Along with my studies, I also kept doing theatre and soon started to branch out and try my luck in theatre companies in Delhi—both amateur and professional. At some point, I realized how much I loved the stage and started dreaming of becoming a theatre actor.

Unfortunately, at home, Amlan viewed things differently. Given the times and our upbringing, I think he had always assumed that I would eventually settle down and focus on our family. But I had become a bit too ambitious and didn't see myself ever being a regular housewife. I wanted more from life, and the more theatre I did, the clearer my path became.

During the short time Amlan and I were married, we never quarrelled much. Not about our daily lives, the way our house was run or about my studies and career. We were both very, very young when we dove into marriage, but to this day, I don't have a harsh thing to say about him.

But it soon became apparent that we both wanted different things from life. He wanted someone who could be a solid homemaker. I was a dreamer, a hard worker, who saw herself basking in the validation that came from a standing ovation.

Within a year of our marriage, we mutually and amicably decided to part ways and pursue our own destinies. Amlan finally got a good job and moved away. I moved back home with my mother to whom I apologized profusely.

His uncle who lived in WEA was a lawyer and helped us out with the proceedings. Amlan and I were sitting in the court, waiting for our case to be called, but it was taking some time. I was thirsty, so Amlan offered to go get me a Coca-Cola.

A woman next to me observed how we interacted with each other in an easy, comfortable manner.

'You both are so young. What's wrong? Why are you here?'

'We're just here to finalize our divorce,' I replied.

'DIVORCE??' she practically screamed. 'Why? You both seem so nice and comfortable with each other. He even went out to buy you a Coke. My husband wouldn't care even if I were dying of thirst . . . How can you think of divorce?'

We both laughed at this. She was right though. Amlan was a wonderful man.

'But we don't want the same things any more, so we might as well go our separate ways before it's too late,' I said.

And just like that, we parted ways as a couple and started our lives afresh.

I started my MPhil in Sanskrit at Delhi University and decided to do my thesis in 'Stage Techniques in Sanskrit Drama—Theory and Practice'. After this I really wanted to pursue my PhD in Sanskrit but the guide who was assigned to me didn't agree with my approach to the subject. He wanted me to take a more theoretical approach. But I wanted to get my information first-hand—not just from texts and research in the library—because I was really excited about bringing together my two passions—Sanskrit and the stage. But my PhD didn't pan out because of our constant differences in opinions, and I left midway.

It was very disappointing to get that far in Sanskrit and still not earn a doctorate. But I think whatever happens, happens for the best, because had I finished my PhD, with nowhere further to go, I would have probably been working as a schoolteacher or a college professor today.

Instead, this decision opened up new opportunities for me in stage and acting, with all paths leading to the National School of Drama.

4

National School of Drama

When did I decide to give up on my PhD? How did I end up at the National School of Drama?

I started to drift down this path, I think, when I met a man called Satish Kaushik. He was three years senior to me and a student at Kirori Mal College, an all-boys' institute in Delhi University's North Campus.

He also participated in theatre events, and we met because he was looking for women to act in his college's production of *Aadhe Adhure*, a play by Mohan Rakesh that was very popular at that time. He was introduced to me by some common friends at DU who knew I was passionate about theatre and acted in any and every play I could get a role in.

Satish and I became good friends almost instantly. He was kind, humble and had this self-deprecating sense of humour that really made me laugh. Our backgrounds and upbringings were also very similar. We were both from very humble middle-class backgrounds, both passionate about drama with parents who were supportive but also sceptical about our career choices.

We had a great time rehearsing for *Aadhe Adhure*, in which I played the role of Badi Ladki. I also got to meet Hemant Mishra, a dear friend whom I made my 'rakhi brother'.

Even though it was a student production, it was very well organized. We all worked hard to put up a good performance, which was held in the Kirori Mal College auditorium to a full house. On the day, it felt really good when everything went off without any glitches.

The audience loved us and gave us a standing ovation. We couldn't stop smiling as we held hands and bowed. But just as we were about to pack up, there was a huge commotion in the auditorium. A group of boys brandishing sticks had entered the hall and were rushing towards us.

Hemant immediately grabbed my hand, dragged me to the green room and locked me in. My shock turned into fear when Hemant whispered from the other side of the door, 'Stay here. Don't come out until I come to get you.'

I had no clue what was going on, but I sat in the room, as quietly as I could, while a lot of shouting and screaming continued outside. I knew things had got violent when I heard chairs being broken. At one point, a stone came through the window of the green room, and I cowered on the floor. I started to fear the worst and got very worried for Satish and Hemant.

I was in there for almost thirty minutes—though it felt like hours—before Hemant finally came to get me. He told me, as he escorted me towards the gate, that there was a gang in college who fancied themselves the godfather of campus and had tried to extort money from them to be allowed to perform the play. It was bizarre! The boys had stood their ground and refused to give into their demands and that is why the gang had come to attack them once the play was over.

I ran home that day grateful that we'd escaped relatively unharmed. I also wondered how they had managed to stop the fight. Had Hemant and Satish called the cops? No, I didn't see any uniformed men outside. Had they fought back and overpowered them? Or had they just paid them off? I asked them about it a few days later, but they just brushed it off, saying these things were normal and they happened all the time. 'Don't worry,' they told me. 'Everything is fine.'

Life in theatre, I realized, was going to be anything but dull.

* * *

Satish and I kept in touch after that, and we loved to talk about theatre and drama. He got accepted to NSD after he graduated, and he was finally on the path to success. I loved to visit him on campus because he let me watch their rehearsals. This was an enthralling experience for me because I got to see, first-hand, how students were being groomed to take care of every aspect of a production—from lighting and stage design to costumes and sound. It was also where I first witnessed Mr Ebrahim Alkazi, who was the director of NSD at the time, guide and direct his students.

Had it not been for Satish and our friendship, which is going strong even today, I don't know if I would have applied to NSD. His experiences also made me realize that getting into NSD was just the first hurdle. Surviving it was another big struggle because competition was fierce and not everyone was your friend.

Even today Satish, who is now a very successful film director, a self-made man who came from such humble beginnings, recalls how he was treated with condescension by one of his fellow classmates.

He was in his second year at NSD and Mr Alkazi was asking them all what they wanted to specialize in. Some said dance, music and sound, set design and costume. Many said they wanted to specialize in acting. Satish was among the few who said they wanted to direct. Hearing this, one of the girls started to laugh.

'*You* want to be a director?' her cackling seemed to say, and it really bothered him. He told me later how that laugh echoed through his head for years and made him even more determined to pursue his dream.

This is what I admired about Satish. He was a go-getter. If he wanted something, he would chase after it with single-minded determination and that is how he silenced all his naysayers. This is the one quality I would like to imbibe because it's among the most admirable things about him.

As an insider, Satish gave me glimpses and advice on how to navigate NSD. Even before I thought of applying, Satish knew I had what it took to get accepted.

By inviting me to rehearsals and introducing me to his classmates and teachers, he helped me experience what was in store. I was thoroughly mesmerized.

Mr Alkazi had a great presence on and off stage. He took a scene that seemed to be perfect and managed to elevate it to another level altogether. From the little I saw of him, I realized that he was the sort of director, teacher and mentor who brought out the best in people whether they were on stage or off it.

The seniors at NSD had only good things to say about Mr Alkazi. Under his guidance, the institute had taken on a new life. Students at NSD, regardless of whether they saw themselves on stage or behind it, learnt not just about acting and direction, but also literature, lighting, sound, set design, etc. The more I heard about Mr Alkazi, the surer I became that my career would bloom under his tutelage.

When NSD called for applications for the year 1977, I decided to try my luck. I knew my parents wouldn't approve. My mother didn't think much of the performing arts as a career. She still hoped I would pursue higher studies, get a PhD (at the very least) and then find a stable job as a teacher or an IAS officer.

But I knew that everything in my life had been building up to this. Even my MPhil thesis was on 'Stage Techniques in Sanskrit Drama: Theory and Practice' because it was theatre that interested me the most. I knew there was nothing else out there that could bring me as much joy as drama.

I was lucky that NSD offered a scholarship to promising students. It was competitive and very difficult to get. But I applied for it anyway, because I didn't want to ask my parents to pay for an education they didn't fully believe in. I felt like if this was what I truly wanted to do, I had to earn it myself.

The admission process required one to write a very difficult essay, following which we would be invited to perform a piece from a classic work of literature. If we got through these rounds, we would be invited to give an oral interview. It was a bit unnerving because the interviewer asked me to perform something impromptu that represented my cultural background. This was something that was asked of all students, and I felt like I should have prepared for it. When I stood in front of the judging committee, I was dumbstruck. What could I perform? I was just a regular Delhi girl who grew up in Karol Bagh. What could I present that would truly capture my cultural heritage? Did Delhi even have anything that was worthy of being performed? Many years later I finally found the answer to this and captured it in my National Award-winning documentary *Bazaar Sitaram*. But at that moment, I was blank.

Others, I felt, would have an advantage over me, coming from such varied backgrounds with amazing classical and folk influences. In the end, I performed a song called 'Piche Piche Aunda' from a Punjabi play called *Kanak Di Balli*.

Walking away from the performance, I wondered if it would be enough. But when the list was put up, to my surprise, not only was my name on it, but I also received a letter stating that I had been awarded the scholarship! This was for all three years, including boarding at Mandi House, where one of the school's hostels was located, food and a meagre—but to a student, rather helpful—stipend to cover monthly expenses.

My parents weren't overjoyed, but they didn't make me feel guilty about going against their wishes either. They sat me down and told me exactly what they thought of my decision. They felt I could do better with my life. But when I explained that this was what I truly wanted and they saw how excited I was at getting such an opportunity, they helped me pack my bags—more with snacks and toiletries than clothes, given I could keep coming back for fresh ones if need be—and helped me move into the hostel.

The first time I walked through Mandi House, I couldn't help but marvel at how huge it was. It was a sprawling campus that housed Kathak Kendra—a school for kathak dancers as well as NSD. The hostel and the mess were behind the building. NSD also had another hostel for its students, which was around seven minutes away. There were sprawling gardens as well as an outdoor and indoor theatre. Further out was the Repertory Company, the 'performing wing' of NSD alumni, which had its own campus a few minutes away. Many students who had passed out of NSD were given jobs here to work as set designers, actors and support staff. Many of these staff members also lived with us in our hostel at Mandi House. The Repertory Company also had its own outdoor and indoor theatre, and as students we were constantly recruited as extras, chorus singers or just extra hands to help out with the productions.

The hostels were filled with students from all over the country and even around the world! My roommate for two years was a Bangladeshi girl called Zeenat Ghani. We even had a student from Nigeria called Samuel Babatunde who loved to sing Hindi songs. His favourite was 'Bade achhe lagte hain' from the 1976 film *Balika Badhu*, except he pronounced it as 'Bade adche lagade hain'. He was adorable. A really nice person and very talented. There was also Deepak Kejriwal—now Deepak Qazir—who, for a short time, was more than a friend. But our romance fizzled out quickly and we developed a strong, lifelong friendship.

Deepak was a great guy and a woman's man in the sense that he was so dependable that we would drag him with us to discos—the only boy among five girls—to be our protector.

It looked like a very promising new chapter in my life. But just as I joined, Mr Alkazi resigned from his post after a group of students got together to form a union. I don't know exactly what happened, but my seniors told me that some students were not happy that all our plays were performed either in Hindi or Urdu.

'NSD has students from all over and many of them don't speak Hindi, not even as a second or third language,' they said. This meant that all the main roles went only to Hindi-speaking students, leaving the others feeling short-changed.

I could see their point, but it was also a very difficult issue to resolve. There was no way we could do plays in every language. Maybe the school could have made an effort to stage a few Hindi and English plays which had been translated into regional languages. Or they could have performed regional works translated into Hindi so that everyone felt represented. Maybe if this had happened, the union would not have made things so difficult for Mr Alkazi, causing him so much trouble and stress that he chose to leave the institution rather than stay for those who really needed him.

The first six months after the academic year began, NSD had no director. Students were running wild around the campus, doing as they pleased. There was chaos all around. The classes lacked direction, and I wasn't the only student who felt lost during this time.

Hostel life was a huge adjustment for me given how comfortable and protected I had been in my parents' home. My batch had twenty-four students, out of which only four were girls. Now I had to deal with being a minority in a hostel which housed boys who had never lived in such close proximity to girls who weren't their mothers or sisters.

A bizarre thing happened one morning when I was going to the bathroom. There was a man sitting in the courtyard. It looked like he was meditating. When he saw me, he stood up and started following me. There was a look in his big eyes that made me feel like he wasn't completely right in the head. He had a manic energy around him and his broad jaw, tall stance and wide shoulders gave him the air of someone dangerous. I was scared.

He was at my heels till the door to the bathroom appeared. This was when I turned around and almost screamed.

'*Kyun peecha kar rahe ho mera?*'

He looked into my eyes and smiled. I still haven't forgotten his response because it was among the scariest things you can say to a woman.

'*Jahan jahan aap jayengi, hum aapke peeche peeche chale aayenge,* Madam.'

I slammed the door in his face and didn't come out for almost an hour. When I finally couldn't stay in there any longer, I snuck out and ran back to my room. All day long I kept looking over my shoulder to see if he was following me. After a while it got too much and by evening I was almost in tears when I told my friends what had happened.

But, to my surprise, they just laughed.

'That's just Prabhu,' they said.

'Prabhu?'

'His real name is Rajesh Vivek but everyone calls him Prabhu,' they said. Apparently, he was a very spiritual guy, always spouting philosophical sayings at completely inappropriate times. He was also into tantric practices and was constantly meditating in the courtyard. If anyone asked him what he was up to, he'd look them straight in the eye and with a serious expression say, '*Hum athma shuddhi kar rahen hai.*'

Athma shuddhi? Really? No wonder everyone called him Prabhu.

'Don't worry,' they said. 'He's harmless. He won't do anything.'

For days I kept feeling his presence around me. Rajesh was part of the Repertory Company and sometimes alumni who joined the company were allowed to put up in the hostel for a while. His presence there made me uncomfortable. But as my friends had said, he was strange but mostly harmless. So eventually I got used to him and even found humour in the things he did and said.

I had to make a lot of adjustments in the first few weeks. I had always been independent, thanks to my mom, so I had a lot of practice in washing my own clothes and keeping my room clean. But the toilets posed a problem.

The houses I lived in growing up only had Indian toilets and squatting was all I was used to. NSD had only Western toilets, so for the first few weeks, I would climb up on to the seat and squat to do my business.

Thank God I wasn't the only one because Western toilets were not all that common back then.

'A lot of students climb on to the commodes and then squat to do their business,' one of my seniors told us. 'Mr Alkazi was the sort of man who didn't shy away from resolving such problems. He once took a group of people into the toilets and explained how it works. He even sat on a commode—fully clothed obviously—to demonstrate how to use them.'

I missed Mr Alkazi because I had heard he was a wonderful director as well as a guide. He was vested in every student's growth and well-being. If, say, a student bunked classes but was sitting in the library to complete a project or catch up on work, he would let them be. But if he found out that someone had skipped class to go grab a chai at the *nukkad*, he ensured there were consequences. But, in addition to all of this, he was the sort of man who took it upon himself to help students with their grooming and habits, especially those that affected the student community at large.

That first year, I seriously questioned my decision to come here. I wondered what I would do if the institute failed, and I had to go back to my parents' house covered in the stench of failure.

So I used that free time to write tests and audition for Doordarshan—TV as well as radio—and became an approved artiste, which was a very big deal at the time. Not everyone who applied became an approved artiste. It was very competitive. One had to take two tests—one for TV and one for radio—and depending on their talent, they would be approved. In fact I'm still an approved artiste for DD and it's something I feel very proud to flaunt. I did announcements and advertisements. The money wasn't great but as a student it felt like a lot, and, yes, being on TV was very thrilling.

Thankfully, after half the year was over, we finally got Mr B.V. Karanth as our new director. He was a well-respected director, actor and musician who had done some great work in Hindi and Kannada theatre and cinema. He also had great experience in cinema theatre. We were very excited to have him with us initially because he brought some semblance of order to the institute. Classes began as per schedule, teachers were motivated once again, students were pulled up for faffing around, and we started creating and performing stage productions.

Unfortunately, Mr Karanth, while being a very talented artiste and creative head, wasn't the best administrative person or a very tactful people's person. The union continued to make life difficult for him which affected all of us. He also had his own creative differences with the staff and students, because, while he had the experience in the arts, he hadn't really run an institute of this scale before.

But at least, I thought, our classes had started and we were doing what we all loved: theatre.

The three years I spent there were among the best of my life. Like my seniors, I received a good education in the performing arts, which included lighting, set design, carpentry, dance, literature and, of course, acting. Our days were busy, most spent attending classes. The free time went into rehearsing. If we had a play coming up, we would spend an hour or so after dinner reading lines with each other before retiring for the night.

We had amazing teachers who encouraged and inspired us in unique ways. There was Robin Das, my stagecraft teacher who was artistic and passionate. He spoke passionately about Salvador Dali and taught me all about his paintings. I had the biggest crush on him, nothing sexual, more like a fangirl admiring an authority figure whom she considered inspiring and erudite.

There was also Nibha Joshi who taught me English literature. She introduced me to Shakespeare and Euripides for the first time. Kirti Jain taught us Hindi literature which I was already familiar with, but her lectures made me look at texts in a completely different way which translated into how we interpreted them on stage in our performances.

We had some funny characters who would make us laugh. Our yoga teacher, Mr B.S. Sharma, was so—there's no other way to say this—fat, we often wondered how he was selected to do yoga. But he was quite strong and bendy when he wanted to be. He pushed us to go deeper into our asanas and was known to even sit on students to push them further. This probably wasn't the safest way to get us to do yoga, but at the time we found it so funny we'd laugh about it after class.

We also had a teacher named Rita Ganguli who instructed us in dance and mudras. I really admired her and tried really hard in her classes. Dance has been such an important part of my education, and it's something I use even today.

Ms Ganguli was a wonderful instructor, but she was also quite strict. She didn't like us faffing around and would scold us if she felt we weren't taking things seriously.

Once, she actually asked me to leave her class because I was wearing kajal.

'What are you trying to do?' she shouted at me in front of the whole class. 'Are you here to dance or show how fashionable you are? Get out and don't return until you've washed it all off.'

That was the only time I ever got scolded by her, and I never gave her another opportunity to do it again. I was honest, dedicated and tried my best so she was always satisfied with my efforts.

The boys, however, were always getting on her wrong side. I think they felt silly doing classical steps and standing in elegant poses because they felt that they lacked the grace us girls had.

Ms Ganguli didn't let them off easily though. If they tried to fool around in class or crack self-deprecating jokes, she would also, as they say, take 'phirki'. 'Phirki lena' was a common thing back then among peers. It meant pranking the other person who didn't even realize it was just for laughs. Ms Ganguli knew just how to embarrass them. She would make them stand in Nataraj pose for a long time just for a good laugh.

The boys absolutely hated this and once decided to make a statement. They all shaved their heads and stood right in the front row where she couldn't miss them. When Ms Ganguli entered, they waited eagerly for her reaction, but to her credit, she didn't even blink. She just went about directing the class as usual and didn't spare the boys for a second when they tried to faff around.

At the time, I didn't realize how lucky I was to get the exposure that came with being a student at NSD. We were being trained to look at simple things in many different ways. It's exactly what I had seen Mr Alkazi do when I had visited his rehearsals, but when you're that young, you take things for granted.

There were some experiences I fully appreciated and knew I wouldn't have had them if not for NSD. Like, one semester, a guest lecturer called Fritz Bennewitz visited us. Mr Bennewitz was a noted German director who taught us about Bertolt Brecht and his works. His visit ended with us staging a wedding sequence from one of Brecht's plays called *The Threepenny Opera*, in which I played the lead role. The performance was in Hindi, a language Mr Bennewitz didn't speak. But he still directed us beautifully and included amazing songs in the script. I loved that part, and how I wish I could sing some of those songs for you in this book.

* * *

At NSD, I made some really good friends who, over the course of three years, became more like family. This included Alok Nath,

Ravishankar Khemu, whom we just called Khemu, Alopi Verma, who is now a big theatre director, and Sanjiv Dixit, who, unfortunately, passed away many years ago.

This was my gang. We were together all the time. We shared a lot of experiences, food being the prime among them. We would all walk down to Bengali Market almost every day. There was a standing joke among us that we walked that path so often that even if we were blindfolded, we would still be able to find our way there. The market would be bursting with sound and activity. But our favourite was the food. There was a small *thela* that sold a cheap but healthy thali of daal and unlimited rotis—perfect for broke students. There were also places selling great chai and chaat. But our favourite, I think, was Nathu's where we went every time we had a few pennies to spare. It wouldn't buy us much. But it was hilarious nevertheless to order one gulaab jamun or dosa and split it five ways.

Years later when I was visiting Delhi, I suggested a lunch date at Nathu's to a few girlfriends I was catching up with. The joint, I was pleasantly surprised to see, wasn't a small shop any more. It had expanded over the years and was now a full-fledged restaurant. I also wasn't a student any more, so it felt good for the first time to eat whatever I pleased without having to worry about sharing or money. We ordered every item on the menu, including my favourites—dosa and gulaab jamun.

But at the end of the meal when I asked for the bill, the waiter refused to bring it.

'*Sahib ne kaha ki aap se paise nahin le sakte hain*,' he told me shyly. Really? They couldn't charge me? Why not?

I was shocked at this. I asked him to take me to his 'sahib'. The owner of Nathu's looked up at me and gave me a warm smile.

'Why can't you charge me?' I asked, recounting how many items we had ordered.

'Kya madam,' the owner smiled shyly. '*Aap se kaise paise le sakte hain?*'

'Accha? When I was a student and had no money, *aapne ache se charge kiya hamein*,' I joked. '*Ab paise hain hamere pass aur aap nahin lenge?*'

'Madam, *hum bhi aap ke saath bade hue hain*,' he said. '*Aap se hum ab paise bilkul nahin le sakte hain.*'

I was so touched by his words that I agreed to let him waive off our bill.

'*Theek hai*,' I said. '*Par sirf iss bar. Agli baar appko paise lene padenge.*'

'No chance, ma'am!' he said with a laugh.

He kept his word. The next time I visited, I tried to sneak in from the back door so that he wouldn't see me. But I had become a known face by then and all the waiters also knew me. So there was no way I could get away with paying the bill because they never brought it to me.

* * *

Our gang, in fact our entire batch, became very close over the course of three years; we were living, eating and having so many experiences together. If we weren't sitting in the courtyard and laughing, we were hanging out in my room where I had a pressure cooker and hotplate to make simple dishes like daal and pulao.

NSD also organized field trips that enriched our experience. One of the places we visited was Ujjain in Madhya Pradesh. We travelled by train, and with so many of us together, it almost felt like we owned the entire compartment. We had a great time on the way there.

When we reached, we set up camp in a large field, very close to a river which was nice and scenic, but the ground itself was very dusty. At night, we had to slide into our tents and subsequently our sleeping bags very slowly and gently because any heavy moves would kick up a cloud of dust.

NSD had taken us there with the intention of helping the folk artistes, practitioners of Maach—a traditional folk theatre. We were to organize a festival to celebrate the art form. Artistes from all over MP were to come in bullock carts to participate.

The NSD students were in charge of the whole festival from setting up the stage to organizing the seating and erecting the mandap. We did everything from scratch right on that big, open field. We all lifted the heavy bamboo for the stage and the boys climbed up tall ladders to tie them into place. Even the girls did a lot of the heavy lifting because we were taught to work as a team and do everything that we were capable of.

It was because NSD made us do everything during our productions, it instilled in us a great sense of dignity of labour. I never felt like I was above a task—be it carrying heavy equipment or even sweeping the floor—because it was drilled into me that every job, every task, no matter how small or seemingly menial, served a bigger purpose.

In Ujjain, we spent our days rehearsing for the skit that we were performing in collaboration with the Maach artistes. It was an educational experience for all of us because we got to work on a more traditional form and technique of folk dance and storytelling.

The audience came from the neighbouring villages, and we had different troupes performing Maach skits and dances for them every day.

Our evenings were spent by the riverbanks. Some of the boys from our class would go down to the market and get a local fermented drink called gulaab. It was delicious and heady, but any high we experienced also came down quickly.

We also visited a temple nearby which had a deity who apparently preferred alcohol over the usual offerings of sweets and flowers. Devotees would stand in long queues to pour gulaab over the idol and would watch, gobsmacked, as the liquid disappeared beneath her feet as if by magic.

The boys and I laughed heartily when one of us suggested that the alcohol perhaps didn't just disappear. That maybe it was collected somewhere below the idol and that the pandits perhaps drank it at night.

A day before we were to leave, the authorities requested that we perform our skit for the inmates of a nearby prison. Apparently, it was close to our camping site and they had been curious about the songs and dialogues they had heard during our rehearsals.

I will never forget this experience because the inmates, starved of any sort of distractions, were very grateful for our performance. The applause they gave us once we finished was something else altogether. It was thick, loud and so powerful that it hit my very soul. For me, this was one of the most validating experiences because that applause still echoes in my mind.

* * *

The three years at NSD not only honed my skills as an actor, but also helped me grow as a person. Living in a hostel with peers was a lesson in humility as we all lived modestly, humbly and adjusted to make community living comfortable.

But there is one train of thought that has haunted me throughout my life. What if . . . if only . . . Mr Alkazi had never left . . . I wondered, still do. Would my education and experience have been better, more enriching than they were? Because let's face it, a lot of changes were made to our curriculum under Mr Karanth.

In previous years, students were allowed to choose electives, specializations in their second year. But in my year, that option was scrapped, and we just did a bit of everything for all the three years. This was a bit disheartening for me, because I didn't see how learning about lighting and sound could help me when I only wanted to be an actor or director.

There were times when we would complain to each other about how the whole institute was managed.

'This is such a waste of time,' I would say to myself when my lighting teacher, G.N. Dasgupta, yelled at me for not even trying to understand how it worked or when Goverdhan Panchal, my theatre architecture teacher, critiqued my haphazard designs. My sound design teacher loved my enthusiasm for singing but didn't like that I made no effort to understand the technical aspects of his course.

I took everything they said through one ear and pushed it out through the other. But looking back, a lot of things they said stuck with me. I don't think I learnt a lot from those technical classes, but some key lessons stayed with me.

I realized this during the lockdown when I had to do interviews and shoot ads in Mukteshwar. I did so much with just my phone or my iPad. I had to do my own make-up, find the right angles for the perfect lighting and do my own tech and sound checks. My NSD teachers' voices kept playing in my head. I just couldn't believe I had dismissed them as a foolish young woman. At times I wish I had paid more attention to what they taught us because there are so many times when I struggle to get things right.

I know I had my reasons for faffing around in technical subjects though, because the experience I had at NSD was very different from the ones my seniors, like Satish, had. A lot of modules were shortened, a lot of experiences scrapped.

In previous years, a handful of NSD students had been sent to the Film and Television Institute of India (FTII) in Pune on an exchange programme for a period of six months! But to my complete disappointment, this programme was scrapped the very year I joined.

I had heard a lot about FTII and was keen to go even if it wasn't part of the programme at NSD. So, I let lose my rebellious streak, and with the help of a friend, arranged a week-long visit to FTII. I made up an excuse to Mr Karanth, pretended to have a family emergency, and took off to Pune.

The week I spent there was hardly enough to soak in all that FTII had to offer. But it had to be enough because I couldn't risk sneaking into their classes or bunking my own back in Delhi.

I came back to Mandi House happy and full of inspiration. But before I could even settle in and unpack, I was summoned to Mr Karanth's office.

'You thought I wouldn't find out?' he shouted. 'How could you lie to me?'

I felt so guilty that I just stood there, bumbling like a little girl who had been caught stealing. I hoped that a scolding was all I would get but Mr Karanth was so angry that he suspended me for one whole week. I found it utterly and completely unfair.

'He hates me,' I vented to my friends after leaving the office. 'He utterly and completely hates me and wants to make my life miserable.'

I was young, I'll admit, and prone to overreacting. Whatever I felt, I felt with great passion and conviction—I truly did belong in the drama business. But I know now that Mr Karanth may have been strict and at times a little lost in managing his staff and students, but he was also doing his best. Especially when we didn't make things any easier for him. The union was constantly going after him and the students, including me, were constantly complaining to or about him.

Over the years, Mr Karanth and I clashed a lot, and he either threw up his hands at my behaviour or punished me for my actions. The worst time, I felt, was when he forced me to go on stage and perform my best when I was struggling with a fever and bad throat.

'How did you fall sick?' he asked me suspiciously. I lied that I didn't know even though I did. A few days before the performance, a Parsi play in which I had to sing, I went out to Bengali Market with my friends and drank a glass of sharbat filled with ice.

'Neena, your body is your instrument and I see you constantly disrespecting it by eating garbage from the streets,' he said. 'Your voice is your medium as an actor. If you want to have a long, successful career in this field, you have to take care of yourself.'

'I'm sorry,' I mumbled. 'I won't do it again . . . '

'Good. Now go get ready for rehearsals.'

'Rehearsals?' I asked, shocked. Surely he didn't expect me to perform. He could see how sick and miserable I was, how badly my voice had been affected.

'Yes, you will still perform,' he laughed, and at that moment I thought him to be so cruel. 'The show must go on.'

I hated him for making me perform. His whole attitude towards me seemed biased and unfair.

But years later when we met at a party hosted by a mutual acquaintance, he seemed so happy to see me that he came over and gave me a hug. I laughed and started ribbing him about the hard time he gave me during my years at NSD.

'Why did you hate me so much?' I asked.

'Neena, I did not hate you one bit,' he said. 'I loved you and saw so much talent in you. But you were an exasperating student who did as she pleased, not caring about the consequences. I was a teacher and I had to discipline you.'

He was right, of course. I was young, foolish and like so many people at that age, I thought I was above the rules. I also realized it couldn't have been easy for Mr Karanth either to manage a bunch of rowdy drama students, a union that kept staging protests, and teachers who came with their own issues and complaints.

* * *

You cannot live in a hostel and not forge strong ties with your peers. My gang, Alok, Alopi, Khemu and Sanjiv, was very close and you rarely saw any one of us without the others. But we also had a sense of loyalty towards our fellow hostellers even if we weren't in each other's intimate circles.

I was and still am an early riser, and I used to wake up and go downstairs to sit alone in the courtyard. One day, as I was sitting and meditating on a production we were working on, a girl entered the hostel looking hysterical.

She wasn't a student at NSD, but I knew her. She was dating one of my classmates, who also lived in the same hostel, and I had met her a few times. She was frantically looking for her boyfriend. When she saw me, she asked if I knew where he was.

I did, in fact, know his whereabouts because living together in such close proximity meant we couldn't help but keep tabs on each other's flings, affairs and indiscretions.

The boy in question had spent the night in another girl's room, and I suspected he was still there. Covering for him was probably not the best thing to do, but a sense of loyalty made me spring into action and pacify his girlfriend.

'Stay here,' I said, taking her up to my room. 'I'll go look for him.'

I ran straight to the other girl's room and knocked on the door.

'Come quickly, your girlfriend is here,' I whispered when he emerged from inside. The speed at which he ran down was hilarious but I tried to keep a straight face as I followed him. I stood at a distance as he assuaged her fears and convinced her to go out for breakfast. They continued dating for a few more months after that but eventually she broke it off. I'm sure she caught him being unfaithful again, because this particular boy, a fellow Delhi resident like me, was known far and wide as a flirt and player.

There were many things I turned a blind eye to at the time. But there was one injustice at NSD that didn't let me look the other way. It was about a teacher getting romantically involved with a student and it left a mark on my psyche.

The teacher in question was our hostel incharge, whom I will not name here out of respect to his surviving family and refer to only as D.

D was a nice man, though not much to look at. He taught us a few classes and was extra friendly. He would always insert himself into our activities and conversations outside class. I didn't think much of him, but I respected him as a teacher and authority figure. It was also tough to avoid him because his quarters were just outside Mandi House, when you entered the hostel gate.

One day, we heard a rumour that D was having an affair with a young girl, one of my juniors. I won't reveal her name here either because I respect her privacy and want to preserve her dignity.

These rumours were confirmed soon enough because they were often spotted together, and a few times we even saw them go into his quarters together. It made me very uncomfortable because the girl was young, pretty and very innocent, while D was much older and an authority figure. I could see how a young girl could get smitten by a teacher, but, honestly, the fact that D was taking it to another level made me wonder if he was using his power and influence to coax her into something undesirable.

When I heard from fellow students that D and the girl had quietly got married in a mandir somewhere, I was shocked and didn't want to believe it. But the next morning when I saw him in the courtyard, boasting about it to a few students, my stomach churned and I felt sick.

'Have you heard the good news, Neena?' he asked, gesturing me to come over and join the conversation.

'Yes, yes, sir,' I said, trying my best not to show my disgust. 'Congratulations.'

D then started to tell us how it happened. Some of the students were laughing and clapping while a few others, like me, seemed visibly uncomfortable. But this was nothing compared to what we felt next when D started to say things about her that were not very nice. This even included some intimate details. I was shocked and felt nauseated because I just couldn't believe the things he had coaxed the girl into on their 'first night'. Worse still, he kept telling us about how inexperienced she was and how unsatisfactory he had found the whole 'session'.

That was it for the girl because word of what D said spread far and wide. Suddenly she was tainted and considered immoral. Someone who should be avoided. The fact that she was much younger than D or that he was a teacher, an authority figure who probably took advantage of her innocence and vulnerability, didn't matter. He was a man after all. He was just doing what comes naturally to men. Right?

Over the new few weeks, it felt like every person in NSD, and beyond, had heard about this and was judging her. It was so unfair, but I couldn't say much because I didn't have the guts to speak up against a teacher, something I regret to this day.

Things got worse for the girl because one by one, everyone in the hostel stopped talking to her. D didn't waste any time in giving people more details about their private life and painted her to be some sort of villain. Soon, even those who were polite and cordial to her stopped acknowledging her presence and pretended any chair with her in it was empty.

Every time I saw her sitting by herself in the mess or holed up in the library, it made me want to cry. I always made an effort to talk to her and ask how she was doing. She would hide her pain behind a smile and say, 'Fine, thank you', but I knew from her eyes that she was in pain and had been crying in private.

'Why can't people treat her nicely,' I asked my friends. 'What's her fault in all of this, other than falling in love with that wretched, manipulative man?'

'What can we do?' they asked. 'He's an authority figure. We don't want to get into trouble.'

Such cowards we were . . .

As human beings, our morals and principles are very twisted; our double standards are off the charts. This has never been more evident to me than in the way this girl was treated. Used and discarded by an older man she had faith in. Tainted for life because everyone trusted D over her. Exiled by peers to whom she had been nothing but kind.

It's not like we were any better. Every resident had his/her own affairs and indiscretions . . . vices and faults. No one was perfect. But it was disgusting to watch the glee on my fellow hostellers' faces as they spoke about this girl's character, her personal life and her intimate moments that no decent husband should ever reveal. For those few fateful months, every person I met was drunk on schadenfreude: a word I learnt which means pleasure derived from another's misfortune.

D was in charge. He was our teacher and responsible for us. He was supposed to protect us. But instead, he used his position to seduce a young girl and then slander her hatefully before discarding her.

Throughout this period, I was one of the few people who spoke to her and tried to make her feel better. I felt sorry for her because, somewhere, I identified with her. Until then, I hadn't been treated that badly by anyone. I know it's contradictory to be called a 'bhenji' and 'shameless' in the same breath but these two words have been most descriptive of my life. I was a Sanskrit-loving girl who wore tops with spaghetti straps and that confused people. So, depending on the day, based on what I said or wore, I was either a 'bhenji' or 'shameless'. I had also been called a slew of other names for being in relationships previously, not to mention a marriage that had ended with us parting ways.

I didn't know the extent of this girl's pain. This sweet, innocent person was caught in the eye of the storm and the environment D had created for her was nothing less than a cyclone. I tried to help in any way I could, but I knew it wasn't enough. I still remember the look on her father's face when he came one morning to drop off some clothes and supplies for her.

In that moment, he reminded me so much of my father, because Papa too came to the hostel almost every week to give me food and other supplies. So, I went up to him to say hello and noticed he had tears in his eyes.

'What's wrong, uncle? Is everything okay?' I asked.

'What can I say?' he sobbed. 'My daughter is going through a very bad time. Nobody here accepts her any more.'

'I'm sorry,' I said, not knowing what to say to make him feel better. As parents, we experience our children's pain and injustices a lot more intensely than they do, and I could see that this man's pain was a hundred times worse than that of his daughter. His helplessness teared me up.

'What can I do to help?' I asked. 'Please let me know.'

'Will you take care of her? It will help me sleep better knowing there is somebody watching out for her,' he said. He looked so sincere and vulnerable in that moment that I promised with all my heart that I would do everything in my power to help her out and ensure she came out of this okay.

I would like to think I did all I could, but we lost touch once I passed out of NSD. Much later I heard she and D split up (thank God) and she moved to Bombay (now Mumbai) where she eventually found work and remarried.

5

New Beginnings

After I passed out of NSD, I was offered a full-time job at the Repertory Company. This was a great honour, and I knew many seniors who had taken this up.

This meant I would get to do theatre professionally and get a steady salary for it. But it also meant that I would not get to explore other avenues of acting and I would only be working with one troupe.

I was young and filled with ideas and there were many, many different things that I wanted to do. So I turned down the offer and started to explore opportunities in the Delhi theatre scene. I went to a lot of places, met with talented individuals who were doing amazing work, and started auditioning for roles.

It was a whole new world of possibilities. At NSD, we had been sheltered and supported. Everything, right from our costumes and make-up to set designs and scripts, was handed to us. But out here in the real world, we didn't have experienced teachers to guide us. If we wanted to perform independent scripts, we had to shell out money for our own costumes and make-up. If we failed, there were consequences because we weren't students any more. We were supposed to be trained professionals. We were on our own. I felt like I was stepping out of a cocoon.

I got a lot of work with local troupes, some paid, most unpaid, but I found the experience exciting and learnt a lot.

One play that I distinctly remember from this time was *Sakharam Binder*, written by Vijay Tendulkar and performed by a local troupe. Sachin (name changed), an actor with whom I was having a serious affair, was also cast in this production. He played the lead, the titular character, Sakharam, and I played Champa, a destitute woman who is rescued by the protagonist and becomes his mistress.

It was an intense play and the role of Sakharam took its toll on Sachin. There's a scene where Sakharam smothers Champa with a pillow. When we got to it, Sachin, who played the part with great conviction, suddenly felt like he'd been taken over by the character. Instead of pressing the pillow down on my face like we had rehearsed, he put all his strength into it and started to smother me for real.

I couldn't breathe and it felt like my eyes were going to pop out. Another minute and I would have pushed him back, without caring that the entire performance would have got ruined. But luckily, the stage went black and nobody saw me shove him.

'What was that?' I asked once we were backstage. 'You almost killed me!'

'I'm sorry. I'm so so sorry,' he said, and it seemed like he meant it. 'I got too caught up in my emotions.'

It was shocking that this had happened because Sachin was a very professional actor. I couldn't understand how he had been capable of such violence. But I also understood why he had slipped. Theatre can have that effect even on the best of us. We get so immersed in our roles that very often we roam around with the baggage of our characters. We feel their emotions with such intensity that until the performance ends, we don't know who we truly are—ourselves or our characters.

But, for some reason, even though I know he didn't do it deliberately, this incident has stayed with me all these years. It's probably because after that incident I never saw a single actor lose themselves to that degree on stage.

* * *

My very first film was *Aadharshila*. It was produced, written and directed by Ashok Ahuja and the cast included a lot of actors from the local theatre scene—Naseeruddin Shah, Anita Kanwar, Raghubir Yadav and Annu Kapoor. Satish Kaushik was also part of the film as Ahuja's assistant director as well as an actor.

I landed this role along with many other students from NSD who were cast in smaller parts.

Aadharshila is a film within a film, so the shooting was very exciting. This was the first time I was acting in front of a camera, and I loved every minute of it. They didn't have a very big budget and I wasn't getting paid. But it didn't bother me. I did my best on screen and even behind it because NSD had instilled in us a good work ethic. When I wasn't acting, I was either assisting the others on set or silently observing and trying to learn more about this new medium.

In one scene, I had to ride a cycle while wearing a one-piece swimsuit. It was funny because I did not know how to ride a cycle and, having never learnt how to swim, I didn't own a swimsuit either. I used to go to Ashok Ahuja's house every evening so that his brother could teach me to ride a cycle in the tiny *galli* behind their house. My mother, once again, proved how good her sense of style was by buying me a really stylish swimsuit. On the day we were to film, I rode the cycle, a skill I hadn't yet mastered fully, while feeling thoroughly exposed in the swimsuit. It was awkward and everyone kept teasing me, but we finally got a good take. I wish I had a picture from behind the scenes because it was quite an iconic moment of my life. Interestingly, once I got off that cycle that evening, I never got back on again and, sadly, I still haven't learnt how to swim.

Our crew was nice, small and very closely knit. In the evenings, once we wrapped up, we would all go over to Ahuja's house where we would eat, chat and generally reminisce. We would also joke and laugh a lot at the things that took place on a daily basis.

Like, one day, Satish arrived on set deep in thought. He kept muttering, '*Main kuch cheez bhul gaya . . .* ' over and over. It wasn't until the director asked him, 'Neena *kahan hai?*' that he realized that the '*cheez*' he had forgotten was me. He used to pick me up every morning on his scooter and we'd go to the sets together. That morning, he didn't pick me up and I just waited for hours without being able to get in touch with anyone because there were no phones to call. Everyone had a big laugh that evening and kept teasing him for days.

Filming *Aadharshila* kept me very busy and I barely got to meet Sachin. We were quite serious by then and had started talking about moving to Bombay to become 'strugglers'—a notion that was as romantic as it was misguided—so that we could get our big breaks. We honestly didn't know the extent of these 'struggles', but we told ourselves that as long as we had each other, everything would fall into place.

So, one day, after we'd wrapped up the shoot and everyone was preparing to leave for Ahuja's house, I requested to be excused so I could spend the evening with Sachin. We had a standing date, and I was really looking forward to seeing him. I had so much to tell him about my experience, the crew and the kind of work that went into filming. It was so different from what I had learnt at NSD, which was centred mostly around theatre, that it had opened my mind to several new possibilities.

Just as I was entering the hostel, high on life and giddy with excitement, I stopped to say hello to a common friend of ours who told me something that brought me crashing to the ground.

Sachin, he told me with a pained expression, had been seeing another girl while I was busy with work.

I was so shocked that I didn't know what to say. I walked to my room with my head lowered because I didn't want to make eye contact with anyone. Could this be true? Did everyone in the hostel know? Of course they knew. Everyone knew everything that went on behind closed doors in Mandi House. I locked myself in my room and cried well into the night.

The next day, Sachin came looking for me because I had stood him up the night before. I didn't want to see him, but I also wasn't going to let him go so easily. So I opened the door and stepped out. The sweet, innocent smile on his face, I knew, hid a deep, dirty secret. I couldn't help myself and burst into tears.

'How could you do something like this?' I yelled. 'We had so many plans and dreams.'

Sachin and I had been, at least I thought we'd been, very serious. We had discussed how we would both move to Bombay together. How we would struggle together and, eventually, once one of us got their big break, we would get married and spend the rest of our lives together.

He didn't deny my accusations, and this made me feel even worse. I broke down again and started sobbing. We were in the courtyard, in full view of the entire hostel and everyone stopped to stare.

'I'm sorry, I'm sorry,' he kept saying. 'I made a mistake. You are the only woman who matters to me. The only woman I love.'

He told me that the girl he'd slept with had come on to him and he had tried to push her away but she was persistent. He didn't mean to but, in the end, he was a man and it could be so difficult to back off when women were so forward.

When he said this, I suddenly found myself getting angry with the girl. That wretched girl with loose morals and no principles, I thought. Which man would say no to a woman who so willingly came to him to initiate sex? It was her fault. She was to blame.

This happens too often, even today. We forgive our cheating partners and instead direct our hatred and anger at women. Why do we do this? Do we really think that only one party is to be blamed? That men who cheat are actually saints who were led astray by devious women? I ask myself today, 'Would Sachin have forgiven me so easily had I been the one who had cheated?'

I know now that blaming the woman had not only been wrong but also outright stupid. Sachin was the one who had cheated. But at the time it had been so much easier, socially acceptable too, to blame the woman because I wanted to believe this man whom I thought I was in love with. But I didn't know that he would go on to cheat on me and break my trust again and again and again.

I forgave Sachin. But I never forgot this indiscretion. I became jealous and insecure, the kind of woman who gets told that she's being crazy and making things up in her head. In time, I also started to believe that I was imagining things. So, I let things slide even when the signs were right in front of me and instead turned my attention to my work.

I stayed with Sachin, but every once in a while, jealousy would raise its ugly head. When he started doing a lot of work with the Delhi-based troupe Samarth, I heard from someone that he and Mandira (name changed), the founder of the group who was also an actress, seemed to be getting very close. She had founded the troupe with her husband—a big movie star at the time—and was very well known in Delhi's theatre circles. I was not a part of Samarth and was busy doing work with other companies. So I relied heavily on what I heard from mutual friends and from Sachin himself. Nothing had happened between Mandira and Sachin, to my knowledge, but I still didn't feel comfortable. I kept questioning Sachin about his whereabouts, Mandira and started to panic that he would slip again.

When I heard that Samarth was doing a play called *Desire Under the Elms* by Eugene O'Neill, with Sachin and Mandira in leading roles, I finally put my foot down. The play has a very adult theme with lots of sexual scenes, and I did not want Sachin to participate in it. In retrospect, if he wanted to do something with her, he could have easily done it offstage and not wait for an onstage excuse. But I wasn't thinking straight. I insisted that he back out.

'No way you are doing this,' I told him again and again.

'Okay fine,' he finally agreed. 'I won't do it.'

This made me feel better and, in my head, it strengthened our relationship. He gave up a role for me, I thought. He must really, really love me, right?

* * *

When *Aadharshila* was about to release, we started to strategize how to promote the film. There was no marketing budget for PR and press or to place an ad on billboards. So all of us—cast and crew—went all over the university and promoted the film. With social media and all, you won't see this happening today. But this was such a fun exercise for me and also a very humbling experience.

On the day of the release, we all sat outside on the steps of Regal Theatre, waiting to see the reaction of the audience. Well, the response was lukewarm, and the film was taken down in a few days, but it didn't disappear. It was screened at film festivals over the next few years and the response was fairly good.

As for me, seeing myself on the big screen for the first time in my life gave me a high. Until then, I had only acted in plays and the experience had been satisfying. But what I felt after *Aadharshila* was nothing like what I had ever experienced on stage. Suddenly, I started to see possibilities everywhere, and I knew if I worked hard enough all that I had dreamt of would become a reality.

* * *

Soon after, there were calls to audition for a Hollywood film called *Gandhi*. At the time, I honestly didn't know the scale at which it would be made or how iconic it would become in world cinema. I definitely didn't think it would become world famous and win eight Academy Awards.

I just knew I wanted to be on the silver screen again. So I went for the auditions and did my best. At first, I read for the role of Kasturba Gandhi, Mahatma Gandhi's wife. But they cast me in the role of Abha because they thought I suited that character better.

This was the very first film for which I got paid, and I decided to put all my earnings towards moving to Bombay with Sachin, who was also part of the cast. In fact, there were many actors from Delhi who used the money from this film to move to Bombay. It was almost like a movement.

The assassination scene was the very first one they shot, and I was among the cast who was right in front as one of the walking sticks of Gandhi. We were in this open ground, just waiting for the shoot to begin, when it started to rain. This happened for almost three days and we kept starting and stopping and starting again. I know I should feel bad that it took so long to finish the scene, but our payment was per day so the delay meant that we would get paid more and we could save more for Bombay.

With Ben Kingsley in the film *Gandhi* where I play Abhaben

When we had finished the sequences that were to be shot in Delhi, we were all asked to report to Bombay where the rest of the shoot would take place. This was our chance, Sachin and I decided. After our work in *Gandhi*, we had absolutely no doubt in our minds about where we wanted our careers to go. We would book one-way tickets to Bombay, and once the filming ended, we would finally become those strugglers we had heard so much about.

I decided then that I would pack my bags with the intention of moving permanently. We were given a date to report on set. I had become very close to the film's crew, so I decided to take the same flight as them. My fingers and toes were tingling as we boarded the flight to Bombay. Throughout the journey, I kept looking out of the window trying to guess which part of the country we were over. It kept my mind occupied, so I wouldn't let myself rethink the decision I had made to stay back.

The closer we got to our destination, the more excited I got. I couldn't help but feel that there was something big and exciting waiting for me. When the plane began to descend at the Bombay airport, I started to feel jittery, and it had nothing to do with the air pressure. My stomach was filled with butterflies. Was I excited? Was I nervous? A bit of both.

When the wheels finally touched down on the runway, I felt something shift in me and I couldn't help but smile. I thanked God for all the opportunities he had given me that put me on this aeroplane. Everyone on the plane started cheering and clapping, and I couldn't help but join in.

When I walked out and breathed the salty air of the Arabian Sea for the very first time, my eyes welled up. It was like nothing I had ever felt before. It was like I had just come home. For the very first time.

Part 2

Bombay Girl

1

Homeless

I got off the plane and went straight to baggage claims. I walked out of the airport and stood in line for a taxi. The drive to Santacruz West was short. It was either January or February in 1981. I breathed in the air and was hit by a smell. It was pleasant. I cannot describe it. But I only get it once every year. It's the smell I associate with Bombay in those months. It's the smell I associate with new beginnings.

After I reached my destination, I walked up two flights of stairs with my baggage. I rang the bell and was greeted a minute later by a middle-aged lady wearing a cotton sari.

'Hello, Aunty,' I said. 'I'm your son's friend's sister. I'm supposed to stay with you.'

With a smile that didn't quite reach her eyes, she welcomed me in. The apartment was small, and I would have to sleep on the sofa. Hope I didn't mind. Of course not. Accommodation was free, and I could hardly afford to make any demands. Good. Very good.

This was my first house in Bombay, and I don't think I have ever tried so hard to be invisible. The only reason I had even been allowed inside was because their son, a close friend of my brother's, who was studying in Delhi, had requested them to let me stay. As I guessed on the day I arrived, Aunty wasn't happy with having me in her home. She didn't like the idea of a virtual stranger living under her roof, eating her food and using her bathrooms. She never said much to me. But I often heard her complaining about the inconvenience; about having to be mindful of this stranger living in her house.

I felt so lost and alone, I often locked myself in the bathroom to cry. I tried really hard to be a good guest. I made my bed the minute I woke up and put the sheets, pillows and blankets away. I ate very little because I didn't want to be a burden on her. I didn't make any phone calls back home because I didn't want to block any of their incoming calls. I was miserable.

My mother called me almost every day and Aunty would just say, 'Humph . . . ' and hand me the phone. I didn't tell my mother for the longest time about how miserable I was. I just talked about *Gandhi*, the people on set and what I had eaten that day.

But, one day, when Aunty wasn't at home, I just let it all out. My mother was telling me what she'd cooked for dinner and how she'd seen some clothes that would look perfect on me. The dam just burst, and I started crying. I told her the truth about how uncomfortable I was, how I tried to make myself scarce so that they wouldn't notice my presence and how they just didn't want me there.

My mother just couldn't bear hearing my distraught voice and not being able to take me in her arms.

'*Chalo*, move to a hotel right now and I'll pay for it,' she said. But I refused her offer because I knew it would be too expensive. 'Okay. Hang on. I'll see if there is someone else we know in Bombay.'

The next day, my mother called and told me there was an old family friend of hers, Mr Dayal Setia. He lived in Bandra East and would be happy to have me.

'He has two daughters, Deepa and Neeru,' she said. 'Deepa is now married and Neeru is studying to become an architect. Very, very sweet girl. Mr Setia says you can go there any time. He will be very happy to have you over.'

So I packed my bags, said my thank yous and goodbyes, and left that house the very next day. It was such a relief to reach Kala Nagar and be welcomed at the door by a smiling man with kind eyes. The house, once again, was not very big. But they made adjustments and put me up in a comfortable bed.

Neeru, like my mother said, was a bright and lovely young girl and we quickly became good friends. She was already used to sharing her space with her sister and was more than accommodating of me.

In the meantime, Sachin found a room in ESIC Nagar, Andheri West. We were pretty serious, but we didn't want to live together because our parents would absolutely not allow it. So we took up separate accommodations. But we met as often as we could. As both of us were in *Gandhi*, we also got to meet on set. When we had days off from shooting, we would meet on Juhu beach. We didn't have much money to eat in restaurants so we would just walk on the sand while holding hands. We didn't care what time it was. Even in the afternoons, when the sun was at its hottest, we'd be at the beach, looking for some shade.

It wasn't ideal, but it was what we had. We were happy. Even now when I see couples holding hands or sitting under trees or in the shadows of buildings on the beach, I'm taken back to my own youth. It makes me appreciate how we made the most of what we had even when we had very, very little.

I settled into my new life in Bombay, but it wasn't without its glitches. I could take a taxi to the set of *Gandhi* because it would get reimbursed. But if I had to go anywhere else, I had to take the local train.

It takes a lot of time getting used to the local trains for someone who is new to the city. Neeru would find my misadventures hilarious. On some days, I missed three to four trains at a time because I couldn't part the crowd and get in. On others, I missed my stop because I wasn't standing close enough to the door.

'I said "Excuse me, side please" so many times. But nobody moves. Can't they hear?'

Neeru patted me on the shoulder and said I had to stop being so polite. That I had to forget everything I had learnt about public transport in Delhi because in Bombay nobody cared.

'Don't stop to think so much,' she said. 'Just close your eyes and push your way out as hard as you can and do the same while getting in.'

So I took her advice the next day and pushed as much as I could. It worked and I mentally gave myself a pat on the back. But then I made another rookie mistake. When I reached the overhead bridge, I forgot which way to turn for Bandra East and walked down to Bandra West instead. It took me a long, long time to figure out the whole concept of East and West.

* * *

Mr Setia was a wonderful man and his wife was warm and loving. But as much as I liked them as a family, they weren't my own family, so I knew that my time there was limited.

They never made me feel like an outsider. In fact, they went out of their way to ensure I was comfortable and secure. But the thing is that when you're living in a house with a family that isn't your own, you end up feeling awkward at times. The rules are different, the traditions are different, and the food is very, very different. For example, in Delhi, we used a lot of tomato in our food. I liked my daals and curries to be rich and tart. Here, they didn't use much tomato and it took me some time to get used to that. That's a small thing to complain about, I know. But remember, this was the farthest I had ever been from home and these little differences, especially in food, kept reminding me how unfamiliar this new place was.

The biggest thing that kept reminding me that this wasn't my home was the fact that they never accepted any money from me. Not for my stay—'How can we? Your mother is such an old friend of ours! —not for the food, and definitely not for making trunk calls home.

These calls were so expensive in those days and I couldn't do that to him. But nothing I said changed his mind.

One day, I was missing my mother and really wanted to speak to her. Aunty saw my face and understood that something was wrong.

'Uncle won't take money for my phone calls,' I said. 'So I don't feel right about making phone calls any more.'

Aunty laughed. Okay, she said. 'Make all the calls you want and give me the money. I won't tell Uncle.'

This made me feel much better. It also felt good to have a confidante who was like a mother in this strange, new city.

Eventually, the filming of *Gandhi* got over, and I started spending my days trying to make new contacts and find work.

Around that time, Aunty and Uncle decided to sell their house and shift to Agra. They were followers of the Radha Soami community and wanted to spend the rest of their lives doing seva. It was time for me to move out.

Neeru also got married to the man she loved. I was so happy for her because I was often present when she sat in front of her recorder and recorded loves notes on cassettes. It was just so romantic!

A lovely, positive girl, Neeru had a good life with this man but passed away a few years ago. She wasn't old, and I cannot even imagine what her family and kids must have gone through. As for me, I remembered all the advice she gave me about surviving the local trains and her voice . . . such a lovely voice, pouring her soul into countless cassettes.

I sometimes wonder . . . does her husband still have those old cassettes with her love letters to him? I sincerely hope he does.

* * *

I finally left Kala Nagar with mixed feelings. The Setias were lovely and I knew I would miss their warmth. But I was also happy to finally move into a house where I would be paying rent and buying my own food.

I found a nice enough accommodation in Khar West. It was a 'PG', and I would be sharing a room with another girl. The house was right in front of railway tracks, and when the trains went by, it felt like the whole house was vibrating. In the beginning I found it hard to sleep, especially at night when the area was quiet and trains sped by every three or so minutes. I'd stay up until the last local had passed before finally drifting off. Eventually, I got used to it. A few years later, when I moved out, I even missed the noise that used to lull me to sleep.

My landlady was a Sindhi lady. She was a widow and lived alone. She had three children, but they were all grown up and married. They lived in the city itself but rarely visited.

My rent was Rs 500 per month but this didn't include meals. But years of cooking for a big family had left Aunty incapable of cooking for just one person. She made big, lavish meals and always offered me a plate. We became good friends. She was the closest thing I had to a family during this time.

She wasn't in the best of health. She was overweight and found the climb up and down three flights of stairs very difficult. She trusted me and always gave me errands to run. Once, she was having a silent stand-off with another family in the building over who would get more water from the tank upstairs. It was one of those old buildings where water came only once a week, and there was a tap on the terrace which directed water to only one house at a time.

This particular neighbour, she told me, was cheating.

'They keep going to the terrace and turning the tap, so all the water goes to their house,' she huffed. But since the terrace was always locked, she would need to sleuth around to get access to the key. So, one day, she made up some excuse to get the key from the building's secretary. I watched with fascination as she pressed the key to a fresh bar of soap. She then handed me the soap and asked me to run to the key maker in Khar Market to get a copy made.

I was thoroughly impressed by this lady and did as I was told. She treated me to home-made badaam halwa when I returned. It was the best badaam halwa I had ever tasted.

We rarely suffered from water problems after that.

* * *

On the work front, I soon realized that being a struggler was everything they said it would be and much, much more. It was almost impossible to meet commercial film producers and directors. But the Art House Cinema directors were much more accessible. They were also making beautiful films in those days, so I started looking for ways to approach Shyam Benegal, Govind Nihalani and Saeed Mirza.

Everyone I met told me that as a newcomer, I needed to get a good professional photo shoot done. This is what we would take to our meetings with industry professionals.

This was a really expensive affair, and I didn't have much money. But there was a big photographer at that time, Jagdish Mali, whom I had met through some common friends. He lived in the same area as me and we were good friends. I begged him to take just a few pictures for a nominal fee, and because he was fond of me, he agreed. So, I finally got a good set of pictures that we shot on Versova beach.

I was finally feeling good about my chances of getting work thanks to these pictures. But turned out every director had their own way of selecting actors.

Subhash Ghai, whom I finally got an appointment with thanks to friends of friends of friends, didn't even glance at my pictures.

'Photos are not a real representation of how you look on screen,' he said, explaining how one could manipulate them to show only the best angles. I left feeling dejected.

I met Mani Kaul whose films weren't commercial successes but very intellectual on the whole. He set my picture aside without even glancing at it and asked me, 'Why should I cast you in my next film?'

'Because I'm a very good actor,' I said, confident of my abilities.

'Too bad,' he shrugged and looked away. 'I don't need actors in my films.'

I left feeling very confused. What did he mean? Was there an intellectual point he was trying to make that went over my head? What was I expected to say?

I was also introduced to Govind Nihalani whom I visited very often. He was a very nice man who was doing good work. I hoped that if he saw me enough, he would cast me in his next film. I would sit with him every day and we would chat for hours. When he started casting a play he was doing with lots of female actors, I was hopeful he would include me too. But he did not cast me, and I felt discouraged. He was a nice man and was very fond of me. So why didn't he want to cast me? When I think about it now, I realize none of my friends or acquaintances ever gave me work. We would sit together, chat and drink tea for hours. But when it came to their projects, they always chose other people.

I soon got to meet Basu Bhattacharya, whom we called Basu Da. He was a lovely man—very kind, encouraging and supportive. He had a beautiful sea-facing bungalow in Bandra with a lovely garden.

His wife and him had separated a few years ago but she still lived in the same bungalow. They had divided the house into two parts. It was on the first floor and she lived in the part that faced the road. His part had a spectacular view of the sea.

She was a lovely lady whom I was very fond of. But there was always some tension in the air and I often felt like they were asking us to pick sides. I didn't have the luxury of dilly-dallying and picked Basu Da because my only focus in life was to get work and he was a better candidate for that.

Every morning at 6.30 a.m., me and another struggler, Anuj Kapoor, Pankaj Kapur's brother, would go to Basu Da's house. He would serve us tea and biscuits and sit down to talk about his life, work and experiences. Anuj and I would listen, hanging on to every word he said. Every day we would tell ourselves that today is the day . . . the day Basu Da would say, 'I am making a new film and you will star in it!'

Anuj eventually gave up, but I continued to visit him, because I had grown very fond of our morning chats and who knew? He was a big filmmaker. Something had to come along eventually.

Along with this, I also started frequenting Prithvi Cafe which was a hub for strugglers in Bombay. It was where we got to meet producers, directors and, at times, even successful actors. My regular gang at Prithvi included Aditya Bhattacharya (Basu Da's son), whom we called Babla, and Aamir Khan.

In fact, Babla, who also aspired to be a director like his father, once made a silent short film that starred me and Aamir. Recently, I tried very hard to locate that film online because it would be amazing to revisit our younger, struggling selves, but I have had no luck so far.

Prithvi Cafe was run by Prahlad Kakkar, who was already a big adman at that time. He gave me small parts in his ads. One close-up here, one shot there and I would walk away with Rs 500–1000 for a day's work. This really helped me make rent and afford commutes to meet different people in the industry.

I was so regular at Prithvi that I would even help out with the running of the cafe in return for free food and tea. During the intermissions, I would make the famous Prithvi Irish coffee and serve snacks to customers. Once I made bharta and gave some to Prahlad. He loved it so much that he added it to the cafe's menu.

I was thrilled because for a while my bharta was almost as famous as the Irish coffee.

'Have you come to Bombay to be an actress or a waitress?' Sachin often asked me snarkily.

I hated when he said this because it demeaned the work I was doing. But I didn't let him affect me because in my heart I knew I was living on my terms and earning my own money.

'At least I'm not in debt,' I told him one day when I couldn't take it any more. 'I earn my own living and food. Unlike you who even borrows money for cigarettes.'

Eventually I did an ad that made me famous! Well, temporarily anyway, but it was great while it lasted. Prahlad cast me as the lead in an ad for Hawkins which became so famous, it actually went 'viral' by 1980s standards. It was a catchy song accompanied by a little dance that I did. The catchphrase went something like this:

'Hawkins ki seeti baji
Khushboo hi khushboo udi
Mazedar, lazzatdar, khana hai taiyar!'

Everywhere I went, people sang this part of the song to me. In schools and at birthday parties, kids were enacting the whole ad—the song and dance steps—in talent competitions. It was my first brush with fame, and I loved it.

Thanks to the money I was making from ads, I asked Aunty to let me rent the whole room instead of sharing it. For a while I had been uncomfortable with my roommate because I felt there was something shady about her.

She told us she worked at a beauty parlour nearby but refused to tell us the name. She often came home with bags of expensive clothes, shoes and jewellery. How much could one make at a beauty parlour, I wondered. I had to be really careful about money because I had to pay rent and take care of my food and travel. I couldn't remember the last time I went shopping because my mother, as always, bought all my clothes for me. In fact, even though my mother stuffed my bags with enough toothpaste, soap, dry fruit and snacks to see me through till my next visit, I barely had two pennies to rub together.

And here was this girl, coming home with something new every day. It didn't seem right.

I finally got my answer one day when the phone rang. There was a man on the other end, and he was asking about my roommate. She wasn't home so I asked him to call later. But before I could hang up, he started asking about me. What I did, how old I was . . . what I looked like. It was so strange, and it scared me a little.

'Oh don't worry about him,' my roommate told me later that night when I told her about the phone call. 'He's just my boyfriend. He owns a hotel nearby.'

I still felt uneasy, and, more importantly, I was scared for our safety. So I decided to do some digging. I visited a few parlours in the area and inquired about her but nobody knew her. I asked around some more and even dared to go towards the hotels she had mentioned the other day. That's when I found out that my roommate wasn't a parlour girl. She was a hotelier's mistress, which is why she could afford all those clothes and shoes.

I immediately told Aunty and begged her to let her go, and, because she trusted me, she did. I never saw that girl again and, thankfully, her boyfriend didn't call the landline either.

* * *

My patience and persistence with Basu Da finally paid off when he informed me that he was making a new television series called *Anveshan*.

It was a docuseries hosted by me and Javed Jaffrey. Followed by a filming crew, we would travel on a bike and visit different villages across India. The idea was to showcase how simple, pure and beautiful villages were as opposed to the cities which were fast gaining a reputation for being harsh, inconsiderate and corrupt.

The unit was small. We travelled in one van with the cameramen and crew. During filming, Javed and I rode ahead on a motorbike.

The show didn't have a big budget. Actually, it was pitiful. On good days we got to stay in a guesthouse that probably belonged to a collector or some well-to-do friend of Basu Da. But on others, we slept in a villager's house on the kitchen floor.

Even the food we ate was arranged from the homes of Basu Da's friends or bigwigs in the villages. The whole situation was far from comfortable. But when you're young and just starting off, you have to adjust and overlook these struggles. I filed them away as stories and adventures I would share with friends and family later on.

But there were some uncomfortable things about the shoot and the overall experience that even I could not ignore. The villagers, whom we were portraying as wonderful, generous and innocent on camera, actually expected to be paid to be featured in the series. The days we spent shooting weren't exactly what I had expected (far from it, in fact), so I was glad when we finally packed up and started the drive back to Bombay.

We woke up at 4 a.m. that morning and immediately filed into the van. We drove for hours without stopping at a rest stop for tea. It had been hours and we were all really hungry. Every time we asked Basu Da when we'd stop for breakfast, he would say, we'll stop ahead. But he just wouldn't let the driver stop.

What happened then is something I will never forget.

Finally, the driver stopped the van and got out.

'What happened?' Basu Da asked. 'Get back in and start driving.'

'No,' said the driver. 'I won't. I work really hard to fill my stomach. Why should I work if my stomach is going to be empty?'

We were all shocked by what he had said. Nobody spoke to Basu Da like that, ever. But in my mind, I agreed with him because

I was really really hungry and needed my morning cup of tea just as badly as he did.

To this day I remember this driver because what he had said was so amazing and innocent.

I empathized with him because for the past ten days we'd worked really hard and lived in uncomfortable conditions.

Basu Da stared at him for a while. I think he was shocked. But finally he laughed and said, 'Ok fine. Get in and drive us to the next dhaba.'

They say everything tastes like a feast when you are ravenous. Looking at us that morning, you'd think that we were having the biggest feast of our lives.

When we returned to Bombay, I slowly stopped visiting Basu Da because it felt like we were going back to our old ways. I would sit with him, hoping for work, and he would talk about everything under the sun, his garden especially, except projects. Who knows how many years I would have had to wait before he offered me another job? And what if the experience was as bad as the one on DD?

It was time now for me to focus on new prospects, different directors to get some work—if not my big break. My persistence paid off eventually as I got my first role in a full-length feature film that made me famous, but perhaps not in the way I was hoping.

2

Lallu Ladki

When you're young and a struggler like I was, all you dream of is your big break. If that doesn't happen, then you just pick the next best thing. Which is basically anything that puts you on the silver screen.

In 1982, I got cast in a film called *Saath Saath* starring Farooque Shaikh and Deepti Naval. It also starred Satish Shah and me in supporting roles. I was working with a lot of theatre groups in Bombay at that time and had met Satish and Farooque on multiple occasions when they were performing something with their troupe, Ipta. This was how I came to be recommended for this role.

My role was really small, but I was determined to make an impact. I was to play a young, nerdy girl in a gang of friends who wore big spectacles and kept saying, '*Main na kehti thi?*'

She was a Lallu Ladki. Cute, endearing but also slightly annoying in a know-it-all way.

I did a spectacular job of it. Everyone found my performance memorable. Everywhere I went, people mimicked the way I said 'Main na kehti thi?'. I enjoyed it for a while. Because it felt good to be on the big screen and get such great feedback on my acting.

But little did I know that Lallu Ladki would also kill me as an actor and would become one of the biggest regrets of my life.

At a party organized to celebrate the film's success, I met Girish Karnad. We knew each other from NSD where he was on the board.

'Did you like my acting in the film?' I asked him, giddy from all the compliments I had been getting all evening.

'You can do so much better than *that*, Neena,' he said seriously. 'Why did you take up this role?'

All evening, everyone had been saying what a good actor I was. How wonderfully I had played the part. Seeing Girish react like this, I didn't know what to say. I had taken the role because it was in a Bollywood film, and I thought it would lead me to my big break.

'You are now going to find it really hard to get cast as the lead,' Girish told me. 'Playing this role is going to typecast you as that nerdy, bespectacled, comic character and nobody is going to see you as a heroine.'

And to my utter dismay, that's exactly what happened. Every role I was offered after that was a variation of Lallu Ladki, wearing different outfits but saying the same catchphrase. Nobody could even picture me playing another character.

I can't remember how many of these roles I turned down, but there were so many that it made my head spin. I regretted *Saath Saath* every single day and often cried myself to sleep.

When a writer friend called me and offered me a role in a big production starring Rishi Kapoor, I thought I'd finally turned a corner. I agreed immediately and was so excited that I didn't even ask to see the script or what the role entailed.

But after I reached the set and started to shoot, I realized, a bit too late, that it was the same role. Lallu Ladki was still haunting me and there was absolutely nothing I could do about it.

I came home that night and cried. I cursed my luck and I cursed myself. I also cursed the person who had offered me the Lallu Ladki role to begin with and then I fell asleep still cursing the writer of the big production, whom I knew meant well but couldn't see that I was capable of much more.

He was and still is a dear friend and a wonderful man for what he did for me thereafter. I called him a few days after the shoot and begged him for the biggest favour. I asked him to cut me out of the film.

'Cut the role or recast it with someone else,' I said.

'Ok,' he said and removed the character from the film.

Thinking back, I realize I had paid more attention to my photo shoot than thinking about what roles I wanted to play. I just thought I'd come to Bombay, someone would spot how talented I was, and I would get good work.

But, after this film, I kept cursing myself because it wasn't the photographs I needed. I needed a guide. A mentor. I kept thinking about my interaction with Girish and what would have happened if I had spoken to him before accepting the role instead of after the film had released.

Even today, after reaching a good place in my career, I cannot get over this mistake I made because it feels so foolish and naive. I also wonder how many young men and women aspiring to be actors fall prey to this 'Lallu Ladki/Ladka curse' because they foolishly think that to be seen is more important than how they are seen.

In retrospect, I know it wasn't just the big break I was after. It was also the pay cheque because, lallu or not, the role helped me pay rent and buy food.

But if there's one piece of advice I can offer to young, upcoming actors, especially women, is not to be blinded by the here and now when accepting roles. Think about who you are and where you want to be in the future. Don't take up a role that offers you up as comic relief just for a pay cheque if that is not who you are. Back in the 1980s, we had few options in our career. Films and, to an extent, even television were limited back then.

Now, there are so many options for young actors. You have options in film, television and even the web. You can do shorts that are significant, and you can do videos online that showcase your talent. It's important to set the terms of your career and stick to them. But, more importantly, if you can, please find yourself a good, sensible mentor or guide.

Whatever you choose, don't just aspire to see yourself on the silver screen. Stop, breathe, consider . . . look at the bigger picture.

* * *

Sometimes I wonder whether '*Lallu Ladki play karke main actually lallu ban gayi*'. There's no other explanation I can think of for why I stayed with Sachin for as long as I did.

For a long time, Sachin and I were not doing too well. He was facing his own issues as a struggler and was finding it even harder than me to find work.

So, when Mandira moved to Bombay, he went back on his promise to never meet her again.

Her husband, a famous actor at the time, was doing really well and lots of actors approached her to act in a play with her troupe. They thought that if they played a role well and her husband happened to be there with a big producer or director, they would finally get spotted. Sachin also felt the same way.

'This could help me get noticed by her husband,' he would tell me. 'I have to be in her good graces.'

Soon Sachin told me that Mandira had given him a huge opportunity. Samarth was putting up *Desire Under the Elms* once again in Bombay and Sachin had been offered one of the lead roles. It was going to be performed at Prithvi Theatre.

'Her husband might attend, you know,' Sachin retorted to my protests. 'He might even bring a director.'

'Fine, go ahead,' I said, because I was honestly getting tired of the same fights over and over again. 'Maybe I will also join Samarth.'

And that is how I found myself, pride swallowed, standing in front of Mandira, asking to be part of the troupe.

'I'm sorry,' she said. 'But you're dating someone in my troupe, and it could complicate things.'

I knew this rejection wasn't because I had no talent, because I did, or experience. Mandira explained that because of my relationship with Sachin, it could create drama in the group.

I have faced a lot of rejection in my life, but Mandira's brush off still stings because I knew she was lying. She didn't want me to be a part of Samarth, not because of my relationship with Sachin, but because she didn't want me in her path when she went after him herself.

Sachin could work with her because she liked him. But I couldn't work with her because it would create tension? The whole situation struck me as bizarre.

As time went on, I continued to hustle for work to make ends meet. Sachin, on the other hand, got even more immersed in the troupe's activities and in Mandira's circle. The situation started to get worse when Sachin's friends, who were also my friends, started to tell me what all went on when I wasn't around. Rumours of Sachin having flings with multiple women would emerge, and I would be left feeling scared and shattered.

'Those are just rumours. There's nothing going on,' Sachin would say.

About Mandira, in particular, he would always say: 'It's all in your head. Remember, I'm not doing this for myself. I'm doing this for us and our future!'

But then one day, I clearly heard that Sachin and Mandira were together. That things had been 'happening' at rehearsals and at Mandira's house where the cast and crew hung out after the show.

'This has to stop,' I shouted. 'You have to tell me the truth.'

Sachin still maintained that nothing was going on between them. When I threatened to walk away, he promised me, once again, that he would cut all ties with her. He said that we were going to be together forever and that's all I should focus on.

So, I made him promise, once again, to cut all ties with her. Only then would I stay with him. He did.

Now, dear reader, you might think why did I continue to stay with a man who had proven time and again that he was a cheater. This is something I wonder about even today, so many years later. Why do we, as women, do this to ourselves? Was my sense of self-worth so low that I didn't think I could find someone better? Was I so in love with him that nobody else would do? I can't say for sure what the exact reason was. Maybe a bit of both—low self-esteem and love. But also maybe laziness? I didn't feel like I had the energy to try again.

But this question always haunts me. Every time I hear about women who are with men who cheat and/or abuse them, my heart breaks. Because I know what it's like to have someone come crawling back the next day with tears in their eyes and so many loving and apologetic things to say . . . I know what it's like to melt and say to yourself, '*Chalo, maaf kardo*. Everyone makes mistakes. Look at how sorry he is. He says he can't live with himself for doing this to me. He says he can't live without me.'

We got engaged a while later in a small ceremony in his house in Delhi. Before the ceremony, he promised me, once again, that he would never see her again. He also said that he would take me along to every event and social gathering to ensure my peace of mind.

What an idiot I was. Honestly, the signs of his infidelity had always been there, not for months, but years, and yet I had ignored all of them. When I couldn't turn a blind eye, I would confront him, and he'd tell me there was nothing and I would believe him. Why did I let it go on for this long? Why did I so readily believe him? Was I so desperate to hold on to what we had (whatever it was) just because I didn't want to lose him?

When you're young and you think you're in love . . . when you are with someone just because you don't want to suffer another break-up, you think differently. So, I just closed my eyes and said that I had to look ahead. I had to be positive. We had to get past this.

'We missed you at the party the other day,' a friend I ran into told me a few weeks later.

'What party?'

'The birthday party for Mandira's daughter?'

'Why would I be there? We're not friends,' I said and laughed to lighten the mood.

'Really? But Sachin was there. We thought you would come with him . . .'

My jaw dropped. Sachin went to Mandira's daughter's birthday party and didn't even have the guts to tell me?

This, for me, was the final straw.

'It was a child's birthday,' he said later that day when I confronted him. 'She personally called me. How could I refuse?'

I saw my future with this man then. Clear as day. This would never stop. The promises he made with a hand on his heart would be broken again and again. Mandira would always be part of Sachin's life. I would never be good enough for her troupe. She didn't like me and didn't want me around. Moreover, if it wasn't Mandira, it would always be someone else because over the years it hadn't been just one woman. Not to mention the fact that he had already cheated on me in the past and got caught.

If I married Sachin, this would be my life. I would be constantly suspicious, prone to gullibility and living in denial.

This wasn't the kind of person I wanted to be. Even when I narrate this part of my life today, I feel like whatever happened back then was strange, bizarre and very, very wrong. And I'm glad I decided to walk away from Sachin.

When you love someone with your whole heart, it doesn't matter even if you break up. Eventually, you're able to appreciate all the good times you had together because that love, though not as intense, was such a big part of your life and it never really goes away.

I have been in several relationships in my life. And I look back on all of them fondly, even if they did end, because there was some positivity while they lasted and they helped me in some way or the other. Unfortunately, this isn't the case with Sachin. We shared so much, even when we were just friends and rookies in Delhi and then as lovers and strugglers in Bombay. When I look back on this chapter of my life, I realize I only have bad memories of our time together.

The lying, the cheating, the manipulation . . . the affair with Mandira that almost broke me as a human being and made me question my talent as an actor. I am incapable of feeling anything but contempt for those memories.

Once I parted ways with Sachin, I didn't bother to keep in touch even though we still had many common friends. I would hear about him from friends. Occasionally, we would run into each other at parties, but while it was cordial between us, it was never warm.

When I moved on with my life, leaving Sachin to his own devices, I didn't bother to look back. I still wouldn't if I wasn't writing this book.

* * *

In 1983, I finally got cast in an Art House Cinema film. Shyam Benegal was making *Mandi* and he offered me a role. I was so happy because I felt like I could finally leave my previous mistakes in the industry behind. This was my chance to step out of the

With Om Puri in *Mandi*

garb of Lallu Ladki and don something new.

More importantly, after all that time of doing the rounds of directors and producers' homes and offices, which amounted to absolutely nothing, I was very excited to land a role in a Shyam Benegal production, which always had been a dream.

Mandi was a niche film and didn't draw crowds out in droves. But those who watched it, in fact cinema lovers even today, really liked the set, the story and the message.

It was a star-studded affair with Shabana Azmi, Smita Patil, Naseeruddin Shah, Kulbhushan Kharbanda, Om Puri, Saeed Jaffrey, Annu Kapoor, Satish Kaushik, Anita Kanwar. Among the newer artistes were Soni Razdan, Ila Arun and many others.

In the film, Shabana Azmi plays the madam of a brothel in the bustling part of a city that's visited by men from all walks of life, including politicians. Smita Patil, Soni Razdan, Ila Arun and I play prostitutes who live and work there. When a group of social workers takes up a morcha against the brothel, saying that it corrupts society and is detrimental to children, the politicians, including the ones who visit the brothel, eventually succumb to the pressure and force them to move. The women are given land in a remote area that has nothing around for miles. But slowly we see that men start visiting them again. Shops and establishments crop up. Soon, the area becomes a full-fledged township with public transport. The message is that wherever these women go, society follows.

The film was shot in Hyderabad and we all stayed at a hotel called Rock Castle. Us junior actors shared single rooms and, while it was a tight squeeze at times, it was a lot of fun. Soni was my roommate, and we soon formed a friendship that has lasted to this day.

I played a dancer in the film and had a very intense dance sequence to practise every morning in my room. I obviously couldn't do it while Soni was still asleep, so I would go up to the terrace with my loud ghungaroos on to practise. I can imagine what Soni must have gone through hear me practise on the terrace right above our room, but what to do? We were both so junior. We had to somehow tolerate each other.

I learnt a lot from Shyam Benegal. He is such a wonderful man, and also very curious and learned one. He would speak eloquently about art, world cinema, history and life. We used to joke that he knew everything. That if we asked him about the history of a safety pin, he would know that too.

He treated us young actors courteously but it took him some time to truly let us in. What I mean by this is that very often, he would host the senior actors in his rooms in the evening where they would discuss profound topics. How I longed to be part of this elite crew.

Shyam Benegal directing me in *Suraj Ka Satvan Ghoda*

Through the course of the filming, I did get opportunities to be part of some of these sessions. Shyam introduced me to a lot of fascinating subjects, including whiskey. It was with him that I took my first taste of whiskey—I wasn't much of a drinker before that—and while I didn't enjoy it at first, I soon came to appreciate it.

But of course, it wasn't all fun and parties. *Mandi* required us all to be very diligent and punctual. The schedule literally demanded that we arrive on set every day and sit through the shoot even if our parts were not being filmed.

So, all of us would arrive on set every morning and change into our nylon saris and pointed bras and hang around. When we got bored, we played cards or volleyball—yes, in those saris and bras. Satish Kaushik, who was constantly cracking jokes and making us laugh, would get very serious during these card games. 'It's the only time you have a straight face, Kaushikan,' I used to joke with him because he took these games very, very seriously.

We all needed to pass the time somehow because we had to wait for days, sometimes weeks, for our turn to shoot. But we didn't mind because we had such good company.

Speaking to Shyam could be quite intimidating, and I often found myself shying away from saying anything or making my opinions heard. Once, when I came down with high fever, I actually asked a friend to pass on the message to Shyam and request him, on my behalf, to postpone the shooting of my dance sequence.

Shyam, however, said he was not having any of it. The schedule was set, and there were a lot of other actors who had limited dates and had flown down only to be part of this sequence.

'I'm sorry, Neena,' he said. 'But you're going to have to work through your fever. The schedule cannot be changed.'

This took me back to NSD, when I had come down with a sore throat but Mr Karanth had still insisted that I perform. I just couldn't take it. I got very upset because I was in a very bad way. I cried to Shabana that Shyam was being unreasonable and inhumane. But Shabana consoled me and said it wasn't his fault. For actors, especially ones as new as me, it took time to appreciate the effort and coordination that went into a production like this. Some difficult choices had to be made to be a team player. Shabana too had had to work through sickness a few times in her career. But she had done it for the sake of the whole production.

This made me feel better, and while it was really difficult to look bright while feeling weak and miserable, I gave it my absolute best.

Shabana and Smita, two very different women with very distinct personalities, were wonderful to work with. I learnt a lot from them. I also admired Naseeruddin Shah immensely. I used to watch his scenes being filmed intently, because I felt there was just so much to learn from him.

Our evenings were often spent in Kulbhushan Kharbanda's room whom everyone called Kulji. He was doing really well, and, among all of us, he was the richest. He was very sweet and generous, so we'd make our way to his room where he'd treat everyone to alcohol and cigarettes.

I also developed a crush on Sujoy Mitra (name changed), who was assisting Shyam. Sujoy was really nice and very handsome. I was single at the time, so it was good to have this attraction to take my mind off the rigours of filming.

The bus ride from our hotel to the shoot location was where I first tried to catch his attention. The seating arrangement on the bus was more or less set. People usually sat in the same seats. So, one day, I got on the bus really early and got a seat to myself. Anyone trying to sit next to me was asked to go elsewhere because I wanted Sujoy to sit there. When he finally climbed on, I waved to him and said, 'You can sit next to me if you want!'

So he did. We had great conversations and shared lots of laughs during our commutes over the next two days. I thought his place next to me was set, but then one day he went and sat next to someone else.

I felt rejected and wondered what had gone wrong. Did he not like me? Had I said something stupid? Did I come on too strong?

I spent way too much time deliberating over what had gone wrong. Sujoy steered clear of me for the rest of the shoot.

We eventually became good friends. In fact, we're still very good friends even though we speak maybe once every few years. But it was only once we started getting more friendly and I summoned up the courage to ask him why he had stopped sitting next to me that Sujoy laughed and said that it wasn't something I had done that had put him off. It was just that he preferred men.

* * *

My landlady had a lot of rules about how we should live, what time we should return and, of course, her number one rule: no boys in the house. But I learnt that this rule was flexible depending on who the boy was. Or rather, how the boy looked.

Once Babla had some urgent work that couldn't wait. So he came to my house and rang the bell. Aunty opened the door and gave him a big smile. She asked him to sit in the hall and came to fetch me.

'Will you have some tea? Coffee? Snacks?' she asked.

But Babla politely refused because he felt if he stayed for too long, I might get into trouble.

'Such a nice boy,' she said after he left.

A few weeks later, Satish Kaushik rang the bell. He said namaste to Aunty when she opened the door and asked for me.

'Stay here,' she said and shut the door in his face. She came to get me and said, 'You know boys are not allowed, no? Please take him and go outside.'

So, Satish and I stepped out and had our chat at the juice stall down the road.

'I don't know why she was so rude to you,' I said to Satish after apologizing. 'She was so nice to Babla. Even offered him tea.'

Satish laughed at this and said he knew perfectly why.

'Babla is a tall, *gora chitta* boy, and I am short and *kala kaluta*. Aunty *ki chai sirf gore ladkon ke liye hai*,' he said. I laughed at this too. Satish has always been able to laugh at himself and make others laugh too. It's one of the many things I like so much about him.

Aunty suffered from a lot of health issues. But the most prominent one was her weight. She was obese and had trouble moving about too much. She also walked with a limp.

Also, in the 1980s, there was still a lot of stigma attached to widows. They were meant to wear only white and conduct themselves a certain way.

The station area where we lived was bustling with shops, restaurants, carts and stalls. I used to love going out in the evenings when I was home to get a glass of juice. One evening, just when I was about to leave, Aunty stopped me and handed me some money to bring back some juice for her.

'Why don't you come with me?' I asked, suddenly excited at having her for company.

'No, no. I can't. What will people say?' she brushed me off.

'What do you mean?' I asked, confused.

'People will say, look at this widow, going out with her young PG to drink juice and have fun.'

I was shocked when she told me this. My heart also broke for her because I realized that even though she was very active and independent, not to mention earning her own money by renting her room to me, she still felt she was answerable to society. That she had to watch what she did, or rather didn't do, so people didn't get the impression that she was living a good life even though her husband was no more.

From then on, I started to feel even more affectionate and protective towards her. I started bringing her juice even when she didn't ask for it. She showed her love for me by frequently making me badaam halwa, which was her specialty.

This, however, changed soon enough when my parents came to visit me in Bombay. They came to the house, and Aunty was really nice and pleased to meet them. They chatted for hours, and Aunty fed us all really well.

I was very comfortable in that house. But my mother looked around her and couldn't take that I was living like 'that'. Born and brought up in Delhi, we always lived in a house, not an apartment. We had enough rooms and bathrooms for everyone. We had running water 24/7! And we most definitely didn't live adjacent to a very active and loud railway track.

My mother was a very practical woman. She realized that if I were to live in Bombay, I would need my own house.

'Why do we need to wait to give Neena her inheritance,' she told my father. 'She needs it right now!'

And that's how they bought me a house in Sher-E-Punjab colony, and I moved out and started living on my own.

* * *

In 1983, when I was cast as Priya in *Jaane Bhi Do Yaaro*, I honestly didn't know I would become part of one of the most iconic films in Indian cinema.

The film, directed by Kundan Shah, starring Naseeruddin Shah and Ravi Baswani, was funded by the National Film Development Corporation of India (NFDC) and was made on a shoestring budget.

But we all had such a ball filming it! Most of us had a theatre background so our approach to work was very similar. We were used to giving every scene our best, even if it was just a rehearsal. In fact, even before we got on the floor to shoot, we were made to rehearse the entire script much like we would do for a play. This actually helped Kundan edit a lot of parts, because he was able to better visualize the film as a whole.

My character was originally cast opposite Ravi's, and I was very excited at the time, because it meant I'd have a bigger role. But that development was cut out of the final script, because the film was getting too long and it added no value to the story. I was a bit disappointed, but it hasn't ruined my memories from that time.

We shot all over Bombay, in Film City and even went across the bay to Alibaug. In fact, our schedule in Alibaug was so tight that we once shot for thirty-six hours straight. This was where the cake scene—'*thoda khao, thoda phenko*'—was shot. Since this was a small-budget film, there were only two rooms that were split between the actors and the crew. Whenever we got a few hours between our scenes, we would go to the rooms and grab a corner to get some shut-eye. But in no time at all, we would be shaken awake to shoot again. Not everyone got to take naps though. At one point, when they were testing out the lights, we saw our cameraman rest his forehead on the camera and fall asleep briefly.

Kundan Shah had a very clear vision of how he wanted the film to turn out. This meant that he thought of little to nothing else during the entire time. He was constantly pushing us to do better, move faster and, in general, keep up with him—and he was difficult to keep up with.

'Chalo, chalo, chalo, chalo,' got engraved in our brains and we'd dread hearing those words. One time, at Film City, I had just picked up a plate to eat lunch when I heard him shout these words. I left my plate untouched and so did many of my co-stars. We didn't moan or bitch about this though because Kunan was a great man and wonderful to work with. Also, we would have so much fun on set.

That Mahabharata scene, which many people tell me is their favourite, was so much fun to shoot because even though it depicted chaos, it was very smoothly done. We honestly had a blast!

Even now when I watch the film or just a clip once in a while, I'm always struck by how young we all looked and, yes, the fact that all my costumes in the film were my own clothes.

Diehard fans of *Jaane Bhi Do Yaaro* still find it hard to believe that the film got a lukewarm response at the time. 'We can watch it 100 times and never get bored,' they say.

But once the film wrapped up, it was back to reality for me. By the end of that year, I was struggling to get work once again . . . Looking for my next role that would hopefully land me a lead role in future.

3

Home, At Last

Having my own house was liberating. I could come and go as I pleased and didn't have any restrictions. I missed Aunty, but I also knew that living in my own house was a step closer to growing up.

I was still struggling to find steady work, but having a place that I could call my own really lifted my spirits.

The house, a one BHK in Andheri East's Sher-E-Punjab colony, was on the second floor and really, really tiny. I mean, it was so small that there was barely any room to move around once I shifted in my furniture.

The drawing room was small. The kitchen was just a little kitchenette. The bedroom was as big as my four-poster bed. It was just too claustrophobic.

So, I decided to tear the walls down and make everything part of one room. It came to resemble what would now be called a studio apartment, and I absolutely loved it.

Andheri East in those days was still being developed. In fact, the colony itself was not fully built. Buildings were still being erected and there were barely any residents.

But I was lucky because an old friend from Delhi, Rajesh Puri, lived in the apartment right opposite mine on the same floor (there were only two apartments per floor) with his wife. The apartment on the floor above us was occupied by Rajesh's uncle, who would in time become like my own uncle.

We even had actor Shekhar Suman, who was quite famous at the time and doing very well, living in one of the apartments on the ground floor of my building with his wife and children.

The colony, though sparsely populated at first, was very active in organizing *kirthans*. The residents loved to attend these because it gave them an opportunity to exchange news and gossip. They especially loved to discuss Shekhar Suman, who was often visited by famous actors, producers and directors.

'Do you know who came today?' they would ask while the kirthan was going on. 'Did you see what she was wearing?'

Things were still a bit difficult because I didn't have a telephone and had to walk fifteen minutes to the main road—to what's now the Western Express Highway—to make phone calls. The neighbours could also be very nosy and judgemental at times.

I honestly don't think about what people will say when I decide to do something. Especially when I know in my heart that my intentions are good and I have nothing to be guilty for.

When my old friend from NSD, Deepak Qazir, needed a place to stay for a few days, I didn't even blink before opening my tiny home to him. It was cramped with two people in it. But we still made it work. I didn't think what people would say.

Deepak is one of the most wonderful people I have ever met. Even in college, he was always there for us girls. He would be the sole boy in a group of girls in a disco, protecting us from strange, unknown men. He had been living in Bombay for a while and looking for work. He was also struggling like me. Very briefly, he had been without a home and had to sleep on a train station platform. One morning, he woke up on the platform and found that the person next to him was dead. This incident shook Deepak, and he went back to Delhi to recover from the trauma. After he returned to Bombay, still looking for work and a home, he stayed with me. Deepak had always been there for me, and now I wanted to be there for him. I would never let a friend of mine go through something like this if I could do something to help.

But even though Deepak slept on a mattress by the door, and I slept in my four-poster bed, tongues began to wag in the colony. Young, unmarried woman living with a man? Some nasty things were being said about me. But I did not care one bit. My intentions were pure, and my conscience was clean.

Overall though, I was happy in Sher-E-Punjab. It felt like a very grown-up phase of my life had begun and being surrounded by more mature people and having a good, positive support system was amazing.

I was still going around trying to meet industry bigwigs, spending time at Prithvi and getting some work. Thanks to my mother, who ensured I had a lot of kitchen duties and did chores around the house while growing up, I was also able to cook for myself very well. I would wake up in the morning, cook and then spend the day out. Somedays I would eat out, but since I have a very delicate stomach, I would try to cook as many meals as possible, or eat what had been sent over from Rajesh or his uncle's house.

Even though I had been living on my own in Bombay for a while, this was the first time I truly felt like an independent and responsible adult.

But one day, when I visited a parlour to get my waxing done, the parlour lady noticed some bumps on my arm.

'Can I see your stomach?' she asked, even though I only wanted to get my arms and legs waxed. I was a bit stunned but also worried because the bumps she was referring to weren't there the night before, and I had barely even noticed them.

When she saw the same bumps on my stomach, she said, 'You cannot get your arms and legs waxed today. You have measles.'

Measles? How? Didn't I have measles as a kid? I was fairly certain I did. At least that's what my mother had told me.

So, I quickly walked over to a phone booth and placed a trunk call to my mother.

'Did I have measles as a child?'

'Yes, you did. Why are you asking?'

I told her that I might have measles and she immediately asked me to go to a doctor.

'Do you want me to come there?' she asked.

'No, it's okay. Don't trouble yourself,' I said, but in reality I really wanted my mother around. To take care of me, feed me and pamper me like she did when I was a child. But I also didn't want to trouble her. Coming to Bombay had been my decision, and I needed to prove to my parents that I could make it on my own. That I was grown up and fully capable of taking care of myself. Asking my mother to come and take care of me felt like an admission that I didn't have my act together.

I went to a doctor who confirmed that I did have measles. It was rare for the virus to recur as an adult, but it wasn't unheard of. And that's how I found myself quarantined in my house for almost a month with nothing to do.

I couldn't read or watch TV, because the virus had spread painfully to my eye. I couldn't meet anybody and nobody could come visit me, because it was contagious. I couldn't call anybody on the phone because I didn't have a phone. I couldn't cook because I had absolutely no energy.

My kind neighbours supplied me with food, so I didn't go hungry. But I was starving for some company. A bit of love and affection.

One afternoon, I was lying on the mattress I had put on the floor of my living room. I had left the door ajar and was listening to the sounds of a radio playing somewhere and trying to catch any signs that indicated that there was still life outside in the world.

Right then, I heard something that drew my attention, wandering everywhere and nowhere at the time, to the staircase.

I heard someone say 'Ufff . . .', and I understood it was someone elderly person who had trouble climbing up the stairs. Then I heard a sound uttered in a voice that unmistakably belonged to someone I knew.

Could it be? I didn't dare get my hopes up.

A few seconds later, my mother emerged from the staircase and stood there with her bags and baggage, smiling broadly at me.

She had come after all! She had come all the way from Delhi and up two flights of stairs to take care of me.

I hadn't realized how alone and miserable I had been during my illness. I felt like a child again when she took me in her arms—reassured by her presence. She spent the next few weeks taking good care of me. She cooked for me, kept me entertained with stories from our neighbourhood in Delhi and ensured I was always comfortable. Having her there really speeded up my recovery, I felt.

I have many memories of my mother from the time I was a little girl to when I grew up. But I think this memory of our time together because of my illness is by far the best.

* * *

In *Trikal*, which was released in 1985, I had my heart set on playing the lead character, Anna.

The main star of the film was, of course, Leela Naidu, who had been a big name in the 1960s, making her mark with films like *Yeh Raaste Hain Pyaar Ke*. It also starred Naseeruddin Shah, Nikhil Bhagat, Anita Kanwar, Soni Razdan, Ila Arun and Kulbhushan Kharbanda.

Anna's role wasn't very challenging, but playing it wasn't about showing off my acting abilities. It was about the prestige of being the main heroine in a film.

With Nikhil Bhagat in *Trikal*, directed by Shyam Benegal

It meant that people would get a chance to see me without their 'Lallu Ladki' glasses.

We lived in Goa for two months and filmed in the house of an iconic artist, Mario Miranda. What a beautiful house it was! It was very reflective of the Portuguese style of architecture and even had a basement where they said people were sometimes hidden during the Portuguese colonization.

The film is a love story, but also has very strong themes about family, secrets and ancestry. Set during the Portuguese colonization of Goa in the 1960s, it revolves around Dona Maria Souza-Soares, played by Leela Naidu, the matriarch of the family who comes unhinged after the death of her husband. She uses her maid, Milagrinia, as a medium to call forth her husband's spirit, but instead the wires keep getting crossed and only spirits of those wronged by the family come forth.

I was very excited to be playing the role of Leela Naidu's character's granddaughter. I had worked with Shyam in so many films, and I'd been patiently waiting for a lead role. It felt like I was finally getting my dues.

But a few days after we arrived in Goa, Shyam called me aside and said that he wouldn't be giving me the role of Anna. I would instead play the maid, Milagrinia. At the time, I was very scared to ask him why he had changed his mind, but a few years and many films—including an hour-long ad film on the benefits of soya bean oil for DD—later, I summoned up the courage to ask him.

'Why didn't you give me the role of the main girl?' I asked him, still stinging from the rejection. 'Did you not think I would do a good job?

'Not at all,' he said. 'I just thought the role of Anna would be very easy for you. This role was challenging for an actor of your calibre.'

Mollified and also a little flattered, I tried not to let my bitterness get the better of me any more.

The role of Anna finally went to Sushma Prakash, and I ended up playing a maid who is also an illegitimate child of the malik of the house. In those days, it was very common for maliks to have affairs with their house help, and while many would chuck the maids out if they got pregnant, it wasn't uncommon either for them to keep the children in their homes, take care of them but also use them as slaves.

My character also ends up having an affair with Anna's love interest, Ruiz (Nikhil Bhagat played him as a young man and Naseeruddin Shah the older character, who is also narrating the story). She gets pregnant but, of course, doesn't have a happily ever after because she is, after all, a servant.

I was very put off having to play this role because Girish's words after *Saath Saath*—that I would never get the lead part—kept ringing in my ears.

It stung even more because everyone in the film was dressed in very stylish clothes from the 1960s Goa—floral frocks and cute skirts with blouses. A lot of the outfits had once belonged to Leela Naidu, a very elegant and stylish woman, who donated her own personal collection to the film. I, on the other hand, got to wear only a black-and-white pinafore dress with an apron.

But once the filming began, as usual, we lost ourselves in our work and soon the unit was like a proxy family again.

As with all of Shyam's films, we all had to report to the set every day dressed and ready to roll. Many of us had to wait for days and weeks to shoot, so we spent our time enjoying the sounds and scenes of Goa. Some days, the boys would bring chilled beers to the shoot and at night, we would go to a shack to enjoy some music and great food. Our house also had a cafe-like setting right outside where they sold kaju feni. They sold a peg for Re 1. Feni, I think, is a very acquired taste. The smell was just too strong for us. But we didn't have much of a choice because we were all short on cash. So, we used to buy pegs of feni and gulp them down with RimZim, a masala cola drink that is sadly not available any more, which cost Rs 2.

My dear friend Soni was also part of the film, so we often found ourselves walking on the beach. One day, Soni suggested we go sunbathing. I was a very conservative girl and didn't really know what sunbathing was.

'It's when you put on your bikini and lie on the sand,' Soni told me.

It didn't sound like the most comfortable thing to do, but I agreed because there was very little to do anyway.

So, we wore our bikinis and took off to the beach when the sun was at its peak. By evening, I was really uncomfortable. The prickly heat was making me itch all over and, to Shyam's utter horror, we had tanned.

'This is going to be a continuity problem, you know that right?' he said. We got a verbal lashing that evening and were banned from visiting the beach, except in the evenings when the sun had set.

One day, while filming, a senior actor on set, with whom I was working closely, had a change in attitude towards me. I didn't know if she just got too immersed in her role and started taking it too seriously, but, for some reason, it seemed like she was picking on me.

She started ordering me around, and speaking a bit rudely. She kept asking me to follow her even when the cameras weren't rolling. I didn't like it one bit. So, I went to Shyam and requested him to intervene.

'Why?' he asked. 'She's gotten into her role. The scenes are coming out well. Go with it. It'll be good for your role as well.'

I didn't want to argue with Shyam over this, so I bit back my retorts and just went with it.

This actor, we all knew, had once been among the greats in Indian cinema. But her life hadn't been easy. She had married a man who had abused her and the trauma of that still showed in her mannerisms. She also had a drinking problem, which is why Shyam had warned us all that we shouldn't sit with her in the evening— after the shoot, we'd all gather to drink, eat and basically just let our hair down.

He wanted to keep her sane and sober during the shoot, so I understood that keeping our distance would prevent us from unwittingly enabling her problem.

She was also prone to fits of rage and at times would take it out on all of us. One day, one of her lipsticks went missing. Apparently, it was a very special limited edition shade that had been specially ordered from Paris. The actor was livid and Shyam was caught in the crossfire.

She was yelling on the set, asking for it to be returned. Threatening the 'thief' that they would not get away with it.

Finally, Shyam took us aside and asked if any of us had the shade that matched her description. Soni, fortunately, did. So Shyam took the lipstick from Soni and gave it to the actor, who seemed placated.

'I promise I will replace it once this is all over,' Shyam whispered to Soni. It was a crazy thing to happen on set. But it was also a bit funny.

That's just how things are while filming. Sometimes bizarre things take place, and we walk away with stories for life.

Overall, I look back on my time in Goa and know that I had a great experience filming *Trikal*. I didn't get the role I wanted. But I was happy that I got to intimately experience Mario Miranda's beautiful home—something not a lot of people get to do otherwise— and I made some very good friends too.

Nikhil Bhagat, not exactly my love interest in the film, but someone whom my character has to submit to, was a wonderful human being.

The scene where we had to roll around in hay was shot by Shyam with great care and sensitivity. There were only four people on set apart from Nikhil and I, so the whole thing was very comfortable. But once the scene was over, both of us were itching all over. Our naked bodies had been pricked and poked by dry hay and we were going crazy.

'Let's go wash up on the beach,' Nikhil suggested, and I happily agreed.

This was a terrible idea because the salt water stung us even more and our bodies were covered in red patches. We finally decided to head to our rooms and take a normal, cold water bath. This helped a bit, but our skin burnt and itched for days after.

After all that we'd been through, the scene didn't even end up in the final cut. Apparently, some part of my body that shouldn't have been seen was quite prominent on camera, and Shyam decided against using it. It wasn't obscene and definitely didn't involve nudity, but that was the thing about Shyam and many other directors in those days. They didn't use romance, and especially not lovemaking scenes, to titillate the audience and sell tickets. If it worked in the final cut, they would keep it. But if it didn't work or further the story, the scene would end up in the archives.

Nikhil and I ended up becoming very good friends after this film. He was a wonderful person and a promising up-and-coming actor. But due to some family commitments, he quit his career in films and returned to Calcutta after a while and we sort of lost touch over the years.

* * *

I may not have played the lead in *Trikal*, but I did get an opportunity that no one else in the cast got.

Trikal was picked up for screening at a film festival in Rio de Janeiro, Brazil, and Shyam decided to take me along! It was an all-expense-paid trip, which included flights from Bombay (via London) to Rio and stay at a very posh hotel. I was very excited because I had never been abroad before. And the fact that I was travelling to such an exotic location on my very first trip abroad had me dancing for days!

With director Shyam Benegal in Rio De Janeiro for the screening of *Trikal*

We flew British Airways (BA) to London, and after a stopover at Heathrow, we boarded Varig Airlines straight to Rio. It was a funny experience for me, because I was expecting BA, considered a posh airline, to pamper us like crazy. Instead Varig gave us such good service that we just couldn't believe how lucky we were. For example, on BA, we were served drinks that were smaller than the smallest pegs. We had to literally request them to pour a little more. But on Varig, they poured us such large drinks that we had to ask them to stop.

Rio was such a beautiful city that I felt I could just admire it all day. The shopping arcades were amazing, and you could tell that all the clothes and colours were suited exactly to brown and dark brown skin. I also couldn't believe how beautiful the women were. They were stunning, dusky and many were of mixed race. They had the most beautiful skin and stood tall. I should have been jealous, but it was impossible when you saw how freely they smiled.

When we checked into our hotel, the staff gave us a long briefing on the dos and don'ts around Rio. 'Don't carry too much cash. Keep all your valuables in the locker in your room. Stay away from certain areas when going out alone, etc., etc.' It was a long list and we abided by all their rules.

We were met at the hotel by Uma Da Cunha, a dear friend of Shyam's whom I also became good friends with. She was part of the film committee and showed us around a bit.

In the beginning, I felt very shy and didn't want to make too many demands. I tried to keep a low profile even around Shyam, because I didn't want him to regret bringing me along on this trip.

It was hard though, because when I scanned menus in restaurants or our hotel's buffet, there wasn't even a single vegetarian dish to be found. I once found something that I thought was black daal, but it tasted kind of funny. When I asked the waiter what they had put in it, he said it was beef stock, and I almost threw up my entire lunch.

Shyam was very considerate. He tried to take me shopping but I didn't want to buy anything. I didn't have much money and I didn't want him to think he had to do me a favour by paying for any of it. But Shyam was really kind. He sensed how awkward I was and told me, one morning, to go to his locker and take as much money as I liked to buy myself something nice. I told him I couldn't, but he insisted. So, I went to his locker and took very little money and headed out to the markets. I didn't pick up anything too expensive though. Just two or three simple dresses and a skirt.

As the festival was about to begin, we sat down to analyse how to plan our days and which films to watch. But then Shyam had other ideas.

'We can watch these films any time we like. But we will never get to come back to Brazil,' he said. And so, we decided to skip a few days of the festival and go travelling. *Trikal* wasn't being screened until the end of the festival, so we decided to return before that.

I'm so glad we made that decision because we got to go to Manaus, Brazil's home to the Amazon river. We took the most amazing trip down the river, an experience like no other. The water, black as cola, would suddenly shift into a different colour because of the sediment and soil run-off. For a while, it would be completely black, and then, without so much as a shade change, it would turn bright yellow.

We returned to Rio via Sao Paulo a few days later and started preparing for our premiere. We spent a sleepless night when we found out that our film was still stuck in customs, which was quite strange because a film being held back was unheard of. But Uma Da Cunha stepped in and pulled some strings to get it released.

Our premiere was underwhelming because there was hardly anyone in the audience. Uma said this was okay, because the local crowd preferred more commercial films to Art House. But we still felt bad about it at the after-party.

Our trip finally came to an end and it was, to date, the best I have ever experienced. Shyam Benegal was, as I have mentioned before, very intellectual, worldly and knowledgeable. Having him as a travel partner not only enriched my experience but also left me with a whole new perspective of this beautiful world. For this, I will be forever grateful to him and *Trikal.*

* * *

I was starting to feel good about myself as an actor and, having put so much into my roles with Shyam, hoped against hope that he would cast me as the lead in his next film. After every project we did together, I'd tell myself, next time. Next time. Next time. But unfortunately, it was never to be.

After *Trikal,* Shyam cast me in *Yatra,* a fifteen-part TV series for DD, which aired in 1986.

Filming *Yatra* was magnificent because we got to live and film almost entirely on the Himsagar Express—one of the longest running trains of the Indian Railways that travels from Kanyakumari to Kashmir.

The journey was an enjoyable experience as we were getting to visit places in India that we would not otherwise get an opportunity to see.

The series starred Om Puri as well and we'd often spend time with Shyam Benegal in his private coupe, which was in the last compartment of the train. We loved to sit in the little sitting area of his plush room and watch the landscape go by. Shyam was also very generous and ensured that the food that was cooked on the train was top-notch.

The actors had been put up in coupes too and soon enough we personalized our spaces with little trinkets and other memorabilia we'd picked up from various stations on the way. The three best things about this experience were: 1) the trip itself because it was all shot while the train travelled up north; 2) the entire train was reserved for us; 3) the fact that we were getting to act in a very exciting series.

I had a double role in this series. I played a pregnant Punjabi woman who goes into labour on the train and also a Rajasthani woman. We didn't just shoot inside the train but also got to step out and film at local attractions and monuments. The best part about this was that we got to pick up a little something from everywhere we went.

In Kochi, when we went to Jew Street, I discovered a quaint little furniture store. I fell in love with an antique piece, triangular in shape, made of solid heavy wood. But I was in two minds whether to buy it because I didn't know how to get it to Bombay. But Shyam just waved his hand at me and said it could travel on the train with us.

'The whole train is ours,' he said. 'It's like we own it. Go ahead and buy it. We'll keep it in storage until Bombay.'

I am so glad he did that because that cupboard is still with me in my house. It's been painted white over the years and is one of my favourite things.

As *Yatra*'s shooting came to an end, the fact that I had been cast by Shyam, once again, but still not as the lead, started to really grate on me.

After years of loyalty and hard work, I really felt like I should be the heroine. I was hungry for bigger roles. But it was also not entirely Shyam's fault, or anyone else's.

I was young and lacked guidance. I kept making the wrong decisions. I also needed the money, so I couldn't afford to be picky about the roles I played. Lallu Ladki was like a curse that followed me around for a large part of my career, and I feel like there's no one to blame for that except me.

* * *

In 1984, I met Shankar Nag for the very first time on the sets of *Utsav*, a period film based on the Sanskrit play *Mrichakatika* (The Little Clay Cart) by Śūdraka.

The film also starred Rekha, Amjad Khan, Anuradha Patel and Shekhar Suman. It was produced by Shashi Kapoor and was very beautifully designed to represent the period it was set in—around fifth century BCE. The director of the film was Girish Karnad.

The film was shot in Manipal, and I was in awe of the detailing of the sets and our costumes. As one of the young women in the film, who was playing the role of a servant, my costume was just a cloth to cover my chest and a tiny skirt at the bottom. The Sanskrit student in me was absolutely thrilled because I knew a lot of the language, the costumes and phrases. Moreover, I had studied *Mrichakatika* as a text and was excited to see how it would translate on screen.

With cameraman Ashok while filming *Utsav*

Shankar Nag, a very well renowned actor and producer in the Kannada industry, played a thief in the film and also my love interest. Thievery was an artform in the century this story was written. They called it 'Chaur Vidya'. Every thief at the time had their own signature move and they left behind signs in the houses they robbed. It was called 'Saindh', which could be a hole in the wall shaped like a bird or something they left behind.

My character, the servant girl Madanika, lusts after Shankar Nag's Sajjal. We had to shoot a very erotic lovemaking scene which was set to the sound of beats, counts and breath.

Sajjal breaks in to steal something and enters Madanika's room. She's stunned to see him and asks him to run away before someone else sees him. He tells her to count till twenty, because it will take him seventeen counts to make love to her and then another three to run away. On screen, the scene was very charged and erotic. In person though, I was really nervous, shy and awkward. Dubbing for this scene was even more difficult because I had to make very heavy, breathy sounds while counting and we had to keep redoing it until Girish was happy with the result.

Shankar Nag was a big name in the Kannada industry, and I was very nervous to work with him. Was he a nice man? Did he have the airs of a big star? What if something made me uncomfortable and I couldn't say anything?

Girish could see that I was very nervous and unsure. He didn't want that translating on to screen. So, he called up Shankar and requested him to arrive on set two days before we were to shoot so that we could get acquainted with each other.

So, Shankar and I met for the first time and had a meal together on set. It was very funny and strange for both of us because while we were courteous, we didn't hit it off or become too chatty or friendly. There was just too much pressure on us, and it made us feel even more awkward around each other.

The day we were to shoot the scene, Girish did everything to make sure that I was comfortable and that the whole thing was treated very tastefully. It also had to look like I wasn't wearing anything on top, so Girish asked everyone who didn't absolutely have to be present to leave. The lighting people had set the scene up in advance. The assistants did their part and left. No still photographs were shot either. In the end, there were only about four people on set, including the sound recordist and the cameraman.

Girish was an educated man with a very good eye. This really came through while filming because the end product was tender and sweet, just the way he had visualized it.

Shankar Nag was a very decent man (I was also very decent, by the way!)

Our interactions before the scene had been cordial, but not very friendly. But after the scene, we sort of became more comfortable around each other. I guess the awkwardness of doing a lovemaking scene with someone you have only just met can sometimes be the start of a beautiful friendship.

We used to joke about our time on set and even laugh at how everyone tried to get us to get too friendly too fast. But there's nothing like an actual sex scene on camera to forge a lifelong friendship.

Shankar Nag and I were dear, dear friends. He was a wonderful human being. He was very famous, but he never put on any airs in front of his friends. He was a *'yaaron ka yaar'*. He never discriminated between friends who were famous and struggling even though he was such a successful person himself.

Utsav didn't do well at the box office. A lot of people found it too erotically charged and panned it. But honestly, I think it was a beautiful film that was way ahead of its time. I am really proud to have acted in it, and till date, I think it's among the best scripts I have ever been part of.

* * *

When I look back to those days, I really wonder how we got any work done without phones. I used to walk for fifteen minutes to the highway to make phone calls. It was a very different time and we managed, but it was also inconvenient and stressful because I always wondered if I was missing out on offers because I didn't have a phone.

I heaved a huge sigh of relief when my application for a telephone in the Sher-E-Punjab house finally got approved and I got a landline. I even got a gas connection at the same time, and having these two finally made me feel more permanent in Bombay. Like I belonged.

My landline rang one morning, and I answered it with a big smile on my face. It was so good to hear that ring which was meant only for me and nobody else. From the other end came a deep, sexy voice that made me feel like a giddy schoolgirl.

'Hello,' it said. 'Can I speak to Neena Gupta, please?'

'Yes, this is Neena Gupta. Who's calling?'

'This is Satyajit Ray.'

Oh my god, my heart just jumped to my throat. My landline rang, and it was a call from THE Mr Ray! He had a role for me, he said. His son, Sandeep Ray was making a series of short films and he wanted to cast me in one of them.

I said yes immediately and spent the rest of the day calling my family and friends to tell them about it.

We shot in Calcutta (now Kolkata) in this quaint little bungalow. They put us up in Kenilworth Hotel, which was plush, green and luxurious. Even Girish Karnad and a few other actors from Bombay's film scene were there so we immediately got together.

We arrived the day before the shoot was to begin. After settling in and freshening up, we went over to Mr Ray's house for tea and samosas. We were then invited to noted theatre personality Shyamanand Jalan's home for dinner.

I came back to my room feeling amazing and went straight to bed. I had to rest up for my shoot the next day. But later that night, I woke up with the worst stomach ache. I quickly ran to the bathroom and threw up. For the next three hours, my guts wrenched out of my system as I had diarrhoea. It was the absolute worst case of food poisoning I'd ever had.

I didn't want to disturb anyone but as I started to feel faint and found my legs giving way under me, I picked up the phone and called Girish Karnad. I told him my condition and asked him to call a doctor.

Girish came over to my room and took a look at me. His wife was a doctor, so he knew a thing or two about these things. He immediately called room service and asked them to send up a home remedy that would control my sickness at least until they could get a doctor.

'Don't worry,' he told me. 'I'll call Mr Ray and tell him the situation. You are in no state to shoot.'

I cried so hard after he left because I felt like this was my fault.
Mr B.V. Karanth's words kept coming back to me. 'Your body is
your instrument. You cannot let it go. You cannot afford to let
yourself get sick.'

The next morning, a doctor came to examine me and asked me
to rest it out. I tried to insist that I should go shoot. I couldn't stay
in bed and inconvenience the whole unit.

But even Mr Ray was having none of it. They asked me to rest
up and see how I felt the next day. Girish even offered to switch his
dates so that he could stay a few extra days if it meant I got better.
I couldn't let that happen. The next day, still slightly ill and weak,
I went to the set to shoot my scenes.

I was so embarrassed and felt like a complete screw up. I didn't
know how I was going to face the cast and crew after having them
cancel the previous day just for me. But everyone was really, really
nice. They got me a chair to sit on, they asked me what I wanted to
eat, kept someone by my side to keep me hydrated at all times. It
brought tears to my eyes.

Mr Ray came to visit the sets to see how things were going and
sat down to chat with me. He spoke to me so warmly, like we were
old friends. I was in awe of him and couldn't believe that the man
who had made such iconic films was sitting next to me and talking
to me like I was an old friend. We had a wonderful conversation and
even gossiped and laughed.

I came home a few days later feeling wonderful about my
experience and thanking my lucky stars for my landline. Without
it, I don't know. I might have missed this beautiful opportunity in
Calcutta.

4

Khandaan

In 1985, I was cast in a series called *Khandaan* on Doordarshan. The serial was way ahead of its time and is reminiscent of shows such as *Dallas* and *Dynasty*.

I was sitting at Prithvi Cafe, drinking an Irish coffee, when I met Sridhar Ksheersagar. He told me the premise and I immediately knew that I wanted to play the role of Ketaki, a modern, strong-willed woman who is trying to break all barriers.

Ketaki was not a character you saw often on screen. She wanted more from life than being a housewife. She wanted a career. She refused to have kids. She wanted to challenge the patriarchy and work in her father's business.

The show had a great cast. Shriram Lagoo, the lead of the show, played my father. Vivek Vaswani, a very good friend of mine, played my brother. And Jayant Kriplani, whom I had worked with in *Trikal*, played my husband.

The series aired on DD. It didn't have a big budget, but Sridhar was very smart in how he did things. We shot in a hotel in Bangalore and also stayed there. This fictional family was supposed to be rich, so it was fascinating to watch how Sridhar projected so much wealth and opulence with such limited means. He was very creative.

Khandaan was well received all over India and shot me to fame. Everywhere I went, people recognized me. I couldn't take public transport because I would get mobbed. I found this funny, because even though I was considered a success, at Rs 1000 per episode, I still couldn't afford to buy a car.

The public was very invested in *Khandaan* and especially in Ketaki's story. They felt that Ketaki was being too stubborn about not wanting children. Sometimes, I felt that Ketaki's refusal to have children affected the public even more than her on-screen family.

Once I was at the airport, waiting to pick someone up. I was sitting in the backseat of a friend's car and waiting for their flight to land.

A man walked by and saw me sitting there. He approached me slowly and rapped the bonnet to get my attention. I looked up and smiled.

'Madam,' he said, in all earnestness. 'Please have a child.'

I laughed. Did he believe I was Ketaki in real life too? In those days, many people found it difficult to separate the actor from the character. So, I just nodded and said, 'Ok, bhaiya. I'll think about it.'

Khandaan was the only show I could dedicate myself to because the shooting schedule took us all over India. We shot four to five episodes a month, and even though my earning was meagre, I managed to save up enough to buy a second-hand Fiat. It was mehendi green—not the most flattering colour for a car—but it worked just fine. I also employed a driver, because I didn't know how to drive; I still don't.

Having my own car and driver gave a deep sense of satisfaction, because it felt like I was finally on my way up. I had my own house, my own car, a driver to chauffeur me to shoots and a career that I loved.

What more could I ask for?

* * *

The thing about serials in the 1980s was that the producers really knew when to call it a day. So, with a very heavy heart, I bid farewell to my role in *Khandaan* as the show was about to end.

Shekhar Kapur had a recurring role in the serial. In fact, our characters had had an affair but it was never spelt out for the audience. The makers had left that detail open to interpretation.

Shekhar and I have known each other for a very long time. In fact, his late wife, Medha, and I were part of the same theatre troupe in Delhi back in the day. I spent a lot of time at her plush home in Connaught Place where our troupe would hold rehearsals in her garden which was vast and, of course, free for us to use. I have the fondest memories of her and our time together.

Shekhar and I weren't very close friends. But we had a good rapport, and I had a lot of respect for him as an artiste. One afternoon, I was at their house, having lunch, when I showed Shekhar a picture of me taken on a beach. It was a simple photoshoot done by my friend Aditya Arya, whom I had met on the sets of *Jaane Bhi Do Yaaro*. I needed some portfolio shots and Aditya had offered to help out. They were really good photos. In fact, to this day, those are among the best pictures I have of myself. Aditya had captured me beautifully.

One of my favourite pictures taken by Aditya Arya

Shekhar loved the picture, and said he was working on a script for a big production. Shekhar, even then, was a man of many talents and was the writer for the film.

'Can I keep this picture and a few more?' he asked. 'I want to show it to the director and producer.'

The requirement was for two girls, and while they had already hired a big star for one role, the second was yet to be cast. I was so excited to hear this!

'This is it,' I thought, for the millionth time in my career. 'My big screen break.'

So, I left their house that day giddy with excitement, my head spinning with dreams.

'It may take a little time,' he warned. 'And the director might not go for you because you are still largely unknown. But I will push for you.'

I flew to Delhi for a few days after this meeting, and after I returned, I sat by the phone every day waiting for Shekhar's call. I waited and I waited and was worried sick that he didn't call because it was bad news. That the director and producer didn't like me.

Weeks later, I would find out that the film had cast its second lead, a big name in Bollywood, and that was the end of my dreams.

I was still sad but put up a brave front when I met Shekhar at a party.

'I read that you found the second lead for the film?' I asked, keeping a straight face.

'What happened to you?' Shekhar asked. 'You met me that day and then just didn't call.'

'I was doing as you asked,' I said. 'I was waiting for your call.'

'Waiting for me to call?' he asked, angry. 'Don't you have a phone? Don't you have my number? You should have just reached out. You said you were going to Delhi, and I didn't even know when you would return.'

It's then I realized I had made the biggest rookie mistake in the industry. I received a lead and didn't follow up.

Why? Because I foolishly thought it was polite for them to make the first move, when it was me who needed the role more than anything. Because I was shy. Because I was stupid and thought that if I called and pushed, they would think less of me and not give me the role.

What a fool I was. What an idiotic thing I had done.

I knew that making that call (once or even fifteen times) wouldn't have guaranteed me the role. Shekhar had been clear about that. But pushing for a follow-up or even saying, 'Hi! I exist and I'm really keen on playing the role' would have kept me on top of his mind. It would have shown him how serious I was.

Instead, I lost out on a golden opportunity because I was afraid of being *besharam.*

I want the whole world to know that you won't get anywhere if you aren't besharam. That you need to push for what you want and not sit back and wait for offers to fall in your lap. If anything, people in the industry appreciate being pushed, and receiving pictures and requests for follow-ups. It keeps you on top of their mind and helps them know who is actually serious.

I lacked common sense back then and have learnt to never repeat this mistake, even now when I've crossed the age of sixty.

5

The Casting Couch

'Accha, Neena, tell the truth,' an aunty would inevitably ask, 'is it true? That all these famous actresses have to sleep with producers or directors to get roles?'

I dreaded this question whenever I travelled to Delhi to visit my parents. During my visits, relatives, friends and neighbourhood aunties would come to meet me and ask about my life in Bombay. As soon as the chai and snacks were served, they would start demanding gossip straight off the *tawa*.

'I don't know, aunty,' I'd respond. 'I have never experienced anything like that.'

'What are you saying?' they'd prod. 'Everyone knows you need to sleep with someone big to get a good role.'

I'd smile and respond with something vague, and my mother, understanding how I felt, would quickly change the subject so I wouldn't get too upset.

But the questions never stopped. Not from the people I knew. Not from the press. Not even from the people on the street.

The casting couch. I hate this term.

What is the casting couch? Well, dear reader, it is a big velvet sofa hidden in a secret room in Film City where young aspiring actors are lured with the promise of a big break. Ok, I'm obviously joking. But whenever I'm asked about it, this is the image that comes to my head.

128

Now, does the casting couch exist, and have I ever had to sit (sleep? sounds uncomfortable) on it?

The answer is: Yes, it exists, and no I have never experienced it. I always saw it for what it was—a sexual favour offered in exchange for something that might not be what you imagined.

What do I mean by this? Let me tell you about something that happened to me a long time ago.

After *Khandaan* ended, I found myself struggling again to find meaningful work. I was back at Prithvi, doing plays, and was receiving offers but they were for negative roles.

Now here's the thing about the 1980s. Most films had very standard roles. The hero, heroine, villain, vamp, comedian, sidekick and so on.

My character, Ketaki, in *Khandaan*—who was strong-willed, independent and rebellious (by 1980s standards because she wanted to work and not have a child)—was perceived as negative. Closer to a vamp than a heroine.

If there was anything I had learnt from my experience as the Lallu Ladki in *Saath Saath* and as Ketaki in *Khandaan*, it was that the audience got really invested in your character.

So, while Lallu Ladki got me a lot of offers for a comic relief, Ketaki fetched me the roles of vamps. Nobody could see me as a heroine. I found this so unfair that it made me want to scream.

If I could go back today and relive the start of my career, I would definitely look for a mentor or a guide so that they could advise me through so many of the decisions I took. A godfather is very important for up-and-coming talent, because they often stagger in their careers by choosing the wrong roles.

So, from then on, I started rejecting the offers I received. Instead, I worked in plays, which were meaningful and helped me feel fulfilled.

I also networked to be noticed by bigwigs, hoping for better roles if not leading ones.

One day, a friend told me to go visit a producer who was a bigshot in the south. He was visiting for a few days and was staying at the Sun-n-Sand hotel. It was really close to Prithvi, so I decided to go meet him after one of my performances.

'I'll be right back,' I told the cast and crew. 'I'm leaving my stuff here. Please watch it for me.'

I honestly didn't think it would take too long.

When I got to the hotel, I called the producer from a phone in the lobby.

'Yes, yes, I've been expecting you,' he said. 'Come on upstairs.'

My basic instinct told me to not go upstairs. That I should ask him to come down to the lobby instead.

But I was also afraid of what he might think of me if I refused. This was my chance to get some work in the south, and I thought if I refused to go to his room, it would offend him. That's the kind of low self-esteem I had. Thinking that I was so unimportant that I would lose an opportunity if I refused.

So, I took the elevator up and knocked on his door. It was a single room. I entered and he gestured me towards a sofa while he sat on the edge of the bed right.

He spoke for what felt like hours. He talked to me about how he had launched so many heroines in the south.

I tried to look impressed but, honestly, I just wanted him to get on with it because I had people waiting for me at Prithvi. I was also uncomfortable and just wanted to leave.

'So what's my role, sir,' I asked him finally when he paused to catch his breath.

'The heroine's friend,' he said. When he explained it to me, it seemed like a very small part.

'Ok . . . I have to go now, sir,' I said. 'My friends are waiting for me.'

'Go? Where?' he asked. He seemed genuinely shocked. 'Aren't you going to spend the night here?'

Suddenly, I felt like someone had just poured a bucket of ice water on my head. *Khoon sookh gaya* (My blood froze).

I started to shiver, and the words left my mouth in a stutter.

'No sir, I have to go now. My friends are waiting. I am going to go now.'

He looked at me with disgust, disdain and also . . . fear? I think he got scared looking at the shock and refusal in my body language.

He reached over to where my handbag lay on the floor, picked it up and thrust it in my arms.

'Ok then,' he said. 'Go if you want to. Nobody is forcing you to stay.'

I took my bag and practically ran back to Prithvi. I tried to make sense of what had just happened. He expected me to sleep with him? And just to get a small part?

That was one of my first brushes with the casting couch, and it taught me three important things.

First: Yes. The casting couch does, very casually, exist.

Second: Young actors often find themselves offered a seat on it.

Third: Whether an actor gets on the casting couch is entirely up to them. Nobody forces them to do something they don't want to do. It's their choice. Are they willing to compromise?

Another thing I learnt from this incident was that this does not ensure a good role. There are no promises made. You could compromise on your values and walk away with a small role or if things don't work out—say the movie's funding gets cut—with no part at all.

Having said that, not every star is made on the casting couch. Not every director, producer or writer demands sexual favours.

In fact, these days, I have seen, Bollywood has become extremely professional. The young talent in the industry works diligently and fairly.

Even back in the 1980s and 1990s, there were some good film-makers who cast roles without expecting sexual favours in return.

I remember meeting the great Dev Anand once for a role in one of his films. I was very excited because he had been my idol since I was a little girl. Just the opportunity to be in the same space as him had me flying.

I went to meet him at Sun-n-Sand, where he had a suite booked throughout the year. It brought back the bitter memory of the producer, but I told myself to be brave.

When I knocked on Dev Anand's door, he answered it himself. It amused me to see that his mannerisms and way of speaking matched his film persona.

He was also warm and welcoming. He offered me tea, snacks, and we had a good chat. I felt the difference between him and the producer immediately. If anything, I felt even more respect for Dev Sahib, because he was such a big legend and yet, so warm and humble.

He would also be starring in this film, he said. He told me about the role he had in mind for me. Once again, it was too small and it didn't appeal to me.

He appreciated my honesty. We exchanged a few more pleasantries and then I bid him goodbye.

When I think about the concept of casting couch, I'm conflicted by many emotions. Do I think it's unfair? Yes, because a lot of young actors who are new to the industry and don't have a godfather, find themselves faced with a choice between getting on the couch and being overlooked.

But the one thing I know from experience is that you can always say no, and nobody will force you into it. Why? Many reasons but the most important of them is: If one girl says no, there are ten standing behind her to take her place. It's a sad reality, but that's how it is.

Honestly, let's take a moment here to reflect on what I've said. I don't think any of us should judge those who do end up compromising to get where they want to be. It's their choice, isn't it? As for me, I felt it my duty to add this chapter to the book and explain to you once and for all what I went through, how I dealt with it and what I think of this matter.

That's all there is to it. #NoJudgement.

6

The Sound of Music

Just as *Khandaan* was about to wrap up, I received devastating news.

My mother, who had been suffering from Multiple Myeloma—cancer of the bone marrow—had passed away. She had been sick for a while but losing her still came like a blow to the gut.

I took three days off from work to go to Delhi and attend the funeral. The schedule for TV shows can be very tight. And with *Khandaan* all set to wrap up, there was a big climax coming up. Three days were all they could give me.

As I was flying back, crushed and heartbroken, I thought maybe my grief would help me shoot the last few scenes of *Khandaan*, which were very emotional and required me to cry.

It'll be easy, I thought, since I already felt that way.

But once on the sets, I just could not perform as well as I would have liked. Taking my personal grief and trying to use it in my work was not a good idea.

It was then that I truly understood the importance of being relaxed before acting. You will notice that most actors who are lauded for their performances are actually very calm, and their acting is effortless. I somehow got through the climax and was so busy grieving my personal loss that I forgot to grieve the show that had shot me to fame.

It was the end of an era. It was the end of *Khandaan*. It was the end of me having a mother. It was the end of life as I knew it.

* * *

After my mother's death, I spent a long time feeling lost and lonely. Yes, I had a lot of friends to turn to. I even had some work to keep me occupied. But I didn't have my mother, who had always been my rock; the person whose shoulder I could cry on even if we lived in different cities. It felt like a part of me had also died.

I wasn't foolish enough to think that I would be flooded with offers after *Khandaan*. But I also hadn't anticipated the kind of offers I would get. They were all badly written roles for vamps in films, and I knew I could do better than that. Money was tight but Girish's voice from the time I played Lallu Ladki kept ringing in my head.

Khandaan's Ketaki pulled me out of the Lallu Ladki mould, but cast me in a different one. In those days, strong women who dressed sexily, were strong-willed and refused to let marriage and children derail their dreams, were considered 'bad'. Rebellious girls. So, the industry obviously felt that I would be better suited to playing negative roles.

This was shocking because I didn't feel Ketaki was a negative character. She was just human. As Ketaki, I also felt like I had proven my skills as an actor. I had played a rebel, a sexy babe; I had shown intense emotion in so many scenes; and I had also been good, kind and considerate when the story called for it. But it was just not to be. I kept getting these offers to play horrible women with no redeeming qualities, and even though I needed the money, I kept refusing them.

I found some solace in the fact that I had finally moved out of my tiny flat in Sher-E-Punjab into a big three-bedroom house in Juhu, opposite AVM School. This house too had been bestowed on me by my loving and caring mother. She had come to take care of me when I was down with measles and didn't like how tiny my flat was. So, when my father sold a property in Delhi, they upgraded me to this wonderful home.

But, very often, sitting alone in the house made me feel even more lonely and unhappy about my loss and all the things she wouldn't be a part of. This home, a symbol of her love, felt truly empty. I needed something to occupy my mind. I needed to rediscover the things I truly loved.

Thinking about all the wonderful memories I had of my music classes at NSD, I decided to learn classical singing. Basu Da told me about Pandit Anadi Shankar (name changed), a renowned classical singer and musician, and said there was no one better than him. Everyone called him Panditji.

Panditji was a very famous singer and was revered in the industry. Hence, I was very nervous as I climbed up the stairs to his third-floor flat in Shivaji Park.

He was a nice man and had a great presence. I took to him instantly. He sat me down and asked me to sing something for him. I sang the song which I had performed as part of the Parsi play in NSD, when I lost my voice after drinking icy-cold sherbet at Bengali Market. I was very nervous about what he would say. But he just sat quietly with his eyes closed, and when I finished, he said that I would need a bit of work.

Panditji worked with a lot of classical singers, but they were much more advanced in their training than I was. So, I started to train with his apprentice, Praveen Da, and was soon absorbed into the family.

I used to call Panditji 'Baapu' and his wife 'Aai'— Marathi for father and mother.

I used to spend a lot of time in their one-room flat and sometimes even spent the night in their humble house. Baapu and Aai on the bed and me on the floor.

Aai often came and stayed with me in Juhu, that's how comfortable we were with each other. She said she wanted to get some time away from home to focus on work; she was engaged in a project to clean the Ganges. But, honestly, I know she also wanted to keep me company and pamper me, because she knew how lonely I was after my mother's death.

I got friendly with his daughter, Simran (name changed), who at the time was married to a man in the merchant navy, but lived with her parents. I became more than friends with their son, Raghav (name changed), also a musician and composer.

None of this happened behind the parents' back, because we were always together. They were a close-knit family, and I loved feeling accepted and included in the fold.

I think after losing my mother, I just wanted to fill the void in my life by having my own family; having people who were closer to me and whom I could turn to for support.

Raghav and I got serious very fast. There were times when I felt that we weren't compatible mentally, but I just dismissed my niggling doubts, thinking it was just temporary because we had had a disagreement or an argument.

But overall, we were very happy. I started spending more time in their house. Simran had separated from her husband by then and had started dating Sudhir Trivedi (name changed), Praveen Da's brother-in-law. He was a nice man and we got along.

Things were perfect. Raghav and I, along with Simran and Sudhir, would go for long walks on the beach and take day trips to different places.

Panditji was a wonderful presence in my life. I loved to watch him sing. He would sit on the floor with a little fan next to him and sing to the sounds of the fan. It was like a meditation for me, more so because I loved classical music.

I knew things were getting very serious with Raghav when I was invited to their family studio for Ganpati Pooja. I was introduced to

Raghav's maternal grandfather, one of India's foremost film-makers. Panditji introduced me as his future *bahu* and asked me to touch his feet. I was honoured to do this, not just as Raghav's future wife, but also as an actor who had admired his work for so long.

A while later, Panditji officially blessed our union and gave me a diamond ring as a token of my engagement to Raghav. It was one of the best moments of my life.

I was going to get married. But, more importantly, I was going to officially become a part of their family. It felt like things couldn't get any better.

* * *

A little while later, I took a brief trip to Russia as part of a film delegation. After returning to India, I flew to Delhi immediately to shop for my bridal trousseau. It was a very exciting time. I missed my mother and wished she was there to help me. I missed the things we would have talked about while shopping. I missed her tasteful choice in clothes. I missed holding her hand and resting my head in her lap.

But I told myself that I would soon have a new life. A new family. A father-in-law who was wonderful, supportive and talented. A mother-in-law who was warm, friendly and a great maternal figure in my life.

Towards the end of my trip though, just as I was about to come back to Bombay, Raghav called me and told me he wanted to postpone the wedding.

'What do you mean?' I asked him. I was shocked. Everything had already been arranged. People had been informed. Even his father, who had been on a tour abroad, had cut his trip short to make it in time for the wedding.

'I have to get a sinus surgery,' Raghav told me by way of explanation.

This confused me, because in all our time together he had never mentioned this problem.

'Is it really that serious that you need to postpone the wedding? Can you not wait until we're married?'

'No,' he said. 'I am suffering a lot. I need to do this now.'

I had no say in the matter, so I agreed to postpone the wedding. But something about this didn't feel right. I felt like Raghav wasn't being honest. Mainly because it's a very big deal to ask for a wedding to be postponed when everything is already set. Also, shouldn't I have known as his fiancée and such a close confidante of the family that he needed an operation?

There was more. When I returned to Bombay, I realized that Raghav hadn't just postponed the wedding, he had cancelled it.

I didn't know what else to do except beg him, and his mother, sister and father, to tell me why he had cancelled our wedding.

But I never received a straight reply from any of them. They all stuck to the same story. That he needed to get a sinus operation. But nobody told me why the marriage had to be cancelled.

This whole situation came as a very big blow to me, and I didn't know what to do except once again immerse myself in work. Somehow, I had to find a way to put it behind me.

* * *

It was around that time that I was cast in *Rihaee*, a film that starred Hema Malini, Vinod Khanna, Naseeruddin Shah and many others.

The film was shot in a village in Gujarat and us junior actors were put up in a rented house—two to three in each room with bedding spread out on the dusty floor and blankets that smelled like things we didn't even want to imagine. Overall, it wasn't a very comfortable experience, but we were young, and we knew how to rough it out.

When we weren't filming, we were rehearsing. We would return every evening so tired that we would immediately drift off. One evening, I returned to the house after filming and found Raghav waiting for me. He had done some work for the film's music and was visiting the sets for two days.

I felt strange and uncomfortable seeing him there and realized I was still very, very angry.

'I'm sorry,' he said. 'I wanted to talk to you, spend some time with you so we could work things out. I really want us to be together.'

So, once again, I asked him why he'd cancelled our wedding and again he gave me the same old excuse.

Eventually, when it was clear we were going nowhere, I asked him to leave because I really wanted to focus on work. I didn't want this entire nightmare to distract me, especially when the experience was already uncomfortable with less than desirable conditions.

After the film wrapped up, I flew back to Bombay and was surprised to see him at the airport. He had come to pick me up.

We went back to my house in Juhu where we talked and tried to work things out. I tried mainly because of the love I had felt for him once and because I respected his parents very much.

But eventually, when he still didn't give me a straight answer for why he cancelled our wedding, I decided to listen to my instincts and call things off. The voice inside my head said something about the situation wasn't clean. Something wasn't right. Don't do it.

So, one day, I told him that it wasn't going to work out between us and that it would be best if we just parted ways. To this day, I do not know the real reason for why he called off our wedding. It used to bother me because I really wanted an explanation; I deserved an explanation. But seeing how things panned out and how they led me to this stage in my life, I think whatever happened, happened for the best. Not just for me but for him as well.

7

How I Met Vivian

Batwara was my first commercial film and what a star-studded affair it was!

The film, shot in Jaipur at Samode Palace, starred Vinod Khanna (my childhood heart-throb), Dharmendra, Dimple Kapadia, Amrita Singh, Poonam Dhillon, Amrish Puri and Shammi Kapoor.

The film was released in 1989 but it was shot in 1986 or 1987. At the time, I was just getting over Raghav, but I cheered up a bit because I had this big, commercial film to look forward to.

I once again played a small part—Vinod Khanna's sister.

Until then, I had acted in mostly art house films and had been very comfortable with my co-stars. This was my first experience in a big blockbuster, one with a huge number of stars, and I think I was awestruck the first few weeks.

Here, for the first time, I was working with people who had shared experiences earlier and had inside jokes that I couldn't understand. It left me feeling like an outsider and, honestly, it wasn't their fault. It was my own inferiority complex that made me want to be invisible. It never struck me to think better of myself because even though I wasn't a big star like them, I was also known in my own right.

But my mind was too busy trying to understand the lie of the land, as they say, because actors from art house cinema were very different from big, commercial stars. There was a lot of jealousy

('Why is her outfit more stylish than mine?'), insecurity ('This
star is just getting way too much screen time!'), competition and,
predictably, bitchiness.

The number of big names on the sets at any given point made
my head spin. It was the sort of environment where I felt that I
couldn't even compete, and I often found myself feeling lost and
lonely.

There was one actress who claimed to be a well-wisher and
pretended to befriend me but in time I realized she was just using
me as a stepping stone to get closer to another actor. I found this
really awkward.

In my previous films, the cast and crew would always grow
close and become a tight-knit unit by the end of the production,
but here there was no sense of warmth or family. In fact, my only
solace during the filming was Kulbhushan Kharbanda, who had
always been kind, friendly and supportive of me. And, in time, very
surprisingly, and much to my delight, Vinod Khanna.

How Vinod Khanna and I came to be good friends is another
story altogether. A very awkward one, but, in retrospect, also
hilarious.

After I reached Jaipur to start shooting for *Batwara*, I went
straight to the hotel where we would be staying and asked at the
reception, 'Has anyone else arrived yet?'

'Yes,' they said. 'Vinod Khanna, as of now.'

I jumped. I was a huge fan. Almost like one of those crazy fangirls
who would do anything to be in the same space as him.

So, I got his number from the reception and called his room.

'Hi sir,' I said. 'This is Neena Gupta. I don't know if you
remember me . . .'

'Neena,' he boomed (what a strong, powerful voice he had). 'Of
course, I remember you! Come on up. Let's meet.'

I was giddy with excitement. We had both been in *Rihaee*, but
I didn't know if he knew me because we didn't have any scenes

together. I also didn't know if he'd seen any of the other films I had done.

When I got to the room, he was nice and polite. He didn't seem to notice how enamoured I was of him; or maybe he was so used to women fawning over him by then that he was oblivious to it.

He offered me a drink which I refused. So, he gave me some snacks and we talked for a while.

He told me about his days at the Rajneesh ashram and spoke about a lot of different things. I was literally sitting on the edge of my seat, drinking him in. In that moment, I would have done anything for this man.

I sat there for hours talking and listening. He asked if I wanted to step out for dinner or if he should order room service. I was comfortable and felt safe with him, so I agreed to dine in the room.

After dinner, as it was getting late, I decided to finally take my leave.

'Already?' he asked. 'I'm having such a good time talking to you. Stay a while longer. Let's watch TV.'

I froze. Not because I was uncomfortable or that anything he said was suggestive. If anything, Vinod Khanna was a wonderful human being who had been nothing but kind and polite to me throughout the evening.

I hesitated because I was scared that I might slip and do something that would embarrass one or both of us.

I started to wonder then if this was something that happened to girls when they were sitting face-to-face with their girlhood crush and were willing to throw themselves at them.

So, I smiled and politely made up an excuse.

'No,' I said, forcing myself to laugh a little. 'I'm really tired. I think I'll go back to my room and sleep.'

'Sure, of course,' he said. 'Come, let me walk you to your room.'

So, he walked me to my door and was a thorough gentleman. He wished me goodnight and said, 'If you change your mind, call me.'

'Sure, sir,' I said. 'Goodnight.'

I was hit by a mixture of emotions the minute I closed the door. There was sadness, regret and confusion. But as I lay down in bed to sleep, I was also suddenly gripped by fear.

Vinod Khanna was a big star. He was THE star of the film, along with Dharmendra, another icon. I had just spent the evening with one of the biggest actors in the movie, and I started to second-guess everything I had said. Had I been well behaved? What if he found me stupid and naïve? The next time he saw me, would he see an actor, or would he see the naïve schoolgirl who had such a big crush on him?

I couldn't sleep all night and kept tossing and turning, convinced that I had made a fool of myself. What if he now hated me and made my life hell for the rest of the shoot?

Worse: what if he got me kicked out of the film?

The next morning, I arrived on set scared and nervous. I already felt like a misfit in the film, coming from an art-house background and trying to learn the ropes in a commercial setting.

But later, I realized, I shouldn't have worried at all. Because as soon as Vinod saw me, he came over and gave me a big hug and warmly wished me a good morning.

What was happening? I didn't know. But going by the way Vinod was treating me, it felt like the previous evening hadn't ended as badly as I had thought.

In fact, on the sets, when there was cut-throat competition between actors and tempers and tantrums flew, Vinod was still the same warm person I had met that first day and always helped me out as much as he could. He befriended me and took me into his fold when none of the other stars even acknowledged my presence outside of the shoot. And he taught me a thing or two about how things worked in commercial films.

One day, we were shooting a scene on the terrace of the palace. Vinod, playing my big brother, was supposed to slap me.

In art-house films, a slap is a slap, a real one, right across the face.

Turned out, commercial films did it differently.

Vinod recited his line, and when the time came for him to raise his hand and hit me across the face, I just stood there, in character, waiting for the blow.

But his hand swerved just before it made contact with my face.

'You foolish girl,' Vinod shouted. 'Why didn't you move your face? I could have really hurt you.'

I started to fumble. 'I'm sorry,' I said. 'I was waiting for you to slap me.'

The look of anger on his face turned to one of confusion, and then when he realized I was actually waiting for him to slap me, he started roaring with laughter.

'If I had really slapped you, Neena, you would have fallen off the terrace,' he said.

And then he took me aside to explain how they shot a slap scene in commercial cinema. The actor delivering the blow brought their hand down and the person receiving it had to time it perfectly and move their face away. The sound of the slap would be inserted in post-production.

We always laughed about this moment when we hung out.

This friendship with Vinod really helped me survive *Batwara*.

After a long day of filming, on some evenings, we'd sit in Vinod or Kulbhushan's room (because their rooms were much bigger than mine). I was very shy and reserved around Vinod initially, but since he was so friendly, I started to emerge out of my shell.

I told him how I had a big crush on him and how I had thought I had made a complete fool of myself on our first meeting. He laughed and called me a foolish girl who gave herself a sleepless night by overthinking something that wasn't even true.

'You were absolutely wonderful, Neena,' he said. 'Else I wouldn't invite you to come join us here every evening.'

It's true. I was among the very few people who were asked to come hang out with them every day. These meetings also taught me a lot of things about big productions. Until then, I had always judged big actresses for travelling around with their posse. Some came with their mothers and sisters who got their own rooms. Others brought their own hair and make-up artistes. It just didn't make sense to me. I always wondered if they were just being pricey and demanding because their status and fame allowed them to.

But then one evening, I realized why actresses travelled with so many people.

We were in Kulji's (Kulbhushan) room after a gruelling day of shooting. I didn't drink much at that time, so I was just sitting and chatting while waiting for room service to bring our dinner.

I suddenly caught the eye of a man, someone famous who was also the husband of someone on the cast, who gestured me with his eyes and a nod to come outside.

At first, I was surprised and thought I was mistaken. But, after a while, I looked at him again and he repeated the gesture. It seemed to me that he wanted me to come out to the hall. I tried to ignore him, but it was really hard, because every time I so much as glanced his way, he did the same thing.

So, I did something that was truly stupid. I decided I'd had enough and excused myself.

'I'm really tired,' I told Kulji. 'I don't think I'll stay for dinner.'

I left the room and the man obviously thought it was all part of 'our' plan.

I hurried to my room, locked the door and hid under the blankets. I was still pondering what I had done to give this man ideas when I heard a knock on my door.

Knock. Knock. Knock. Knock.

I peered through the peephole, and sure enough, he was standing there, running his fingers through his hair.

I didn't say a word. I went back to my bed and pulled the blankets over my head.

Knock. Knock. Knock. Knock. Knock. Knock.

It went on for what felt like hours until he finally stopped. I thought he must have given up and gone back to his room when my telephone rang.

I didn't know what made me answer it. But I did.

'Hey, what are you doing?' he asked.

I froze. I didn't know what to say. So I lied.

'I'm sleeping ya,' I said, making my voice sound heavy and groggy. 'I'm so tired.'

'Oh, is it? Ok. Ok. Next time.'

I couldn't believe this man. I couldn't believe my luck. But I finally understood why actresses often travelled with a big troupe. And I wished I too had the liberty to bring someone along who would act as my guardian or an excuse to reject such advances without offending these men. Because, at the end of the day, one wrong move, one rejection and they can make your life very difficult. They can slander you and even ensure that you never work in films ever again.

Needless to say, the atmosphere on the sets of *Batwara* was very confusing and I often found myself feeling extremely uncomfortable. I honestly think I survived only because of my friendship with Kulji and Vinod.

To this day, I have nothing but respect for Vinod Khanna because he was kind, humble and a very good human being. That we could laugh about our first meeting on the sets of *Batwara* showed me what a great sense of humour he had.

In fact, years later, when we met at a Chinese restaurant in Kemps Corner—it was a dinner party for a film—we sat and talked about our shared experiences. I had just started drinking beer and we had a great time.

'So,' he asked, suddenly looking very serious. 'Have you changed your mind yet?'

And just like that we both started laughing so loudly that everyone paused to see what the commotion was about.

* * *

While we were still shooting for *Batwara*, I attended a dinner party hosted by the maharani of Jaipur with a few other members of the cast.

A few players from the West Indies cricket team were also on the guest list, including their captain at the time, Vivian Richards.

The team was touring India that year, and I had just watched them play the day before.

I have always been crazy about cricket. Even when I was in college, if there was a match on, I'd sit in class with a transistor radio glued to my ear, concealed by a scarf wrapped around my head. Good thing the matches only took place in winter so nobody suspected me.

The day before the party, I had watched the match between India and West Indies, and I was in awe.

Our team had beaten West Indies by a run or two, and while everyone else was cheering, I had eyes only for Vivian Richards who, I noticed, had taken the loss graciously. I also distinctly remember feeling his pain of missing the win by a whisker because I saw tears in his eyes.

'What a wonderful man,' I thought. 'He isn't afraid to show his emotions on live television.'

When I met him at the party that evening, I shook his hand and mentioned how moved I was by his passion.

We hit it off instantly and decided to meet a few times before he left.

We lost touch once he wrapped up his tour in India and returned home to Antigua. I missed him and thought about him often. We hadn't exchanged numbers, so we didn't know how to contact each other. Also, with my shooting schedule and his matches, we were rarely in one place for long enough to arrange a meeting.

But the universe has a way of making things happen. Life is strange sometimes. You imagine it going a certain way, but something else happens entirely. You wonder if something is meant to be and, when you least expect it, the universe sends you a sign.

I was once sitting at the Delhi airport, waiting for a flight, having forgotten all about Vivian, when suddenly I saw a flash of maroon.

I looked up and saw West Indies cricketers filing into the lounge, and my heart started to pound. There came Vivian.

That's how we came face-to-face once again, started a full-blown affair and the rest, as they say, is history.

I'm going to pause here to request you, dear reader, to please understand why I am keeping the details in this chapter to a bare minimum.

This book of my memoirs is a reflection of the events in my life as I remember them. In a lot of stories, I have changed the names or withheld identities out of respect for people's families, especially their children.

With Vivian

In much the same way, I will skim through this period of my life because I want to protect my daughter.

A lot has been written about this chapter of my life and the decisions I took for love. I would appreciate it, my dear reader, if you could respect my silence on this matter because I honestly don't want to rehash the entire situation and make myself, and especially my daughter, vulnerable to public speculation once again.

With Vivian in LA

So yes, Vivian and I had an affair and I got pregnant. He had already returned home when I found out. I thought about what this meant for me, my career and my entire life.

Should I keep the baby or should I abort it?

I also couldn't confide in too many people at the time because I couldn't risk the media finding out. I was a known figure and Vivian was an international star.

Some people advised me to get an abortion. Others cautioned against the perils of being a single parent. I listened to everyone patiently. They were all very concerned, I know. But once I was back home and alone, I asked myself: What do you think? How does this make you feel?

The answer was: I was giddy with joy! I was so happy to be pregnant. I was so excited to be a mother. My body was ready for the pregnancy. Maybe that's why I got pregnant to begin with, because I sure as hell didn't do this on purpose. Blame it on the pregnancy hormones or my youth and naivety, but I felt like this was really meant to be.

I also understood I wasn't the only person who had a say in the situation. The baby's father, Vivian, had an equal right.

So, I called him one day and spoke to him for a long time.

'I'm pregnant,' I told him. 'Would you have a problem if I were to have your baby?'

Vivian sounded happy and said I should go ahead. This assured me that I was doing the right thing.

As much as I wanted this child, I also did not want to go ahead if the father wasn't on board. So, it came as a relief when Vivian supported my decision.

Celebrating my dad's birthday

With Vivian, celebrating Masaba's birthday

Vivian was as involved as possible, given that he was constantly on the move for matches, that he lived a whole world and a half away and that he was already married.

Our relationship continued on and off for a few years and we had some beautiful moments and also some ugly ones. It was long distance and a very different kind of relationship.

During my pregnancy and for years (even decades) after, people said I was impulsive. That I should have chosen otherwise.

But regardless of what happened, the backlash I faced, the struggles in my life and my career, I was always very, very happy because I got a beautiful daughter out of it. Masaba has been worth everything and more.

Masaba

Part 3

The Princess Arrives

1

Soulmate

I don't have any pictures of myself during the pregnancy. None where I am showing that is. I had to keep my condition hidden for as long as I could, because I didn't know whom I could trust. Looking back, this makes me feel very sad and lonely.

I also couldn't take up too much work. Nothing with long-term commitments, because I didn't know when I would start to show.

The few friends I told oscillated between supporting me and telling me it was going to be hard. Many people begged me to reconsider.

But regardless of how sad and lonely I was, I was still filled with joy and love for this little being which was growing inside me. So, I didn't listen to anyone but myself.

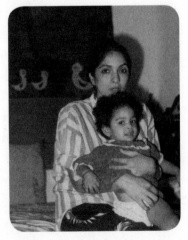

With Masaba

Vivian Richards was married and lived in Antigua. I had a career and lived in Bombay. There was no way I could be with him.

I knew I was okay as long as I wasn't showing. But once I did, I didn't have a plan on how I would handle it.

A few friends suggested I get married to someone so my child would have a name and father figure. Satish Kaushik, such a wonderful friend, called and said, 'Nancy (his nickname for me since college), don't worry. If the child is born with dark skin, you can just say it's mine and we'll get married. Nobody will suspect a thing.'

I found his offer so sweet that I had tears in my eyes. The fact that he was ready to sacrifice his own chance at true love and happiness for me was very touching. But I politely refused.

My old friend Sujoy Mitra also came to me once with a match.

'Do you want to hear the good news first or the bad?'

'Good news,' I said.

'I have a match for you,' he said. 'He is a banker and owns a house in Bandra'.

'Bad news?'

'He's gay,' he said. My heart sank. I didn't know if I should be offended or grateful. Sujoy said that he wanted to marry because of societal pressures. After we married, my child would get his name but we would go about our own lives. I said no straight away.

I received a lot of offers like this. But I laughed them off, because I didn't feel right about getting married just to avoid controversy. I knew I would have to answer very difficult questions. Being a public figure meant that our lives, mine and my child's, would always be up for speculation. But I told myself I would cross that bridge when I come to it. Until then, I would hide behind loose clothes for as long as I could.

Pregnancy can be bliss even if you're going through it without a life partner. Raising a baby without the father, however, is really, really hard. It's possibly one of the hardest things any woman has to do.

Add to this the stress of supporting yourself and your child independently, and you will understand what I went through those first few years of Masaba's life.

But God always provides even if in unexpected ways. I did not have a man. But I had an aunt.

Let's just call her Aunty. I have to talk about her because I would not have survived those first few years of motherhood without her. I can't name her because she ended up hurting me more than any other human being I have ever met. Out of respect for her surviving family, I will keep her identity anonymous.

Aunty was my soulmate, of sorts. She was kind, loving and understood my needs even before I did because she had borne and raised three children of her own.

She wasn't a very close relative. She was an aunt on my father's side. When I moved into my three-bedroom flat in Juhu, my dad, concerned about my well-being, suggested I contact her should I need anything.

We hit it off instantly. In the absence of my mother, whom I still missed every day, she became my friend, my family and my confidante.

When I got pregnant, especially, she was always by my side.

She accompanied me to the doctor's, invited me over for lavish meals and took a personal interest in my health and well-being.

I came to rely on her heavily. One might even say she became one of my closest friends for a while. I could also rely on her to support me like one would rely on their family.

Aunty, in addition to having a big house and three children—all of whom either lived or studied abroad at the time—also had a husband who was very kind. I loved the two of them, and while I was closer to her, I had immense respect for him as well.

Throughout my pregnancy, if I wasn't at Aunty's house, I was with Om Puri. He and I became very close during that time. He was a wonderful man and a close friend.

I used to visit his home a lot, especially when I got tired of eating my own food. Om loved to have me over and give me scrumptious things to eat. He would then drive me back in his car very slowly and carefully, because he was scared the bumpy roads might not be good for me.

Some friends suggested I marry him to give my child a name. He was a wonderful man. But no matter what anybody said or how fond I was of Om, I couldn't do that to him.

'I don't love him, and I don't lust for him,' I said. 'I cannot, with a clear conscience, fool someone and marry them just because I need to legitimize this pregnancy.'

'What does love have to do with it?' my friend Rajesh Puri's wife asked me. 'Just get married now and love will come later.'

But I didn't believe that ideology, so I didn't even consider that course of action.

Soni Razdan, one of my best friends, said that I should think about this very carefully. That a child needed both a mother and father.

'What kind of life will you be able to give this child as a single parent? No husband, no aunts or uncles, no big family . . . It is going to be very, very hard.'

There was also the matter of informing my family. I don't think I was as afraid of what the media, the industry or society would say, as I was of my father and brother.

My brother was quite okay about it when I called him. He said this was my life and I should do what I thought was right.

My father, on the other hand, was dead against me having a child out of wedlock. He wanted me to abort it.

'Don't do this,' he said. 'It is not right. Think about what society will say?'

But I didn't listen to him, because I was genuinely happy about having a child. I was flying!

I told myself and the naysayers that this was MY child. Having this child was MY decision. I was strong enough to do this on my own.

And once my family and friends saw that I really meant it, they supported me with wholeheartedly.

Basu Chatterji, whom I met once at Om Puri's house, told me, 'Neena, if you need anything—money, support, or just someone to talk to—please do not hesitate to come to me.'

I was really touched by his offer and support. I had never met him before, and here he was, offering to help me if I was ever in need.

But I never did ask anybody for money because that's just the kind of person I am. My family would have supported me financially; they did buy me two houses in Bombay. But I never asked them for money.

I also believe that when you truly need it, there is a force out there in the universe—I call it 'God'—that will provide.

I had just Rs 2000 in my bank account, and I had been informed by the doctor that I would need a caesarean. The operation would cost Rs 10,000. I was so scared and upset. I didn't know what to do.

As luck would have it, I got an income-tax refund of Rs 9000 just when I needed it the most and that's how I paid for my C-section.

Over the years, I have had moments of self-doubt and regret, much like any other parent. I am projected as this strong, independent woman by the media. Fans often call me a 'rebel' who is an inspiration to women everywhere.

In truth, though, I think I am the weakest person and a fool for not seeing what was coming my way.

But the one thing about me is that whenever I'm faced with adversity—personal, financial, in my relationships or an unplanned pregnancy—I become the strongest person I know.

* * *

I was almost seven months pregnant by the time we wrapped up the shoot for *Mirza Ghalib*, a historical drama series that aired on DD.

The series starred Naseeruddin Shah as Mirza Ghalib on whose life and works the series was based. It also had Tanvi Azmi, Shafi Inamdar, Parikshit Sahni and me.

Gulzar Sahib had produced the series and had called me personally to play the role of Nawab Jaan.

I was only a few months along when I received this offer but didn't want to lose the opportunity. I really needed the money. But I couldn't be dishonest even if I was a bit desperate. So, I told Gulzar Sahib the truth.

'I'm pregnant and due in November but please let me do this role because I really need the money.'

Gulzar Sahib is a gem of a person and so non-judgmental. He not only gave me the part, but also took extra care of me during the filming.

He would always ensure that I was comfortable and that I had eaten properly. He would even bring me food from his own house, so I would have something exciting to look forward to.

I have mentioned before that I had friends who took special care of me during my pregnancy. I am so honoured to have had Gulzar Sahib among those friends.

We had been friendly for a long time. He used to go to a place in Andheri called Practennis to play tennis every day. I was a huge sports enthusiast, so when I found out I asked if I could join.

Gulzar Sahib picked me up at 6.30 a.m. every day and we'd play together. He even gifted me my first tennis racket. I wasn't very good, but he was a spectacular player. He would play for almost an hour, or an hour and a half every day.

When I started playing, I was so influenced by ace players like Martina Navratilova that I wanted to wear nice tennis clothes like her. You know what I'm talking about? The short skirts and fitted shorts. Perfect to run around in.

In those days, these kind of clothes were not easily available in India, so anyone going abroad was immediately tasked with bringing such clothes for me.

I expressed my desire to dress like Navratilova to Gulzar Sahib and he joked, 'Neena, improve your game first and then start investing in dressing the part.'

I found that funny and yet so true.

Mirza Ghalib was a beautiful series made by a beautiful man. Nawab Jaan, my character, was a dancer and a singer who would sing Ghalib's ghazals.

Gulzar Sahib gave the choreographer strict instructions to ensure that my steps were simple, but elegant. Nothing jumpy because of my pregnancy.

Towards the end of the series there was a scene where I had to sit in a tonga and travel to Ghalib's mazar. The tonga driver was told to go very, very slowly because I was almost seven months pregnant by that time. This scene wasn't shot in a studio where things can be easily manipulated. It was shot outdoors in a village a few hours from Bombay.

By then, the whole crew knew I was expecting, because there was no way I could hide a bump that big. Everyone that day was very nervous because tongas, by nature, are very bumpy and dangerous for pregnant women. But, in the end, everything was fine and the shoot went off perfectly.

You know, I don't think I have many pictures of me when I was pregnant. Om Puri took a picture once, but I don't know where that went. Most of my pictures from that time are from *Mirza Ghalib*. And in so many of them, my bump is hidden. Looking back today, I feel like I should have done at least one photoshoot to remember those wonderful months spent growing this beautiful child in my body.

* * *

Masaba, born on 2 November, suffered the first few days because Diwali was just round the corner and the firecrackers that would go off at all hours—sometimes all night long—would really scare her. I would keep her ears covered and swaddle her tightly because she would get scared of the noise and cry for hours.

One night, she developed a very high fever, and I called three doctors to ask them what was wrong and what I should do. Did I really know what I was doing? Did anybody?

With little Masaba

And on other nights, she was just a regular baby— growing quickly, constantly uncomfortable and testing my competence by waking up multiple times every night. I wondered if I was feeding her enough. If she was comfortable enough. Was she sick? Was I doing something wrong?

I would not have been able to get through any of this if it wasn't for Aunty who was there throughout. She shared her own knowledge with me; she had raised three children, after all, and helped me learn the ropes.

Being a single parent is hard because you have to take all the decisions for your child's health and well-being on your own. There's no one else to share their impressions or opinions.

With Aunty around, I didn't feel so lost or alone and for this I will always be grateful to her. This is why I honestly believe that God may not give you what you desire, but he does compensate in other ways.

Now that I had delivered, I had to, once again, go out and find work. I needed to earn money. Not just for me, but also for my little girl.

Masaba was only three months old when I was offered a small part in *The Sword of Tipu Sultan* which aired on DD. The series starred Sanjay Khan as Tipu Sultan and was also produced and directed by him.

My contract was for one month and would take me to Mysore.

I had just recovered from the C-section and was still coming to grips with motherhood, but there was no way I was going to give up this opportunity.

So, I decided to do the show and take Masaba and my maid along with me to Mysore.

With my co-actor Shankar Nag in *Utsav*, and Masaba

The first few days after we reached were very relaxed because our directors were occupied elsewhere. I didn't complain though because it gave us some time to get accustomed to the new place and meet some of the people we were to live and work with.

My accommodation, along with the other actors, was on the first floor of a house; the landlords lived below. It was modest but comfortable. It was also where I met the actress who would be playing my mother. Let's just call her Actor Mother.

We hit it off immediately and formed a bond. She was very nice and often watched Masaba for me.

Shooting began in full swing a few days later. It was very nice because I could take Masaba with me. She would stay in the green room with the maid. I'd hop over every few hours to nurse her. It would get a little uncomfortable shooting at times because my milk flow was really heavy, and my breasts would often swell up or form lumps where the ducts would get blocked. At times like these I would rush to the bathroom at the first opportunity to express my milk.

A few days into the shoot, Masaba fell ill. I was really worried and struggled to balance my work and time with my child. But Actor Mother was really nice and supportive. She saw how nervous I was as a new parent, especially one who had returned to work so soon after delivery, and did her best to help out.

Masaba had just received a vaccine before we left Bombay and Actor Mother assured me that a fever was perfectly normal at such a time. So, I tried not to worry about it.

This happened on 8 February 1989. I left Masaba home with the maid and went to shoot. It was a big day for my character. I was playing Tipu Sultan's mother, and it was her wedding in flashback.

The set, built inside a studio, was lavish. As we entered through the small door, we saw two rooms built on either side and further inside, in what was supposed to be a grand hall, the wedding was to be shot.

I was fitted for a red nylon lehenga, draped with a beautiful dupatta and decked in faux jewels before the shooting began.

But halfway through the day, I started to get uneasy. How was my baby doing? Was she okay without me? Was she able to sleep well?

The green room, which was behind the studio, was slightly damp and I wondered if it would make Masaba even sicker if I were to bring her there.

But by lunch time, I couldn't take it any more. I needed to be close to her. Even if I were shooting, as long as she was nearby, I would feel better.

So I sent a unit car to pick up Masaba and my maid, and felt so much relief when I finally got to hold her again.

When the production team announced that we would be wrapping up early that day, I was overjoyed. I just couldn't wait to get out of that outfit and into something more comfortable and convenient to nurse.

But then they changed their mind. It was a wedding scene, so they had hired many junior actors to be part of the audience. It would be too expensive if they were to hire them for another day. So, we had to continue shooting until they wrapped the entire scene.

Once this was announced, I decided to sneak out to the green room to quickly check on Masaba and feed her. Actor mother accompanied me.

'What will I do by myself?' she asked. 'I'll come along and give you company.'

They were shooting other parts of the scene, so nobody noticed us as we got out.

I walked into the green room and took Masaba in my lap. But as I was about to feed her, we heard a loud explosion.

We quickly came out to see what the commotion was about, but what we saw scarred us for life.

I think we all have watched at least one film which has a scene depicting a person on fire.

It makes us flinch. But we also know it's not real. It's a stuntman or stuntwoman performing the scene. The environment is controlled. There are special techniques through which the production team creates that effect. That person is on fire, but they aren't really burning . . .

Imagine seeing this happen in real life. Men and women running around frantically, trying to outrun the fire, not knowing they can't because it's become a part of them. It's on their clothes. Their skin. Their hair.

I have no words for what I saw outside the green room that day. I just remember feeling numb and holding my child close to my chest.

A man I recognized from the lighting department ran towards me, his arms and legs ablaze.

'*Behen, meri madad karo,*' he screamed.

I was shocked and clueless about what needed to be done. I just remember saying something to the effect of, '*Main kaise madad karu? Mere haath mein baccha hai . . .*'

I could hear screams from every direction.

I looked down and saw that my maid was pulling at her hair and shouting, '*Mar gaye, mar gaye.*'

I looked closely and realized there was nothing wrong with her. She wasn't hurt. Just frantic. So, I pulled her up and scolded her.

'Be quiet,' I said. 'Stop shouting. We need to leave right now.'

I was so afraid that the green room, which was just behind the studio, though not attached, would catch fire any minute.

So, I pulled her to her feet, clutched my child and set off to the only place I could think of—the office building at the entrance of the studio.

Everything that happened from then on is a blur. We waited at the studio for a long time. I was crying. My maid was crying. Masaba, already sick, tired and extremely hungry, was wailing at the top of her lungs.

Finally, at some point, we were put into cars and sent to our flat.

None of us could sleep that night. We stayed awake, waiting for news of what exactly had happened. We wanted to know if everyone was safe.

All through the night, people kept coming to the flat to take blankets. Mysore Hospital was running short. There were just too many victims and the hospital was not able to cope.

'Neena, you're alive? That's such a relief,' people said to me as they came and went.

The whole scene kept flashing in my mind. It was to be my wedding. I was supposed to be the centre of attention. I wasn't supposed to sneak out, and I didn't tell anybody when I did. That's why everyone assumed I had also died.

At some point during the night, someone suggested we call our families.

'This is going to be big news tomorrow,' they said. 'It's going to be all over TV and radio. We should let our families know we're safe.'

But we couldn't all call home. The landlord living downstairs had one phone and trunk calls were expensive. So, we decided our families could spread the word.

I was one of the three people who were allowed to make a call. So, I called my father.

'Papa, listen, there's been a fire here,' I said, keeping my voice calm. 'I'm okay, so don't worry.'

My father was confused and didn't understand why I was calling him so late. I didn't want him to panic and worry. So, I didn't tell him how big the fire was or the horrible things I had seen. I just told him the basics and passed on the numbers of other family members who needed to be informed.

But, the next day, when the television channels picked up the news, he called me crying. He was very worried about us.

Our director Sanjay Khan had suffered massive burns and had been transferred to Bangalore that very night.

The death toll that night was fifty. The final toll would be sixty-two.

In time, we would put together the bits and pieces of information to understand what had really happened.

The ceiling and walls were covered in gunny bags. They lit an anar, a fire fountain, inside the studio. The ceiling caught fire and it spread quickly. There was a short circuit which resulted in a huge explosion. There was just one exit to the studio and that too was very narrow. When the studio caught fire, there was a stampede. A lot of the dead were found lying at the entrance of this door, crushed.

The next day, it became quite clear that we needed to leave Mysore.

I called Shankar Nag in Bangalore and told him about my situation. He immediately offered to send his car to pick me up. But I told him not to bother because it would take too long.

The production team wasn't around to coordinate with us or arrange vehicles for our departure, so some of us decided to hire a taxi to Bangalore from where we would make arrangements to go back home.

In Bangalore, Shankar and his wife, Arundathi, brought me to their house and, for the first time since everything happened, I let myself truly go.

I was traumatized and the shock had dried up my milk. I hadn't been able to feed Masaba and she wasn't taking formula.

But Arundathi whisked Masaba away and took care of her. I was given a pill so I could finally sleep; I hadn't slept in two days. Shankar and Arundathi insisted I spend the night and fly back the next day.

So I agreed and let them take care of me, my maid and Masaba.

Shankar and his brother, Ananth Nag, were big names in Kannada cinema. Since this tragedy had happened so close to home, the actors made statements, offering all the support and help needed by those injured and stranded.

Shankar also took care of our flight tickets back to Bombay and made all the arrangements. I couldn't thank him enough.

When I arrived in Bombay, I didn't go to my flat. I went to my aunt's house. She immediately took me to a temple nearby to thank God for saving me. I am not a very religious person and I don't go to temples often. But after what I had been through, and the close call I'd had, I just had to stand in front of an idol and say, thank you.

It took me months to get over this tragedy. I was very numb for a long time. People told me I was often unresponsive, lost in my own world. I was also afraid of fire. I couldn't be near a flame. But, eventually, I had to get over it and I had to move on because I had to work so I could feed my baby and myself.

What happened on the sets of *Tipu Sultan* was tragic and I still feel sick to my stomach when I think about it. I also wonder about what would have happened if I hadn't snuck out to feed Masaba. It was my wedding scene. I was covered in nylon. I could have easily been on the list of casualties.

'Masaba saved your life,' people would tell me in the days and years to come. And it's true. If I had let her stay home instead of

calling her to the green
room, I wouldn't have
got out just before the
explosion.

To this day, I believe
that being her mother
saved me because she
needed me and I needed
her.

Love, love, love

2

Lonely, but Not Alone

I honestly don't know how I would have survived those first few years of motherhood without Aunty.

She found a reliable maid to help with Masaba. Aunty was also the reason I could take up small assignments to earn money in those early months after my delivery. Masaba and my maid would stay at her house, which was very close to mine in Juhu, while I went to work whenever the opportunity arose.

I once had a shoot very early in the morning, but Masaba got sick the night before. She threw up and was generally very uneasy. But Aunty handled the situation, staying up the whole night, not waking me up even once, because she wanted me to be fresh for the shoot the next day.

Whenever I had parties or networking events to attend, I would try to take Masaba with me, but Aunty would always offer to babysit instead.

'She's so small, what will she do at these parties?' she asked. 'And you also won't enjoy. Leave her with me and go do your work.'

If I wasn't shooting, I was constantly at Aunty's house or she was at mine, helping with Masaba and overall ensuring my well-being.

Uncle was also very fond of children, and he doted on Masaba, always playing with her.

My aunt also helped me secure a place for Masaba at Jamnabai Narsee School, one of the best schools in Juhu, by calling all her connections and pulling as many strings as she could.

Her own children had attended Jamnabai, and she worked there part time, pro bono, whenever there was a shortage of teachers.

One day, Vivian called me and said that we should meet. That we should go on holiday—him, Masaba and I—and get reacquainted.

I was happy for days after that and even got Masaba excited about our trip. 'We're going to meet your father,' I told her, and she shrieked with glee.

Securing admission for Masaba in a good school had been on my mind for a long time. I had been very stressed because of our unusual situation with her father, not to mention all the negative press we kept getting. It made me feel that no school would accept her.

Masaba and Vivian in Mombasa

But my aunt ploughed through and got me an interview with the main trustee of Jamnabai Narsee School. The date was set, and I was nervous and excited at the same time.

In Orlando

Unfortunately, the interview clashed with the day I was supposed to leave for a holiday with Vivian. So, when he called me a few days later and asked if I was all set, I told him we would have to postpone.

'I have secured this date for Masaba's admission. I have to be there. It's very important.'

But Vivian didn't understand the importance of it. Or maybe I wasn't clear enough in explaining to him how difficult it was for a child in this situation to get admission in a good school.

He thought I was not serious about meeting him and was just making an excuse to drop out. This wasn't the case at all. He hung up on me, dismissive and angry, and didn't call me again for five years.

My aunt was there for me though. She accompanied me to the appointment with strict instructions to not to say a word and let her do all the talking.

During the interview, if I so much as opened my mouth to speak, she shut me up with a stern look and took over the conversation.

Whatever she did worked though. Because on that day we were assured that Masaba would get a spot at Jamnabai. I was overcome with joy.

* * *

One day I came home from Aunty's house in the evening and found that the ceiling of my flat had collapsed.

My flat was on the third floor of the building and, like so many Bombay homes, this one too had cracks in the walls and chips would fall off once in a while. We just filled in the cracks and whitewashed the ceiling and walls so they didn't show.

But this time, when I surveyed the damage, I knew it was serious.

A large chunk of the ceiling had caved in and it was all over the floor. I looked up and saw the iron structure of the building staring back at me.

I got so scared that evening! What if I had been in the house with Masaba and the maid when this happened?

That's when I decided to sell the house. I didn't want to risk living there any more.

'Just repair it,' my father said. 'Don't sell it.'

But I didn't listen to him. I had made up my mind because I was convinced that this was the right thing to do for my child.

I didn't know then that I was making one of the biggest mistakes of my life and that I would suffer for years because of it.

Aunty and Uncle were so nice and kind. I would spend so much time at their house. In fact, every evening when I would get ready to leave, Aunty would say, 'Why are you going home? Just stay back.'

I honestly felt that our bond was unshakable. That we had a strong relationship. So, I sat them down one day.

'I'm thinking of selling the house,' I said. 'I have found another house in an upcoming building, but I won't be able to move in before a year or two. Can I stay with you?'

They didn't even hesitate.

'You are like our own daughter,' they said. 'You're more than welcome. You don't even have to ask.'

But I felt like I did have to ask. I had to tell them what this entailed.

'If anything goes wrong and you throw me out, I will be homeless,' I said. 'I won't have anywhere to go. So please consider this before taking me in because I won't be able to move out for at least a year or so.'

But they were overcome with joy. Their own kids lived in different parts of the world, and I think Aunty was suffering from empty nest syndrome. They were also very fond of Masaba, and they sincerely thought it was a good idea.

But my father was dead against it.

'Even if you stay with them all day, just rent your own house so you have somewhere to go if things go wrong,' he said.

'Why?' I retorted. 'Aunty and I are so close. They would never ask me to leave. You don't know what our relationship is like. She is my soulmate.'

But my father, till the day I moved in, was insistent that it was a bad idea. When I didn't listen, because I honestly thought I knew my aunt and her husband well, he gave up and said just one thing that haunts me to this day.

'Do not trust her,' he said and left it at that.

So, I sold my house in Juhu even though my father was dead against it. I got around Rs 9 lakh from the sale, and I put the entire amount towards booking a Raheja property that was coming up on Yari Road. I had nothing left for myself but I felt secure because my aunt and uncle were very supportive. Their home was my home in the interim. Or at least that's what I thought.

Our relationship was good. A bit too good. Too good to be true.

3

Choli Ke Peeche Kya Hai?

In 1993 I got a career-altering role in *Khal Nayak*. It was a small part, but it would be significant to my future.

Of course, when I first got the offer, I refused.

Satish Kaushik called me one day and said that Subhash Ghai—the renowned Subhash Ghai—wanted to meet me.

I jumped with joy. I remember I had approached him years ago for work and he had told me he didn't believe in headshots. He cast people based on what he thought about them in real life. He had never cast me in anything.

I was so excited that he had called me for a role in his upcoming film, *Khal Nayak*.

I didn't know what it would entail, but I knew I wanted to be a part of it.

When I got to his office and met him, he played me a song. You know which one I'm talking about. It was 'Choli Ke Peeche Kya Hai' and it started like this: 'cook cook cook cook cook cook cook'. This also became a hilarious meme during the first COVID-19 lockdown when all everyone seemed to be doing was cook.

When I first heard the song, I knew it was catchy. But when Subhash Ghai told me what my role would be, I wasn't so keen any more.

I liked the fact that my part was sung by my friend Ila Arun, with whom I had acted in many films. But I couldn't do it. It was

175

only a quarter of the song (at most) and one small scene after that. I could do better. I was better.

I came away very disheartened. I even told him, 'Sir, I'm an actor. I can do better. If it was a full song, I would have thought about it but this, honestly, is too small a part.'

He understood, but a few days later when I met him at a party, he told me I should seriously think about it.

Satish Kaushik called me and said I should do it. But I kept refusing.

I finally gave in when Subhash Ghai called me again and instead of saying hello, actually played the song over the phone.

'Sirrrr,' I whined.

'Listen, Neena,' he said. 'If you don't benefit from doing this song, you won't benefit. But you won't lose anything. I promise you that this song will be a big, BIG hit.'

Well, he wasn't wrong because the song was and still is a massive hit.

I agreed. We shot the whole thing in nine days at Filmistan Studios.

I couldn't help but admire how big the set was the first day I arrived for fittings. They put me in a tribal Gujarati outfit and sent me to Subhash Ghai for approval.

'No! No! No! No!' he shouted. '*Kuch bharo.*'

I was so embarrassed. In my opinion, he was referring to my choli and stating that it needed to be filled. It wasn't anything personal, I knew. He had visualized something . . . bigger for the rendition.

I didn't shoot that day. But the next day I was presented to him in a different outfit, with a bra that was heavily padded, and he seemed satisfied.

Subhash Ghai was very particular about what he wanted, which was why he was such a good director.

'Don't just mime the words,' he would tell me. 'When you're singing "Choli Ke Peeche Kya Hai", say the words and emote like you're reciting a dialogue.'

So, I ended up singing the song and reciting the lyrics like I would a dialogue. The song became a big hit and people loved my performance.

I got very little money from the song, but the live shows that followed, paid me enough to make me comfortable.

It was because of this song that the stage show saga of my life began.

I got to go abroad to perform in many countries. I performed all over India.

I toured with Bappi Lahiri, Asha Bhonsle and many others.

I performed not just my bit in 'Choli Ke Peeche Kya Hai' but also Madhuri's. I could also perform some other songs and sing a full Punjabi number, which is why I became a commodity that the organizers paid for because I was worth it.

In between all this, I got to go for the Manhattan premiere of my film *In Custody*. Again, my part was small, but the film was released internationally and starred Shashi Kapoor, Shabana Azmi and Om Puri among others.

Om Puri was busy with other commitments so he couldn't go to the US, which is why I got the opportunity to fly down. Shabana Azmi and I were on the same flight.

It was a grand, red-carpet affair. We were driven to the venue in a limousine. I had worn my long hair loose and worn a beautiful sari. It was a bit chilly, so I had carried a shawl that I left in the limo so I could use it at the after-party.

But when the premiere ended, we were all ushered into a van and transported to a restaurant for the after-party. The limo had disappeared, taking my stole with it.

I didn't want to make a big deal of it even though I was very cold. I didn't want anybody to think I was a novice and was crying over a little stole.

I woke up early the next morning and went for a walk where I met Shashiji who was also on his morning stroll. We got talking and he asked me how my experience was the night before.

'It was good,' I said, not sounding entirely unconvincing. 'Actually, where did the limo go after the show? I had left my stole in it.'

Shashiji started laughing heartily.

'Madam, this is what happens,' he said. 'We always go in style and come home as peasants. Don't worry. I'll buy you a new stole.'

'No no,' I said. 'That's not what I meant. I was just confused.'

We had a good laugh over this for the rest of our walk.

That was just how things were. We were always taken everywhere in style. The organizers loved to show us off. But it was understood that after the show we had to pick up our own suitcases and make our way to whatever taxi or cattle van they had organized for us.

Even someone as big as Asha Bhonsle understood this and acted accordingly. I was very impressed with her for practising such humility.

Back in India, I was getting more offers for stage shows. My role in *Khal Nayak* wasn't what I expected. But what followed really helped me out financially.

I didn't have an agent or a manager, so I had to take a lot of the bookings and negotiate all of the payments on my own.

I had to learn quickly so that I didn't get taken for granted without someone to guard my interests. I learnt early on that I should ask for my entire payment up front before going on stage.

Once I was flown down to Calcutta for a performance with a very big artiste. The venue was two hours from the city. A close friend of mine was also going to perform and I was grateful for the company.

Before leaving Bombay, I called the organizers to ask about my payment and they assured me that it would be waiting at the Calcutta airport. I took their word in good faith and boarded the flight.

But once I got to Calcutta, I was told by another set of organizers that they didn't know about my payment and that I should just go to the venue and sort it out. Something about this didn't sound right, so I put my foot down and insisted on getting paid.

I even called the artiste and told him the situation. After a while, a surly man arrived with a bundle of 100-rupee notes. He tossed the bundle at me. I counted it; it was not even a quarter of what I had been promised.

I refused to go to the venue and decided to return to Bombay. However, the ground staff told me that the next flight back was in the evening.

So, I decided to book my flight and spend the day at a hotel nearby.

My performer friend found me waiting for a taxi and asked me what I planned to do.

'Have you been paid?' I asked.

'Not yet. They have given me a small portion. I'll go to the venue and see about the rest.'

Even though my friend seemed to be taking things as they came, I didn't feel right. I sensed there was something weird going on and refused to go with her.

As I was getting into the taxi, the organizer who had come to give me the money jumped into the front seat.

'You are not going anywhere,' he shouted. 'We will not let you leave. You will come to the venue and perform.'

'You cannot stop me,' I said.

'Yes, we can!'

His behaviour scared me. He looked angry and desperate.

I saw a policeman and called out to him. He directed us to the closest police station where the inspector heard our complaints.

I also made a quick phone call to a well-connected friend in Calcutta who made calls to the higher authorities for me.

All this while, the man kept shouting, 'She has committed to us. She has to do the show.'

But the inspector saw my side of the situation and tried to knock some sense into him.

'You cannot legally detain her. You cannot physically force her to go with you,' he explained. 'You have to let her go. File a case against her later.'

In all this chaos I started crying. I didn't understand what was going on and why they couldn't just pay me the money in advance, as was the common practice all over the world for live stage shows.

I was finally allowed to leave, and I caught my flight back to Bombay.

A few days later, I found out that the show did not take place at all. Apparently, the organizers had lied about the line-up and promised much bigger stars (who weren't even booked to begin with) to sell tickets.

The crowd had eventually rioted and broken the stage, and all the remaining performers had fled the scene.

This was a really terrible experience and my resolve to get my payment up front, in advance, became stronger from then on.

Months later, there was a knock on my door. It was the organizer who had tried to stop me at the airport. He was in tears when I opened the door.

'Madam, do you remember me? From Calcutta?' I honestly wanted to say no and shut the door, but there was something about the way he was standing that made me change my mind. He looked distraught. So I nodded.

'I remember.'

'The money I had given you that day at the airport was my own,' he said. 'They never reimbursed me. Please, madam, please return that money to me. I am really in need. I have no money to eat.'

I didn't argue. I didn't say anything. I just went in, found my purse and gave him the amount I had received at the airport that day.

I never saw him again. I never did a show with his company or that artiste ever again.

* * *

The set I performed kept me in demand at live shows. It had three numbers, 'Shayarana Si Hai' from *Phir Teri Kahani Yaad Aayee*, 'Choli Ke Peeche' from *Khal Nayak* and 'Peeche Peeche Aunda', the Punjabi song I sang.

It was easy work for decent money. I did a lot of concerts with big singers. Some one-off shows and a lot of weddings.

But even though the money was good for such little time spent on stage, the experience wasn't always pleasant.

I once had to travel to Ahmedabad to perform at a sangeet function. The venue, a club, was just outside the city. I reached there in the morning and went straight to my room, which was just behind the stage, but it didn't matter. It was only for one night.

I had been roped in by a very popular singer who was also a wonderful person. I didn't think even twice before agreeing.

I had my hairdresser with me, so she helped me get ready. It was one of those formats where one set is done by a professional and the second by the family members. I finished my set pretty early, just before the intermission, and returned to my room.

It had been a long day, so I quickly undid my hair and removed my make-up. I slipped into my nightdress and started getting ready for bed.

I was just about to nod off when there was a loud bang on my door. It was late so I got a bit nervous about who it could be.

I opened the door and found a very loud and drunk man standing outside.

'Come out and dance,' he slurred.

'I'm sorry?' I asked. 'I have already finished my performance. I can't go on again. My agreement with them was for the three numbers in my set and it is done.'

But the man was so drunk he couldn't understand even a word of what I was saying. He started to get agitated.

'GET READY RIGHT NOW AND COME PERFORM,' he shouted at me and went away.

I was so scared I didn't know what to do. There were no mobile phones so I couldn't even call any of the other artistes, or the singer who had asked me to come.

At that moment, Vivian called on the landline. I had given him the number in case he wanted to get in touch. I was so relieved to hear his voice.

He had barely said hello when I burst into tears.

'I don't know what to do,' I was crying as I recounted what had happened and what was being asked of me. 'That man was drunk and he's going to come back, I know it. What should I do? I have already finished my performance.'

Vivian told me to take a deep breath and I did. Then he asked if I had someone with me. I did, luckily.

'Then just go and get it over with,' he said.

'What?' I asked. Shocked.

'Just get it over with. You're outnumbered. They won't understand reason at this moment. Just go and perform one song and be done with it.'

He wasn't being patronizing or mean. He sounded like he empathized. Like he too had gone through something like this.

So I decided to take his advice. I changed and went outside. I didn't know anybody there, but having my hairdresser with me gave me some comfort and security in case something went wrong.

I went on stage and performed to a film song. I finished my performance to drunken cheers from the audience, and then I went back to my room and slept.

* * *

Once I moved in with Aunty and Uncle, I found out things weren't as they had seemed. Their marriage, perfect on the outside, had deep cracks in it.

Soon after I moved in, I realized that Aunty was a very unhappy woman. Uncle had been having an affair with a theatre actress for a while.

She would talk about her problems and insecurities. Uncle wasn't as nice as I thought he was, she told me. He was the villain in their relationship.

My aunt's mother also lived with her for extended periods of time. She had her own home in Juhu but that had been shut for almost fifteen to twenty years. Her mother divided her time between my aunt's house in Juhu and my aunt's sister's home in Delhi.

Things were still not terrible, but sometimes I got dragged into my aunt and uncle's conflict. My aunt, especially, with whom I spent most of my time as my uncle was never home during the day, didn't spare a thought before telling me all their intimate secrets.

I felt sorry for her plight and initially found myself taking her side.

But slowly, I started to see that my uncle wasn't as bad as she made him out to be. That he was genuinely a nice man. He was kind and fair to me. He loved Masaba and dropped whatever he was doing when he was at home to play with her.

I think things started to get sour with my aunt when we once had a disagreement about something I honestly don't remember now. Uncle stood up for me and took my side.

This didn't go down well with my aunt. She thought I was turning against her and favouring her husband.

She slowly started to withdraw. She also started an affair with a man. I know this because she sent me a few times to deliver messages to him.

I tried my best to win her love and loyalty back. But in time I realized that it was of no use because I had to, once again, justify my actions, which I thought were honest and right, and prove to her that I wasn't being dishonest. That I didn't have ulterior motives for siding with Uncle during their arguments.

My aunt also started suspecting me of something. I never quite understood what exactly it was. There was no question of me having an affair with Uncle because I thought of him as a father figure. I respected him in much the same way I would a beloved uncle. But the more I tried to prove myself to her, the worse things got.

'I don't know why my aunt is acting like this with me,' I'd tell my friends.

'She must be jealous of you,' they would say. 'She probably suspects you're after her husband.'

'That cannot be the case,' I'd say. 'I have given her no reason to suspect me.'

But that's the thing about some people. They don't need reason because their anger and discontent make them so bitter, they only see what they want to see.

I did what I could to go unnoticed in the house. I started to keep my mouth shut if I disagreed with her. I had nowhere to go if things went wrong. My Raheja flat was still not ready. Our relationship started to get strained. But for the sake of my daughter, I had to bear whatever came my way.

On the work front, I started to get very saturated. I was still not getting any good roles. I had to keep doing live shows to make ends meet. I was in a very bad place and needed something to pull me out of it.

4

Bazaar Sitaram

Once, on a visit to Delhi, my father took me to his old family home in Bazaar Sitaram. He had grown up in that area and we still had some family living there. He took me on a tour in a cycle rickshaw—the roads were too narrow for cars—and we finally reached his house in Takhat Wali Galli, Mohalla Imli, Bazaar Sitaram.

What a melodious address it was! A light bulb went on in my head and I realized I had to capture it in my work somehow.

It took me back to my interview at NSD during the admission process. We were asked to perform something that was specific to the culture of our cities and states.

NSD applicants came from diverse backgrounds, from all over the country, even from abroad.

Students would present something that was specific to their personal cultures. It could be dance, dialogue, folk songs or music. Students got creative here.

But when my turn came to perform, I remember being stumped.

'I'm from Delhi,' I thought. 'What can I do that represents Delhi the way I know it?'

I must have impressed them regardless because I got admission and the scholarship. But my inability to think of something off the top of my head haunted me for years.

Delhi has a good art and culture scene. But a lot of what I was exposed to was borrowed from other cultures and states. I tried and failed for years to find something that was quintessentially Delhi. But that's not Delhi's fault. It's mine. Because until I visited Bazaar Sitaram and saw it through my father's eyes, I didn't realize it was a treasure trove of culture, art, song and architecture.

Bazaar Sitaram was a world unto itself. The lanes were narrow and the houses were built so close together that one could reach out and touch their neighbour's walls. A typical house had an open-air veranda on the ground floor with rooms, a kitchen and a shared bathroom surrounding it. On the first and second floors, the ground was laid out using iron rods so that the light that came through the roof went all the way down, through the house. The first few times I walked on these floors, I was so nervous I'd fall through. But in time and with practice, I didn't even realize they were there.

The day I visited with my father, there was a wedding down the street. We followed the music to find a group of women singing and dancing. I had never heard those songs before, and the music was also new to me. I decided then that I would use these songs, music and culture as my backdrop and make a film in Bazaar Sitaram.

It would be a documentary, I decided, but set to a story so that the audience didn't get bored. I wrote the script myself. I was nervous about pitching it, so I approached Shyam Benegal to take a look at it. He gave me some of the best advice I have ever received. He also said something that stuck with me and I have used it in my writing ever since.

'Every story has to have a clear beginning, middle and an end,' he said. 'Remember that and you will never fail.'

So, I rewrote the script. I made it a love story between a young girl and her neighbour. I drew from my own childhood experience with Babu to write it. The lovers are from very strict orthodox families who are against their union. So, they decide to elope in the middle of the night. Unfortunately, while the girl reaches the meeting point, the boy gets cold feet and ditches her. The girl returns home disappointed. Bazaar Sitaram takes her back with open arms.

I applied for a grant from Films Division and received Rs 4,20,000 for the project. This was in 1993. I took the money and set off for Delhi.

I produced, directed and acted in this documentary. It stars Rajesh Aggarwal and me but really, the main character is Bazaar Sitaram.

This project was a labour of love. I hadn't ever directed anything of this sort before. We stayed in my father's old house. My father was so happy that his mohalla would be featured in my work that he helped in every way he could. He became our production manager. He set up our sleeping quarters with bedding and kept bringing us food from different houses in the mohalla.

The people in the area treated us really well because they had great respect for my father and late grandfather. The boys in the area followed us around to ensure that nobody bothered us. They would take it upon themselves to clear out crowds or bring people in to participate whenever needed. Not a single person took a single penny from us. They were just so proud that their area was finally being captured on film.

I was so careful about how we spent the money, but still overshot the budget because that's just how things are in film-making. In fact, I ended up spending an additional Rs 60,000 from my own pocket, but I did not regret it one bit because it really fuelled my artistic passion.

Bazaar Sitaram won two National Awards—Best Documentary and Best Direction. I was over the moon!

I have to add here that this award would not have been possible without the stellar editing skills of Renu Saluja. I directed the film. I had a good eye for detail and excellent storytelling skills. But it was Renu who brought out the true essence of *Bazaar Sitaram* through her editing skills. I gave her the footage, shot in bits and pieces. She wove it all together, letting the music of Bazaar Sitaram lead the way.

One of the reasons why I have always looked to the future, why I am not jaded by my past, is that I have met some wonderful people who have helped me achieve amazing things. In this case, it was Renu and, of course, the wonderful people of Bazaar Sitaram who with their love, support and faith helped me achieve the highest accolade in Indian cinema.

5

Inaam but No Kaam

After *Bazaar Sitaram* in 1993, I acted in *Woh Chokri* in 1994, another National Award-winning film.

It was directed by Shubhankar Ghosh and starred Paresh Rawal, Pallavi Joshi, Om Puri and me in major roles.

The story is about the rise and fall of Geeta Devi, a well-do-do woman, after she is widowed at a very young age. The main plot revolves around Apsara, Geeta's daughter, played by Pallavi Joshi.

It was a beautiful film, but it didn't get a theatrical release. I don't think many people saw it. I played my part well and received my second National Award, this time for best supporting actress.

It felt amazing to be recognized for my acting talents, and there's no greater accolade for an Indian actor than the National Award.

Mahesh Bhatt once told me that awards are good validation. But they don't necessarily lead to roles. I agreed with him but that didn't stop me from flying high for winning an award for a film hardly anybody watched.

But Mahesh was right. This win did not translate to roles. Well, actually, I did get a lot of work but the curse of Lallu Ladki still loomed large because they were never lead roles.

I yearned for my big break. Yes, I had already got my break in television with *Khandaan* but that didn't get me better roles because of the strong character I had played.

There is a different sort of feeling you get when you are a film star. You're one rung above everyone else. You're in the A-list, and it's something most actors aspire to. So did I. But it would be a long time before I would get anything that was worth the kind of effort I was putting into my work.

That being said, I can't complain how things were going for me either. I had enough roles in television. I was earning a good living. I could support my daughter and myself with no help from anybody. I was successful in my own right, and I was independent.

In the 1990s, I was in a lot of television series. I'd say I really proved my talent as an actor with these roles. I played Kabir's mother in *Kabir*. I played the *gharelu* bahu in *Saans*. I played a sexy babe and I played a strong woman. In television, my characters were vast and varied and really tested my skills as an actor. I loved the challenge.

As for films, well, I did quite a few but nothing significant. I did lots of small parts, short appearances (can't call them cameos because I was still a relative nobody).

I would do so many of these films hoping that they would lead to my big break, or at least a more sizeable role in the future, and would then come home and pray for months that they wouldn't release, because the kind of roles I did, the sort of characters I played, were frankly quite embarrassing.

One such film was David Dhawan's *Eena Meena Deeka* which starred Vinod Khanna, Juhi Chawla and Rishi Kapoor. I was cast as a beggar (yes, seriously), one of many in a gang headed by Shakti Kapoor. If you watch the film again, you will know why I'm so embarrassed to be associated with it.

In my defence, when I took up the role, I thought my part would be a lot bigger than it actually was. But that's how things are sometimes. Especially when you, like me, don't have the self-confidence to speak up for your rights. Sometimes I wonder if I would have got the roles or the lines I truly deserved if I only had the courage to speak up. I had two National Awards sitting on my shelf at home. I sure as hell had proven my worth on TV . . . And yet, here I was, playing a *bhikharan*.

But then again, speaking up can be a slippery slope especially when you're constantly told that you're a nobody. I was told this by well-meaning friends—that my two National Awards and my countless roles on TV meant nothing without a film break—and to an extent that's what I believed too.

During the filming of *Eena Meena Deeka*, dressed like a beggar, I went up to David Dhawan with a request. We had just broken from a scene where all the beggars were running and shouting out different lines. I didn't have a line. I was just supposed to run and shout. I approached Davidji gingerly and asked if he could give me something to say as well.

'Who do you think you are asking me something like that? What lines do you want to say?' he shouted at me. Directors tend to be under a lot of pressure from all sides—producers, actors, the cast and investors—so I knew he was in a bad mood. But that didn't justify the way he spoke to me.

It was a nasty situation. This happened in front of everyone and I just cringed and crawled back into my shell.

This wasn't the first time this had happened and it wouldn't be the last on a commercial film set. And yet I gravitated towards films for two big reasons:

I needed the money.

Being in a film felt slightly better than being on television. Film actors were taken more seriously than television stars.

But then came an incident that would ruin me for all films for a long time.

I was shooting on the sets of a big production with a big director who was known to be womanizer. He was also known for making innuendos.

I tolerated a lot of inequalities which were rampant on film sets. I arrived in Agra and was put up in a small, albeit comfortable, hotel with the junior stars, while the big stars and director were put up in a five-star hotel.

I stood in line with the production and crew for my meals, which again, I was used to.

I sat and waited for hours for my scene to be filmed, while the bigger stars got to go back to their hotel rooms and rest.

Anil Kapoor noticed all I was being put through and offered to speak to the director and get me upgraded. I really appreciated his offer because it came at a time during filming when I really needed a well-wisher. And I will always appreciate Anil Kapoor for this.

But I refused. I just wanted to finish my scenes and go back home.

However, this was not to be, because even though I could tolerate a lot of things—the humiliation, the waiting, the treatment like a junior actor—I still had a breaking point.

The straw that broke the camel's back came one day when the director, jokingly, while directing me in a scene, said, 'Neena Gupta, if you don't use some things, they will get rusted.'

The director was known for saying double-meaning sentences, and I knew instantly what he was referring to.

I was livid. I couldn't believe someone could speak to a woman this way regardless of her circumstances.

So, when I returned home, I did something that I don't regret, but have been told was a big mistake on my part.

I spoke to the press about it.

As you can imagine, the situation escalated because the press printed their version and then the director responded not very favourably. I then retaliated and said some nasty things of my own. It was a disaster for everyone. Well, not for the director who got public sympathy and, owing to his position, most of the industry's support. It definitely sabotaged my career because I stopped getting parts in films from then on.

'You should have just let it go,' a friend told me. 'You are still a nobody and you have a long way to go. You should have just vowed never to work with him again. What did you think? That you would win? That he would be discredited? That everyone would forget how powerful he is and come over to your side?'

I had been a fool, but I stood my ground. In the process though, I left my door open wide to the press, who started to snoop around and find things they could use for their own profit.

When you keep your door closed, anybody standing outside has to knock, take your permission to enter and then scan what they can or cannot touch based on the boundaries you draw. I did none of that. I was an open book.

When you're in the public eye, the press can be an unreliable beast. One that makes you believe they're your friend, gets you to confide in them and then spins your story in a way that will profit them the most.

For all that I have been through with the Indian media though, I do not blame them. They aren't the villains.

They too are trying to do their job. Show biz is their business too. All of us in the limelight profit from their endeavours, but only when we know what to say, what not to say and how to conduct ourselves.

The press is not your friend. I hope young actors and actresses understand this and learn from my mistakes. My media image, how I was portrayed and the losses I suffered were nobody's fault but my own, because I let myself believe that the press was a friend when really, they were just doing their job.

They need to sell their stories and actors who give them the most masala are the easiest and best targets. I was one of those actors, and I thought I would benefit, but really, I just harmed myself.

You may pour your heart out and tell them all your problems. But when the story comes out, it is headlined by a quote that has been taken out of context when not read with the copy accompanying it, which people rarely do. There is usually a picture with a caption that's just as misconstrued as the headline, and you get nothing but trouble.

Star Dust, Filmfare, Cine Blitz were a few of the big magazines at that time, and I gave them enough and more to get by. They wanted masala and I gave them masala at the cost of personal relationships and work. They turned around and wrote rubbish about me.

There's one incident that's more recent. Masaba and I had taken a picture with Vivian and a friend of his, Michelle. Masaba posted the picture on Instagram and a tabloid picked it up and ran a story. But the problem was that they cropped out Vivian's friend so it looked like it was just Masaba and the two of us on either side of her.

It sent out a very wrong message. Vivian's friend, who had been close to us until then—she even stayed in my house when she visited India—thought we had done it on purpose. That we had actually sent the media a photo of us with her cropped out. She cut all contact with us.

We were so hurt and upset. But we also understood that if somebody couldn't understand that this was how things worked with the Indian media, and if they held us accountable for such a situation—accuse us of doing such a thing on purpose—they weren't true friends to begin with.

As for the media, I think I have learnt the hard way that I must be very careful how I conduct myself. That I should think a million times before I say something so that I am not misquoted or my words misconstrued. I have seen that some of the most eloquent actors train themselves and speak only what is relevant and don't add to the fires created by the media.

I am much better at this game now. Well, slightly better because I am still me: open, honest and extremely outspoken.

But regardless of what happened with me back then, I still thank God for giving me whatever I have. That I didn't lose hope. That I didn't crumble under the pressure or hide like a coward, even when the rumour mill was rife with the gossip that I was working as a salesgirl in a showroom. I didn't even know how this started because it was ridiculous. Does nobody realize how highly qualified I am? I always had good career options outside of acting because of my education.

When I was younger, I hated that my mother forced me to do an MA and then an MPhil after my BA. Why did I need so many degrees if what I really wanted to do was act? I used to fight with her about this because I felt like it was a waste of time.

'I don't want to be a teacher or an IAS officer,' I would tell her. 'What am I going to do with these degrees?'

But, later in life, dressed as a beggar or waiting in line with the junior artistes to fill my plate at lunch, I felt really, really grateful to my mother. She pushed me to get the highest degree I could, which meant that no matter what happened in life, I would always be okay. If I ever decided to stop being an actor, I could be a teacher, at the very least. I could teach Hindi and Sanskrit. I could also teach drama if I wanted because I am a gold medallist from NSD. Well, I don't have a gold medal, but I was a topper in my class.

Thanks to my education, I was always okay. Through everything that happened in those years, knowing this always gave me comfort. It gave me courage. It gave me the strength to hold my head high and move on.

* * *

In 1994, I made a series called *Dard* for DD, which I produced, directed and also acted in.

It starred Manohar Singh, one of my favourite co-stars, and Gurpreet Singh who was popular at that time as a model for Siyaram.

My partner in this new venture was Anupam Kalidhar, whom I had met through common friends. He was a stockbroker by profession but wasn't getting any work at that time because of the Harshad Mehta scandal. So, he agreed to partner with me for *Dard*.

Stills from *Dard*

The series follows the journey of a woman who marries an older man out of obligation because he saves her life. She also has a child with him. But then she ends up falling in love with a younger man and faces internal and societal conflict.

It was a success and got very good reviews. It felt great to have achieved this on my own. We were also smart and ended it the minute the story reached its end because we didn't want to drag it on just for the sake of it.

I received a lot of support—investments and expertise—from friends and well-wishers in the industry, including Manish Goswami who was the producer of *Parampara*.

Even Rathikant Basu, who was heading media at DD, was very supportive of our ideas and pitches.

So once *Dard* ended, we started working on *Gumraah*. We had such a good relationship with Basu and were so confident of our work that we didn't really sign a formal agreement before starting work on *Gumraah*.

We had eight episodes of the series in the bank when, one day, we suddenly received word that Basu had been transferred and another person would be taking his place in the media department.

We panicked and flew down to Delhi that day itself to meet him.

When we got there, we had to wait before we were allowed to see the new head. Once we were in front of him, he was dismissive and rude and kept doing other things while we were speaking.

But, at some point, he paused just long enough to inform us that *Gumraah* would be taken off the air. That another show—made my someone with far less experience than us—would be taking its place.

No amount of pleading would change his mind.

'At least air the eight episodes we have already shot,' I begged.

'No. It's over,' he said.

We were ruined. We had put all our money into this series, and we were not even going to be able to finish it.

Our naivety in not getting a signed contract also meant that we wouldn't get paid at all. This was a time before cable and satellite television, so DD had been our only option.

I sat in the lounge at the airport, waiting for my flight. An episode of *Gumraah* was airing on the television. I couldn't hold back the tears that rolled down my face.

A young man came and asked me what was wrong. I was distraught but still managed to point to the television screen and relay all that had happened.

He was politically connected, he said, and would do his best to help me. He also wrote about it to the papers but nothing helped.

The new head of DD's media department had scrapped our show and there was nothing we could do about it.

I lost all my money. My partner had to sell everything, including his office.

We were such small producers, and we'd been ruined even before we got a chance to truly show what we were capable of. I decided to end my career as a producer because I couldn't afford for anything like this to happen again.

* * *

Just when I thought things couldn't get worse, my aunt decided she wanted me out of the house.

Things at home started to become unbearable no matter how nice my uncle was. He was gone all day and I was left alone with her. When the lady of the house doesn't want you around, your life can become unbearable.

So, one evening, I sat my aunt and uncle down once again and reminded them of our conversation before I moved in.

'If you throw me out, I will have nowhere to go,' I said. 'I had asked you before I moved in if this would be a problem, and you had assured me I could stay here until my flat was complete. You had promised that I could call this my home until then . . .'

'Of course, we promised,' my uncle spoke up. I could see that my aunt did not like this at all. 'You can stay here for as long as you need, Neena.'

If my life was uncomfortable before, my aunt made it unbearable after this conversation. She was hostile and stopped acknowledging my presence entirely.

She tied a scarf around her mouth so she wouldn't speak to me even if she was tempted. She retreated to her room and just did 'pooja-paath'.

I wanted to cry every single day.

So, one day, I told my uncle that I could not live there any more and just had to move out.

He offered to let me use my aunt's mother's house in Juhu, the one which had been lying empty for many years, until my flat got ready.

The flat was a nightmare to clean up. There were rat and pigeon droppings and feathers everywhere. The plumbing was rusty and the electric meter faulty.

Masaba suffered a lot for the first few days because she kept getting dust mite allergy. But my maid and I spent a whole week cleaning and managed, somehow, with the help of my friends who sent over plumbers and electricians, to make the place liveable.

But a few days into our stay here, my aunt's mother knocked on the door and announced that she would be living there too.

'You think you can take over my flat just like that?' she asked.

I was shocked and didn't know what she was talking about. But from the way she spoke to me, I realized that my aunt had told her that I had moved in with the intention of never moving out. That I intended to fraudulently take her flat. This was bizarre and completely uncalled for.

That day I decided I would cut all ties with my aunt and not take anything from her.

I went to the Raheja office which was on Linking Road and met Mr Raheja himself. I explained my situation to him very honestly and didn't leave out a single detail.

'Please,' I begged. 'I cannot wait until the building comes up. Please can you return some of my money so I can just move out and buy another house that's ready?'

Mr Raheja was a wonderful man and understood my plight completely. He called his manager and instructed him to give me a full refund; he didn't cut a single penny.

I got my money back and bought a house in Aram Nagar, Versova, and was even able to save up a bit to support myself for a while.

I returned the keys of the house to my uncle and moved to the new house with Masaba and my maid. I never looked back or asked them for anything ever again.

* * *

The place I bought in Aram Nagar wasn't my dream home. The area had a lot of dust which got into every nook and cranny of the house.

It could be unsafe, and hence was not the best place for a single mother with her child.

But it was good in the sense that it was a house, not a flat. It had a backyard and a small garden in front. There was a big maidan right outside, which was surrounded by other residential dwellings.

It was home because it was mine.

Aram Nagar was where I finally started to heal from the events that led to the estrangement from my aunt. Uncle still kept in touch and came by once in a while to see if I was okay and to play with Masaba.

But, one day, when he was visiting, the doorbell rang. I was in the kitchen, so my uncle answered the door.

It was my aunt, and she was livid. I remember she was wearing this white sari and was screaming. 'Come away from here immediately!' she said and my uncle followed.

My aunt had been having him tailed to see where he went. She had found out he'd been visiting us and had been displeased.

I called my uncle the next day and asked him if everything was okay.

'It's the same,' he sighed.

'I don't think you should visit us any more. I know you love Masaba and she loves you too. But it's best if we cut all ties now. I don't want to be the cause of even more distress in your marriage.'

Uncle didn't want to cut ties with us. He wanted to keep in touch. He wanted to see Masaba grow up.

'It's best if we do this now while she's still small,' I said. 'It will be easier for her to forget you.'

And that is how, with a very heavy heart, I stopped talking to my uncle too.

I lost two people who were very close to me. But in Aram Nagar, I met two people who became lifelong friends.

Varsha and Dilip lived a few doors down and they were a wonderful couple. They lived with their big family and had children of their own.

They helped me out because I was all alone and struggling to keep things positive and afloat. They watched Masaba, shared their meals, and, in time, we almost became like family.

During the riots of 1993, there was a lot of trouble around Aram Nagar. There was fighting, gunshots and discord between communities.

Aram Nagar, even on a good day, wasn't the safest place. But because of Varsha and Dilip, I felt secure and knew that help was close by.

One night, when the fighting was at its worst, I took Masaba and went to their home to seek refuge. They took me in with open arms and let us stay the night. The children were together so at least they had some distraction. The rest of us just sat there feeling scared for our children and for ourselves.

Earlier that evening, all the men of Aram Nagar, young and old, had started to take turns to patrol the neighbourhood. They had gone from door to door looking for hockey sticks, bats, basically anything they could use as weapons for self-defence.

It was one of the worst nights I spent in Aram Nagar, and I knew I had to work even harder so I could leave that place.

Varsha and Dilip are still in touch and we're there for each other whenever we need anything. Aram Nagar was not my dream home. But I met these wonderful friends there.

Part 4

Mad Times

Aap Jaa Sakte Hain, Namaste

In 1994, I finally left Aram Nagar and moved to Arshie Complex in Versova. I bought a beautiful three-bedroom home with a terrace, and while I was sad to be leaving some wonderful friends behind, this house proved to be a good thing for my family.

I was getting good roles in television. I was still hopeful that if I did enough small roles in films, I would get my big break sooner or later.

But, overall, this was a good period in my life because I finally had a big, beautiful house again. I had good friends with whom I spent time. And, most importantly, my father left Delhi and moved to Bombay to live with us.

It was absolutely amazing. My father took over so much responsibility that I could go out and work without feeling guilty about leaving Masaba.

I found a good friend in Anuranjan who also had two daughters. So, I would spend a lot of time with her, and Masaba had the girls to play with. Soni was still a part of

Masaba with her nanaji

my life, and we often took our girls out for meals, to parks or just sat at home and discussed parenting.

Being a single parent can be very hard and a lonely journey. But what I didn't get from a husband, I got from my friends and father—a helping hand and plenty of support.

Life for me had finally become 'normal' in every sense of the word. My daughter had friends. I had a family.

But at times I still felt like my career was stagnating. There was so much I wished to do. So many stories I wanted to be part of. So many roles I wanted to play.

Satellite TV was just taking off and I had been doing a serial on Zee TV as well as a celebrity chat show called *Sitara*. But I still felt like I wanted to do more.

As fate would have it, my old contact at DD, Rathikant Basu, who, a few years ago, had been transferred overnight out of programming to another unrelated department in Delhi, shifted to Star TV in Bombay.

I remember meeting him in Delhi a year or two before this move and telling him how much he was missed.

'You were the perfect person for artistes like us,' I told him. 'You should be in Bombay from where all the satellite channels operate. Not here.'

I was really glad to have him back in Bombay, and at Star TV no less. That's perhaps why I ventured into production again. I honestly felt like I had done every role except the ones I really wanted to do. Which, unfortunately, did not exist.

I remember talking to Vivian about my discontent and disillusionment with the industry. Over the years our friendship had grown, and we always turned to each other for support and advise.

'What is it that you want to do?' he asked me.

I told him about a book I had been reading and how wonderful it would be if I could star in a series based on it.

'If you think there's a role you want to play that hasn't been written yet, you need to write it. Go out there and make this show.'

And that's how I came to make *Saans*. I partnered up with Anupam Kalidhar again for this venture and we restarted our production house. Rathikant Basu at Star heard our pitch and commissioned it.

I produced, directed and starred in it. I called up Gulzar Sahib and requested him to compose the title track for the series. Just the antra and the *sthai* because I didn't want to use a full song. He was wonderful and supportive. He didn't even charge us for it. In fact, going forward, he composed the antra and sthai for all my shows, and because he wanted to support my career, he never charged me for any of them.

Life in television was truly good back then. The shows were still weekly, so we only had to shoot four to five episodes a month. The rest of the time we could just enjoy our work, sit back and plan what we wanted to say and visualize where we wanted our story to go. It was a creative person's dream come true.

Saans is the story of a couple, Priya (Me) and Gautam (Kanwaljit Singh), who are happily married with two children. But when a woman called Manisha (Kavita Kapoor) comes into their lives, their marriage starts to unravel and fall apart.

The series ran for four years and I think we ended it in the right way and at the right time. I was on a high after the series became a hit. I won an award for Best Director and Kanwaljit won one for Best Actor.

From then on, I was given free rein at Star Plus. I made quite a few TV shows. There was *Pal Chhin*, which was good, but not in the same league as *Saans* and *Siski*, which was way ahead of its time and didn't do well at all.

But, overall, my relationship with Star was beautiful even though Basu left (again, overnight) and Sameer Nair took over.

We got along well, and he really believed in my vision and shows. We had a good professional relationship and a very comfortable friendship too. I truly considered him my well-wisher and confidant.

I got an even bigger opportunity in 2002 when Star acquired the India rights for the British game show *The Weakest Link*. As the darling of Star TV and having proved my mettle with so many shows, I was among their first choices for an anchor.

It was called *Kamzor Kadi Kaun* and I had to get a full personality makeover to host it. It was a licensed show so the makers were very particular about how the set would look, what the host would wear and, of course, what she would say. So, I had to turn myself into a very stern, no nonsense, some might even call her bitchy, character to play the part.

I rehearsed for almost a month to look, feel and act the part.

The show got great publicity. There were hoardings all over the country. The show's producers had put in a lot of money to promote it and I was flying.

The money I received for this show went into moving out of Versova and back to Juhu. Doing up a new house, buying furniture and setting up the kitchen are some of my favourite things. Some people asked me, 'Why do you keep moving?' I said that's how I am. I absolutely loved a good house, and every time I made a bit of money, I invested it in upgrading property. 'I'm an excellent housewife without a husband,' I'd joke. It made me feel proud that I was able to earn these things for myself.

Unfortunately, *Kamzor Kadi* and my character did not go down very well with the Indian audience. They didn't like me in that avatar.

'*Aap hain aaj ke kamzor kadi,*' I'd say to contestants curtly with what's now defined as a 'resting bitch face'. '*Aap jaa sakte hain. Namaste.*'

Viewers found me rude and dismissive, even though it was all part of the original show's host's persona, and I started receiving a lot of flak.

'You were so nice in *Saans*,' people would stop me at the beach and say. 'Why are you so rude on *Kamzor Kadi Kaun*?'

But there wasn't much I could do personally. The show was licensed and it was impossible to change the character just to appease audiences because that was not allowed.

It was a big blow when the show was pulled off the air. But I wasn't surprised. I understood that it was not working at all. The channel was losing a lot of money. And there was no point pumping in more money to keep it alive and on air.

Things at the channel too had started to change. It started around the time I was still making *Pal Chhin*.

The channel heads had hired a slew of young boys and girls to start intently studying what the market wanted. Those were competitive times and channels were constantly vying for audience attention.

These young kids were called EPs (executive producers) and they answered only to the channel. It was their job to study how well a show was doing, what audiences had to say and then evaluate how they could keep the audience hooked.

This did not work well for us because suddenly we were being told what we were doing wrong. We were told to rewrite scripts to make our shows more juicy, completely disregarding the original vision and narrative.

It became impossible to work in these conditions and I started to withdraw. I stopped going to meetings because I really couldn't understand how someone with little to no experience in writing or film-making could tell us how to run our show. I told my partner, Anupam, that he was free to go to these meetings and listen to the nonsense they were spewing, but I wouldn't do it.

When Ekta Kapoor broke on to the scene with *Kyunki Saas Bhi Kabhi Bahu Thi*, things changed overnight. She had a new format, she tapped into a new kind of market (and audience mindset), and her shows ran every weekday instead of once a week.

I wasn't threatened because I knew there was an audience for all kinds of shows. I was even glad for having her around because it meant a lot more people would look to television for content.

Unfortunately, this worked against me and the kind of shows I was doing, because the channels found a sure-shot formula for what worked with the audience and they were hell-bent on milking it.

But what happened next was something even I didn't see coming.

I was visiting Delhi when I received a call from a senior official at Star. We had been close at one time, but he had eventually left all communications to the EPs. Everything went through them.

He was in complete support of the EPs (I don't blame him). He had targets to meet, competitors to destroy, and just presenting good, thought-provoking content was not good enough any more.

'If I have to choose between my marketing team and EPs and you, I will definitely choose them,' he had once told me in a meeting. Basically, I knew he was, in not so many words, asking me to deal with it or fuck off. But I was too foolish to think the channel wouldn't take any action against me after my years of service.

So, when this official called me that day when I was in Delhi, I was a little surprised and also pleased because his tone was friendly and very open. He hadn't called me personally in a long time.

'Listen, Neena, we're cancelling all your shows,' he said politely. I was a bit shocked but didn't think to argue. 'Don't worry though. We'll find something else for you.'

I said okay, hung up and started to think of new ideas for content that would work during this new wave in television.

But when the official started avoiding my calls and then, eventually, started avoiding me completely, once I returned to Bombay, I knew what was happening.

I was nothing and nobody to him now that he had tapped into a new format.

I was spoken to, instead, by his assistant and subordinates who asked me to back off and move on.

The day this was told to me loud and clear in the Star TV office, I had burst into tears and ran to the bathroom to avoid further humiliation.

I was shattered and couldn't believe this was happening. I was once the darling of Star and now I had been dismissed without even a proper explanation.

The official who had informed me about the cancellation of my shows didn't show his face during the meeting, choosing instead to have his cronies do it for him.

It didn't hurt that they had cancelled my shows and so ungraciously fired me. It hurt that someone whom I had considered a friend, a confidant, someone with whom I had shared a good professional relationship would do this to me without so much as an explanation or apology.

If he had perhaps just called me and told me the situation, if he had just said, 'Neena, your shows don't work any more', I think I would have understood and humbly backed off. But the whole situation was so ugly, so venomous, I just couldn't believe that it had ended this way.

Looking back at this phase of my life—from being the queen bee at Star TV to falling from grace—I don't blame him because at the end of the day he was just doing his job. He was trying to win the television game and he was doing a good job too.

I do, however, blame myself for once again being naive and trusting and opening myself up to someone who pretended to be a friend and then left me battered and bruised without even an explanation or goodbye.

'Aap jaa sakte hain. Namaste.'

2

If I Could Turn Back Time...

Sometimes I find myself wondering what I would do if I had a chance to go back and live my life again. Knowing what I know today, what would I do differently? What would I change and what would I keep the same?

I know I would have spent more time with my mother—talk to her, rest my head on her lap and enjoy her fingers caress my hair. I would have also asked her more about her own life as a young girl, woman, mother . . . wife . . .

I would have spoken to my brother more often; made sure he was okay; that he was making good choices.

I would have told my father how much I loved and appreciated him because I never told him that enough.

I would have taken that young girl, who had just found out she was pregnant, in my arms and told her, 'Your life is going to change beyond recognition. This is going to be the toughest thing you will ever do. But if there's anyone who can do it with grace and courage, it's you.'

But most of the time, when I look back at the things that happened to me in my career, I wonder how I would have reacted to them today.

I took up smaller roles hoping for bigger opportunities, not knowing that I would never get to play the lead. I didn't have anyone to guide me in those early years. In fact, I didn't even have a manager at the time. I took what came my way out of desperation because I needed to earn a living.

I was foolish and didn't know how things worked or how people were. I trusted too easily, and this sometimes came back to bite me. In the early days, when I was still new to the business, a fellow actor from *Jaane Bhi Do Yaaro* called me to discuss something important. We had both been offered an ad film and he wanted to know how much I was going to quote.

'I don't know how much to ask for. What are you quoting?' I asked.

He gave me a number and said I should probably quote the same thing. I honestly didn't know my worth in those days. My instinct told me I should ask for less than what the actor was asking because I wasn't as famous as he was. But I don't know. We'd discussed it and agreed on that number, so that's what I quoted. Turns out my initial instinct was correct. It was too much. I lost the offer entirely.

Later on, I found out the actor didn't quote what we'd agreed on. He quoted a lot less and got the ad film.

Looking back, I know he wasn't trying to screw me over. That he probably changed his quote for a different reason—maybe he was able to negotiate an offer.

But I should never have trusted him because, sometimes, people love to show off; to tell you this is what they're worth and it's how much they can command. I learnt the hard way that everyone is only looking out for themselves.

The industry is a business, and nobody is your friend. They don't necessarily wish you ill, but they don't go out of their way to wish you well either, unless there's something in it for them.

When it comes to determining your market value, remember you know best. If you think you're worth more, then you are. And if you think you need some more roles before asking a higher price, go with your gut.

I have suffered in my career and personal life because I didn't know my worth and sometimes trusted the wrong people.

Everybody likes to show that they're good. They're humble. They mean well. But remember, it's impossible to make everyone happy all of the time. If you meet such a person, tread carefully. If you are such a person, who genuinely wants to be liked and make everyone happy, please know that the only person you can make happy is yourself. If you want to please everyone in the room, you're doomed.

These are some of the things I learnt the hard way. If I could go back in time, I would tell myself to stop trying to please everyone. That I should see myself for what I was worth and not accept any less.

I would tell myself that the only appreciation one really needs is for their own work. But I can't go back in time. I can't change the things that have happened to me or alter the choices I have made. But I am glad I have learnt from my experiences; my mistakes.

Today, I don't care any more if someone says, 'Oh Neena, she's so nice . . . '

The only thing I want people to say about me is, 'Neena is a spectacular actor!'

Of course, that didn't happen when I needed it the most as the gossip around my personal life overshadowed my professional life.

This brings me to a very important thing I have learnt during my long career as an actor.

Never sleep with a married producer or director. Because even though it might seem casual and something that everybody does and is accepted, you will end up ruining your chances of ever working with him again.

Why? Because they don't want to rock the boat. They don't intend to leave their wives for you because, no surprises here, you are probably not the first actor they have slept with.

Some of these men are clear about their intentions. But there are others who make you fall in love with them, much like a student falls in love with a teacher.

They are eloquent and charming; intelligent and talented. They're intellectuals and you are drawn to their wealth of knowledge. Let's say you meet one of these men and find yourself gravitating towards them. Do you think they will say no? I don't think there are many men who will dismiss the advances of a young, beautiful actor. But if you start hinting you want more, you will be doomed.

I know that there are many actors out there who will read this and still sleep with the wrong men in the industry. The married men. The men in power. It's difficult to learn from other people's mistakes, even mine. You learn best from your own mistakes. But maybe make these mistakes outside the industry? Where your career isn't at stake?

Because sleeping with a married director or producer, even if these are just rumours, will kill any chance of you being cast in their films again. Especially once their wives find out.

I had such a bitter experience once, and it mainly happened because I am not two-faced.

If I meet someone I am close to, I hug them or hold their hand while talking to them. I don't pretend to be someone I am not.

This led to rumours of me having an affair with a married director. The media picked it up too.

It got so bad that his wife called me home one day and accused me as well.

I explained to her that there was nothing going on and that I was just the sort of person who was very open about who I was. But she didn't seem to believe me.

'He has worked with so many actors in the industry. Why have there never been any rumours of him with them?'

I honestly didn't know what to tell her. I knew that this director had had affairs with some of the women he had worked with but it had never reached the media.

With me it did because I didn't pretend to be subdued or demure to keep up appearances.

I was stupid and naive to think that this attitude—frank, honest—would be rewarded. That people knew who I really was, when they only saw what they want to see. And unfortunately, this went against me because after that incident, the director never cast me in his films.

If I could go back in time, I know that there are many things I would change about myself and the choices I made. But none of us have this luxury, no matter how rich and famous we get. I guess I can only look at the things I have done right over time and feel grateful for all that I have.

3

Bloody Mary

Writing this book has been therapeutic. It has given me the opportunity to look back on some of the best moments of my life. Reliving some of the painful moments hasn't been fun, but it has given me a chance to reflect.

When I look back on my past, I see a recurring theme. Neena gets shot down. Neena rises from the ashes. Neena overcomes her obstacles. Neena reaches great heights (though still not as the star in a big movie). Neena falls from grace.

So much in my life has left me hurt, disheartened and disillusioned because of the recurring humiliations I have suffered. First from Raghav, who called off our wedding and never gave me an explanation no matter how much I begged.

Then from a director whose wife accused me of having an affair with him, and I lost a lot of work because of that.

But nothing has broken me because if there's one thing I excel at, it's picking up the pieces of my life and career, mending myself, and moving on.

The humiliation I suffered from Star TV hurt me more than anything else. But I moved on. I had to move on. I always move on. But still, I was so depressed from all I had been through, I almost gave up on my career.

I wonder if things would have gone differently had I not retreated, run and hid. What if I had stomped in there, thrown my weight around and said, 'No, I deserve better. And if you cannot give me that, at least give me a straight answer for why you're dismissing me with such malice.'

Sometimes in life, you have to stand up for yourself and demand what you deserve. If you're being treated unfairly, you must at least call out your perpetrators and humiliate them for what they're doing. This will help you in the years to come because you won't look back with regrets. You will look back and feel proud that you didn't take the humiliation lying down. That when you were pushed, you were brave enough to push back.

This wisdom came to me very late in life, and while it would have been more useful back then, at least I know that I won't let this happen to me again.

That was a dark period in my life, and it made me lose interest in everything.

But luckily, something . . . someone new came into my life who took my mind off those atrocities and the loss of interest that followed.

While still at Star, as the host of the India chapter of *The Weakest Link*, I was sent to London for a meeting with the original host, Anne Robinson, along with other hosts of the show from different countries. It was a very interesting experience.

I was flying business class, Air India, back to Bombay. I was sitting in an aisle seat, like I always do, when a gentleman came and occupied the window.

'You like Bloody Marys?' he asked, pointing to my drink, once the flight had taken off. 'I make excellent Bloody Marys.'

The next eight to ten hours were amazing. We drank Bloody Marys and exchanged stories about our lives, kids and work.

He recognized me from *Saans* and knew who I was.

He told me about his life as well. He was a chartered accountant based in Delhi. A senior partner at PwC, he often visited Bombay for business. He had been visiting family in England, and had a stopover in Bombay for some work. He promoted his sister-in-law's paintings on the side because she was a very good artist.

And yes, he mentioned his wife and how they weren't in a very good place in their relationship.

'We haven't spoken to each other in over two months,' he told me.

I felt sorry for him and we spoke about relationships for a while. We also discussed our kids at length, and I told him how much I wanted Masaba to finally go out and see the world.

When we parted ways at the Bombay airport, he handed me his business card.

We started to keep in touch from then on.

The next nine years of my life would be spent solely focused on this man with whom I started an affair. We were very compatible. We had the same ideologies and wanted the same things from life. He was married, yes. But I realized they had their differences.

Sometimes I wonder what I should teach my daughter. Do I teach her to settle down with a man? Start a family? Do the things I couldn't do because of the choices I made? Or should I tell her to work hard and focus on her career?

I see all that my daughter has achieved at such a young age and feel proud. She is talented, hard-working, ambitious and a beautiful human being.

Should I ask her to focus on her work? Or have children?

I honestly don't know. Because it's something I am still figuring out at the age of sixty.

I see many women who love being stay-at-home wives and mothers. They love to nurture their children and take care of their parents and in-laws.

But I also see women who give up very lucrative careers only to find out—a bit too late—that being a housewife is just not for them.

I also see many who balance work and life as best as they can. Things have changed now. Men do help more in the house and with the kids. Such women have the support they need to achieve their goals and dreams, whatever those may be.

But when I think about my own journey as a mother, I often feel bad for Masaba because I don't think I gave her the kind of attention a child needs from a parent. I had no choice but to work hard and hire good help so that she was taken care of. The period my father lived with us also helped soothe my guilt.

I want to ask my daughter countless times: What do you want from life? A career? Kids? Both?

But I feel, in the end, regardless of what she chooses, the only thing that matters is that she has high self-esteem. That she loves herself and knows what she's worth. That she respects herself enough to not chase after other people's acceptance.

I'm not saying I won't make the same mistakes again. But at least I know that no matter what life throws at me, I am excellent at picking up the pieces and moving on.

* * *

So, I spent years dilly dallying. I did a few roles here and there. Nothing major because I was honestly just working to keep my mind young. I had worked very hard to be a mother and father to Masaba, so I thought now that I was married, I should relax and enjoy my married life. So I didn't even think of getting back to the grind.

'They don't write roles for actresses of my age any more,' I told Masaba time and again when she asked me when I planned to return to work full time.

And it was true. While there isn't a dearth of roles for actresses, once they get to a certain age, they only receive offers to play mothers, aunts, distant relatives . . . mostly small supporting roles. Never the lead. Almost never the second lead either.

During this time, I acted in *Ladies Special*, a show I'm proud of. In 2015, I received an offer to play the lead in a small budget film called *The Threshold*.

The film was directed by Pushan Kriplani and shot in Tirthan Valley, Himachal Pradesh.

'The Threshold (. . .) is not a title that suggests a whole lot of action. Neither does a plot précis: this is a two-character film in which a wife decides to leave her husband after decades together. Yet, when you walk out of The Threshold, you feel like you've seen something real and raw and honest, attributes which aren't necessarily present in some of the more heralded Indian films of the festival.'

This was how the *Mint Lounge* described the film, and it's very pertinent.

The film didn't get a great theatrical release, but it got good reviews at film festivals. It was a new and unique experience for Rajit Kapur and I as actors because it was written during a gruelling ten-day improv workshop that we did.

The plot was there, so were the cues for the storyline and the ending. But it was our interactions as actors and our personal experiences in life that inspired the writing of the final script.

In short, the outline existed. Rajit and I added the ingredients with our own interpretations of the story, drawing heavily from our lives. The writer of the film, who was with us throughout these ten days, took what we gave him and turned it into a beautiful script.

The setting of the film, a house in Tirthan Valley, was beautiful and melancholic. It was shot in Pushan's very own family home. It was a small crew and we absolutely loved every minute of it.

I found the house too cold, so I stayed in a guest house nearby called Trout House. We would start filming early every morning and wrap up early too.

Once we packed up for the day, I would head back to Trout House to retire for the night. There was a quaint little cafe on this property, which was covered with a tin roof but open on all sides.

I loved sitting here every evening and taking my meals. They had a small menu for us to pick from, but the food was really nice.

Every evening, I would get back from shooting, order my meal and go upstairs to change into my night clothes. The temperatures would drop quite a bit in the evening so I would bring along a shawl or a warm jacket.

One evening, when I was passing through the cafe, someone called out to me.

'Hi Neena,' I heard him say. When I turned around, I saw a man whom I didn't recognize. He walked towards me and there was something familiar about him. I felt like I knew him but couldn't put my finger on it.

'Hello,' I said politely.

'How are your parents and brother?' he asked and that's when I realized who he was. It was Amlan, my first husband whom I hadn't seen in almost twenty years.

'Amlan!' I shouted. 'How are you? What are you doing here?'

He told me he was a regular at Trout House. He loved to come here for trout fishing, something the area was famous for.

'I knew you were going to be here,' he laughed. 'The room you're staying in is usually the one I request for every time I stay here. It's the best one in the house. But this time when I called, they said they couldn't give it to me because the actress Neena Gupta would be staying there.'

I laughed. Imagine that, I thought. What a crazy way to run into your ex.

We spoke for a long time. It broke my heart to tell him that my parents and brother had all passed away. He had been very close to my brother while we were together and had the utmost respect for my parents, so it pained him to hear of their demise.

We sat and talked for a long time that evening. It was like catching up with a very old friend and I really enjoyed his company. We had both grown older and wiser, but we talked just as easily as we did in the old days. I told him about my life, work and my daughter. He told me that he was also happily married with a beautiful daughter of his own. The joy and ease with which we caught up made me appreciate the relationship we had shared. When you love someone in your past, those feelings evolve into great fondness even if there is no romance between you. I think I was lucky to have at least a few relationships that I still feel good about.

Speaking to him reminded me of the young woman I had been back then. How driven I was. How passionate I was. I had known even then that I was meant for great things. Amlan also saw this in me when he agreed that we should split so I could pursue acting heart and soul.

When I returned to Bombay, and back to my old life, I was once again struck by how much had changed over the years. I felt like I had enough in my life, and yet something very important was missing.

'This cannot be the end of my career,' I thought. 'Quietly disappearing from the scene when I haven't even achieved half of what I want.'

I decided it was time to give it my all or die trying.

4

...Am a Good Actor Looking for Good Parts to Play

I am not a nobody. I have never been a nobody. I am Neena Gupta and since my TV break in *Khandaan*, I have always been a known name. It helped, of course, that I kept myself on the silver and small screens through sheer grit and hard work. But I know now that while I may never have been as famous as Bachchan Sahib or SRK, I have always been a household name in my own right.

Unfortunately, I never became a superstar because I was never offered the main roles in films and the most iconic characters I played on television, barring *Khandaan*, were all produced and directed by me.

My low self-confidence, which I have discussed at length through this book, never even let me fight for what I wanted and thought I truly deserved.

After I married Vivek, still in a slump after the Star TV episode and completely unmotivated to do any kind of work, it seemed as if I had gone into hiding.

For many years, I made this man the centre of my existence and didn't bother to actively network or seek roles. I did a few film and television roles during this time. Small, insignificant roles, honestly, because I just had different priorities then.

I so badly wanted to have a husband and an extended family that it didn't matter that my situation was less than ideal. I was more focused on proving to a different set of people that I was a good and honest person and it was a toxic period in my life, except that the press didn't care for a change and I actually liked that.

Work wasn't a priority, but I did keep myself on top of what was happening in the industry. I played small parts in films like *Hello Zindagi* and *Issaq*. I also played small parts in television shows like *Jassi Jaisi Koi Nahin* and *Saath Phere*.

But while I was trying to build a family, I ignored an important aspect of my work—networking and attending parties and events. I also lost touch with old contacts through whom I would always get some work. Instead, I filled my months and years with birthdays, parties, functions and weddings from Vivek's side of the family.

It should have come as no surprise to me then that whenever I met anyone from the industry, they always asked, 'How's Delhi treating you?' or 'How's married life? You have retired now?'

I didn't think much of it and just went about my business because I had too much drama in my personal life.

But then one day in 2017, I went to meet Zoya Akhtar for a small part in a television series called *Made in Heaven*. It wasn't a significant part, but I really wanted to do the show.

I was just walking in when I ran into her assistant who greeted me warmly and asked when I had returned to Bombay.

'I never left Bombay . . .' I said, suddenly feeling the weight of that statement fully.

The rest of the meeting went well, and I did a small role in the series. But that was later.

I remember feeling so angry and upset after that meeting.

Is this what people think? That I am married now and live in Delhi?

Is this why I am not getting any work?

I was seething by the time I reached home and did something that was extremely impulsive without running it past anybody.

To my 11,000 followers (at the time) on Instagram I wrote:

'I live in mumbai and working am a good actor looking fr good parts to play'

Please excuse the grammar and spellings. I know I made some errors there. I wrote it out of passion and fury. Do bear in mind that I am from the older generation, so texting and social media are things I still work very hard at.

But this is what I posted along with a picture of myself that I thought did justice to how well I had aged over the years.

The post went viral. Two minutes after posting it, I knew it was too late to delete it.

I received a barrage of comments and many of them seemed good. But I suddenly felt choked with guilt and shame because I realized I didn't really know what I had just done. I was scared that the media would pick it up, and the next day, the headlines would state that this actor was in such dire straits that she took to Instagram, a medium she barely knew, and begged for work.

The media I could handle; my friends asking me if I was okay, if my life and marriage were okay, I could handle.

What was scaring me was what my daughter, a widely recognized and famous fashion designer and public figure, Masaba Gupta would say.

'I can't believe you did this, Mom,' I imagined her saying. 'At least think about what you're saying before making it public. If you still have doubts, ask me before posting something embarrassing like this.'

Social media can be so daunting and some of us who are still learning the ropes often make mistakes. Those who think they don't falter clearly don't have grown-up children who care about them enough to tell them how such things are perceived or what a social persona is supposed to look like.

I braced myself for a lashing from my daughter. I kept staring at the phone, waiting for it to ring with her voice on the other end of the line.

Instead, I kept getting likes and appreciate comments from people—both fans and veteran actors—calling me an inspiration.

But deep down I knew I wouldn't feel good about all the love and support, that it would all fall flat if the most important person in my life didn't understand why I did what I did.

As I waited for a call or an angry text, expecting to get yet another lesson in social media, I received a long and beautiful message from my daughter who had shared my post with her followers with the following words:

'Just the other day I was telling someone . . . how I am never afraid/shy to ask for work. It's obviously genetic. My mother put up this post on her Instagram today. I mean, my 62-year-old national award winning mother. She told me I must always work . . . no matter what . . . it keeps you from getting old . . . she told me they don't write for women her age anymore . . . I don't think anyone can replicate what she did for TV anymore . . . she complains that she can't do PR . . . but says 'I do good work, that's my PR' . . . time and again we've spoken about how whatever she asks for . . . in due time, she gets . . . But that's the magic of a pure heart. The universe just can't refuse you . . . the only advice I have the guts to give her is . . . don't work with anyone who won't respect you, at this age, that's the bare minimum & it's a strange strange industry she's in . . . the advice she gives me in return is . . . 'whatever you do, free ka PR mat khaana, your only someone's kid/wife/niece/sister for this long. Prove yourself. WORK. Walk the talk & fly ♥'

I had tears in my eyes. It felt so good to have her say such wonderful things about me. As a single mother–daughter unit, we've always been very honest and real with each other. We don't mince words and we don't indulge in public displays of affection. If you look at our interactions on social media even today, you will see we're honest and real. I tell her, quite honestly, that I find 'holidays' like Mother's Day 'bada boring' and she points out, in my comments section, that I haven't cropped a picture of us together properly.

Sorry, baby. I'm still learning.

This Instagram episode, as you know, changed my life and luck in the industry as a new wave of work started to come my way.

'A second innings' the media loves to call it. But to me, it's proof that good things come your way no matter how old or young you are. Because no matter what anybody says, nobody's a nobody. All they need to do is keep trying.

5

Badhaai Ho!

In 2018, I was cast in a film that not only changed the course of my career but took it to great heights. I had never felt this giddy in my entire career.

Badhaai Ho was the big break I had been waiting for. I got to play the lead in it (though I didn't think so at the time because I was playing a middle-aged woman).

It's a cute story about how a woman in her late forties gets pregnant unexpectedly and the hilarity that follows.

I didn't have to audition for the role, but director Amit Sharma did want to see me in person to see whether I would fit the part. He asked me to bring along some clothes that the character would possibly wear.

I had a kameez, big and loose, that sort of fit the bill of the middle-class housewife. But I didn't have an appropriate salwar to go with it. I got a bit nervous for a while but my helper, more like my right-hand woman, Nirmala came to my rescue. She offered to lend me one of her salwars for the meeting because she felt they might be more in sync with what he had in mind. So, I selected a nice salwar and off we went to meet Amit.

After the meeting, I waited for days hoping against hope that I had fit the part and bagged the role. When they finally called to give the good news, I was absolutely ecstatic.

My experience on the sets was marvellous. The cast and crew were really courteous and professional—miles ahead of any production house I'd worked with in terms of their organizational skills, the processes they followed and the culture they promoted.

Amit was an amazing director. He would get really involved in each and every character regardless of their age or gender.

If he didn't like the way we delivered a dialogue or our body language and expressions, he would come and stand in front of us and enact it himself so that we knew what he wanted us to do.

It was fascinating to watch because in addition to being a great director, Amit is also a spectacular actor!

'You should be standing here and acting with us,' we'd often joke. He'd just laugh.

In one dance sequence, while the actors all did their bit in front of the camera, Amit stood behind the monitor mimicking our steps, jumping with us and, in general, having a wonderful time.

Watching him enjoy what he does so much and being so passionate about his craft gave us the added boost to give the film our best.

Badhaai Ho also gave me the opportunity, for the first time in my career, to go touring all over for promotions. Earlier, my part was never big enough for me to be taken along, but this time, I was the showstopper. In all the studios and halls where we did interviews, for the first time I had significant questions directed at me. In the past, even when I was taken along, people never asked me questions. I would just be sitting and smiling in a corner. This would make me feel bad at times but I understood.

With *Badhaai Ho*, for the first time since I started my career, I felt like I was promoting MY film. And the attention I got was very flattering.

Ayushmann (Khurrana) would often say that Gajraj (Rao) and I were the lead actors of the film and that the rest of them were just supporting us.

I'd laugh at him.

'Are you mad?' I would say. 'Look at us. We're so old. Who's going to see us as the leads of the film?'

But I was wrong on that front because thanks to *Badhaai Ho*, I received my very first Filmfare Award for Best Actress. Not Supporting Actress. BEST ACTRESS. I was so thrilled! It was the first time I truly started to wonder if my age wasn't a drawback after all . . . That the industry had changed over the years and there was still place for me along with everyone else.

I was shooting for *Panchayat* around the time the Filmfare Awards were scheduled. But I flew back for just that one night from Bhopal hoping that maybe, just maybe, I would win.

Holding that award was the best feeling I've had in my career. I really wanted to stay back and attend the after-party, bask in all the attention and glory and eat some good food, but my flight back to Bhopal was at 6 a.m. the next morning. So, I took my leave and went home to catch a little bit of sleep.

I think it's also okay for me to put this in writing because I have said this time and time again.

I love Amit Sharma. I love him! I love him! I love him! I say this every time someone gives me an award for *Badhaai Ho* and when I get praised for my work in the film.

He has talent, yes. He knows how to bring out the best in his characters and crew. But most importantly, he is a good human being. It's very rare to find someone who has all these traits.

So once again, thank you, Amit. I'm really fortunate to have worked with you! Thank you for finally giving me my big break.

6

The Last Colour

A few months after I finished *The Threshold*, I met a stranger on a plane.

I was sitting in the first row. When I got up to use the restroom, a man called out to me. I didn't know him, but I was courteous nevertheless. He said he was a big fan and his grandfather had loved my work in *Mirza Ghalib*.

He was really nice, and it felt good to hear him say such appreciative things about my work.

'What are you up to now?' he asked.

'I've just finished shooting a film called *The Threshold*,' I said, and told him all about the plot and the setting. 'You can watch it on Hotstar.'

He seemed fascinated by this and asked for the number and email ID of the director.

That man, now a dear, dear, friend, turned out to be the famous Michelin-starred chef Vikas Khanna and it was because of him that *The Threshold* was screened at festivals in New York. I even won an award for the film there. Vikas Khanna, an artist in his own right and a great lover of cinema (more on this soon), pulled strings and promoted us out of sheer passion.

I think I'm fated to meet some of the most important people at airports and in aeroplanes. Like I met Chef Vikas Khanna. After this encounter though, we went our separate ways.

Then suddenly one day he got in touch to tell me about something very, very different he was working on, and I immediately got excited.

Vikas had written a book called *The Last Colour* and was turning it into a movie that he was directing and producing. He wanted me to play the lead role.

The Last Colour tells a beautiful story. The plot revolves around a nine-year-old tightrope walker called Chhoti, who befriends Noor, a widow on the ghats of Varanasi, and promises to bring colour into her life.

The story was very well-researched by Vikas, who had spent months in Varanasi understanding the place, culture, the spirituality and rituals. He was deeply affected by the plight of the widows of Varanasi, who spent their lives on the banks following conventions and being pious.

I play the widow, Noor, who is befriended by Chhoti, played by child actress Aqsa Siddiqui. A little boy named Rajeshwar Khanna played Chintu. A local, he would run amok along the ghats and was in general a very street-smart and free-spirited character. He was a very, very good actor which is why he got cast, and I felt like he acted even better than us.

A few days before I was scheduled to start shooting, Vikas called me and said he was already in Varanasi, filming montages. He asked if I could come down for just one day to get into the spirit of things.

My schedule was very tight because we were shooting the ending of *Badhaai Ho*. But I managed to take one day off and fly down.

Vikas greeted me very warmly when I arrived, and I was absolutely intrigued to watch his command over the camera. He was shooting one of the last scenes in the film—a Holi scene which had lots of colour flying around.

'I have an idea,' he said. 'Can you please wear your costume and get in the shot?'

I agreed and promptly went to the hotel to change into the widow's attire—white sari, white blouse, hair combed back simply and no make-up. Not even kajal.

In this scene, there were colours flying everywhere, people were dancing, playing Holi and celebrating. The set-up was beautiful. I could see that Vikas had a great eye. At one point, he asked me to get up and play *Kikli*—a game that involves holding hands and spinning around and around—with another actor who was also playing a widow. This shot came out perfectly and was actually used as the last scene in the film. My picture from this shot was even used on the cover of the book.

By the end of the shot, we were all covered in colour. My sari, which had been white a few hours earlier, was multicoloured now. Even my hair was filled with powder. I could feel it on my scalp.

I had packed only a tiny bag with one change of clothes. I was meant to return to Delhi in less than twenty-four hours, so I hadn't even brought along my toiletry kit with shampoo and conditioner.

We were staying in a very modest hotel in Varanasi, and I tried my best to get the colour out of my hair with the tiny hand soap they had provided. But it was of no use. I laughed and gave up. I couldn't get the colour out until I reached Delhi the next day and was reunited with my hair products.

But I was glad we had done this because it really helped me see what kind of director Vikas would be and get into character.

It was a small unit, only ten people, but I knew the film was going to be very, very special.

Once the shooting began though, things moved quickly, but it was also very strenuous. We would start shooting around 6 a.m. so I would wake up at 4.30 a.m. It was the middle of April and Varanasi was hot. A lot of my shots had me walking barefoot and I could feel the soles of my feet burning and forming blisters.

But Vikas and the crew really took care of me and ensured I was as comfortable as I could be. Every day, after shooting all morning,

I'd excuse myself after lunch break to take a thirty-minute nap in my hotel room which was on the ghats. I really needed the rest because the heat and work would drain me completely.

We'd end the day dirty, sweaty and hot but thoroughly satisfied. It was a low-budget film, but it was Vikas's baby. He would get so immersed in his work that he would forget everything and everyone around him. Sometimes he would even forget to eat. Luckily, his mother had come along. She and I got close during the filming and I was glad to have her there.

'Only you can take care of him [Vikas] at this time,' I'd say because Vikas was only interested in capturing the visuals for the story.

Vikas always told me that it was Ganga Maiya, the Ganges, flowing through Varanasi, that had served as his muse to create this beautiful film. After spending nearly a month there, I could see what he meant. In fact, all of Varanasi was a muse for Vikas Khanna.

The film finally finished on time and I came back home.

Soon, Vikas invited me over to see the first cut of the film. He had completed the post-production and music in New York. When we sat down to finally watch it, I was floored. The film was beautiful, vibrant and filled with so much emotion. I knew it would be deeply appreciated when it came out.

The Last Colour was screened at almost every festival in the US, and is now on Amazon Prime.

I couldn't attend all the festivals, but I did go to as many as my schedule allowed. But there was no way I would miss the premiere of the film at the Palm Springs International Film Festival in California. Even Vivek accompanied me to this one. We were well taken care of. We even flew on a private jet to one of the festivals. I had never flown private, so it was a very exciting experience for me.

Thanks to *The Last Colour*, I won awards for Best Actress at a few festivals. It felt absolutely amazing. I felt happy for myself and for Vikas, as the film was his labour of love.

Thanks to this film, I also got to live my dream of going to Cannes. *The Last Colour* got a book launch and teaser release at the festival, and I was jumping with joy.

I had always watched actors from India and around the world walk the red carpet and admired their beautiful attires. But I had never thought of going myself just to experience the festival.

'I will only go if I have a film being screened there,' I said to people over the years. Before *The Last Colour*, I had almost given up any hope of ever going there. When would I get the opportunity, I thought, to play the lead?

But *The Last Colour* turned all of that around because Vikas and I got to go along with two of the producers of the film.

We didn't have the budget to stay in a big, luxurious hotel close to the festival, but we were more than comfortable at a beautiful boutique hotel even if it was a bit far away.

Every day we would set off with the whole kit and caboodle. We'd carry a change of clothes if the occasion called for it. I carried my make-up bag and hair equipment.

I didn't get my hair and make-up done professionally until the day of *The Last Colour* launch. Most actresses come with their own hair and make-up artistes but I didn't take anyone along. Vikas tried really hard to get me an artiste from the festival but the person wasn't free that day. So, I went to a little salon near the hotel to get dressed. I wasn't too happy with the make-up because they made me a lot paler than I am. I also had these white patches under my eyes. I was feeling very self-conscious about getting in front of the camera, but, in the end, I looked good.

My career had finally taken a turn for the better. It seemed the only direction I was going was up. I wish I had got these opportunities and fame earlier. But I am not complaining because I never thought I'd be able to scale such great heights at this age and stage in my career.

Vikas is a wonderful person and a very dear friend. I am still in awe of his many talents—as a chef, a public personality, a writer and, of course, a film director. Vikas is also a wonderful photographer. In fact, the two pictures I love most of myself at this stage in my life were taken by him. And they aren't set up in a studio, with the correct lighting and background. They were taken by him just as we were walking together—*chalte chalte*.

* * *

Sometimes I just cannot believe the range of work I'm getting. The subjects are vast and varied, and the platforms on which they air numerous.

Badhaai Ho changed the course of my career and I am eternally grateful to Amit Sharma for that. I have mentioned it before, and I will keep saying it again and again.

After *The Last Colour* I worked on a web series called *Panchayat*, which released on Amazon Prime early in 2020, just as the lockdown hit. In it I play the pradhan of a village, but in reality my character's husband runs the show while I obsess over 'housewifely' things like my daughter's marriage.

We shot this in Bhopal and it was a wonderful experience. The series is so well written and executed that everyone—from the most discerning of viewers to hardcore film buffs—loves it. I have received so much love from fans all over for this role. As I write this, we're still in lockdown and I'm really looking forward to it lifting so we can get back to filming season two.

I also played a small part in *Panga* as Kangana Ranaut's mother. The film has been done really beautifully and I'm a great admirer of the director, Ashwiny Iyer Tiwari.

I also bagged a very big role in *Shubh Mangal Zyada Saavdhan*. When director Hitesh Kewalya, who had written *Shubh Mangal Saavdhan* (a 2017 film also starring Ayushmann Khurrana) came and narrated the story to me and told me what my character would be, I knew instantly I wanted to play the role. I was really proud of

Hitesh who had stepped up and not only written *Shubh Mangal Zyada Saavdhan*, but also directed it.

Shubh Mangal is hilarious and has a beautiful message about love. It's the story of two gay men who are in love but of course have to fight to stay together when their families disapprove.

I thought the subject was very pertinent and I loved how the story was treated without pandering to critics or resorting to stereotypes. When you watch this film, you really fall in love with Kartik and Aman. You find yourself rooting for them and experiencing their struggles and pain too.

The film, in which I played Aman's (Jitendra Kumar) mother, got great reviews, but it didn't become a very big hit. It wasn't widely accepted because of the subject of homosexuality. I think it's very sad because our society, though so much more educated and aware of these things now, can still be quite homophobic. In the film, I truly felt the subjects of homosexuality and homophobia were dealt with sensitively, using humour and kindness.

We shot the film in Varanasi for almost two months and the cast and crew became so close that we still meet even today! This has to be one of the most satisfying roles I have ever played.

Another film I did was *Gwalior*, a thriller which is yet to be released. We shot in Bhopal for around forty-five days and it was really, really tough because it was hot. The budget, again, wasn't great so we had to live in rooms in the club house of a residential society. The crew was very nice and tried its best to make us comfortable.

It was extra hard for me because I found the schedule very, very tough and the climate was harsh. I lost a lot of hair because of this.

But luckily, I took along my maid, Nirmala, who has over the years become my right-hand woman. She is so wonderful to have on outdoor shoots because she cooks and looks after me.

Food on shoots can be very dicey so I prefer to take Nirmala along with a little hotplate and pressure cooker. In Gwalior, Nirmala would always have some rice, sabzi and khichdi waiting for me.

Her food became quite popular among the crew as she always cooked enough to feed two to three people.

I feel like I survived Gwalior only because of Nirmala and her home-cooked food.

I started writing this book during the lockdown in 2020, and by the time it hits the stands in May 2021, another film of mine—*Sandeep Aur Pinky Faraar* with Arjun Kapoor and Parineeti Chopra—would have released. Also, on 18 May, another very interesting film called *Sardar Ka Grandson* will be released on Netflix. This role, with Arjun Kapoor and Rakul Preet Singh, has been one of my most challenging. The filming for the second season of *Panchayat*, my very popular series on Amazon Prime, will also start in May/June 2021. During the lockdown, I finished shooting for the film *Dial 100* with Manoj Bajpayee and Sakshi Tanwar. This will release soon.

I also played myself in *Masaba Masaba*. This series aired on Netflix and is really close to my heart because it was Masaba's first stint as an actor. I will start shooting for the second season in May/June 2021.

Over the years, I have been her biggest critic because I am always honest with her. I really didn't know if she would be convincing as an actor, but when I saw her screen test I was floored. She was really really good. I guess some things do run in the family.

Overall, things are nice and comfortable. I am getting to play good parts, significant parts. I am being challenged and I am receiving a lot of praise and recognition for my talents.

I am also receiving a lot of offers. Well, let's see how those pan out, but I'm quite optimistic.

My big break came when I was sixty years old but at least it came. I am so thankful to myself for not giving up hope.

It also helps that this is a golden age for writers, directors and us actors. There are so many interesting parts available for all of us now.

Sometimes, I do wish I were still young. Sometimes, I feel envious of the younger actors and how much potential and possibilities they have.

Yes, I know I'm being greedy and that is why I'm trying to be happy with whatever I have because without *Badhaai Ho*, I wouldn't have even that.

Life is good. I am more active on social media. I have almost 5.3 lakh followers (at this time) on Instagram and I really enjoy hearing from them. They write the most wonderful notes to me.

But every so often, I find myself pausing and reflecting on where my life is going.

Why do I still work? Why am I still acting?

I think I truly like it when people appreciate me. I want more people to see how talented I am, and I want to give stellar performances to keep up my reputation.

This is the case with everyone, I think. Not just actors. Whether you have a corporate career or you are a housewife, you wake up every day and you do what you do best to get appreciation.

Getting what you want from life is often not easy. Ask me! I don't think I knew what I really wanted until I was over sixty years old.

Even Ben Kingsley, who was around thirty-eight years old when he got his big break in *Gandhi*, said to me that it was with this role he realized what he really wanted.

Some people are lucky that they find what they want to do at a young age.

But I sincerely feel that no matter how old you are, or how old you think you are, it is never too late to start.

What I have today is because of a lot of hard work. But it is also destiny. And I thank God for leading me here.

I don't know what tomorrow will bring. But, as of today, I am grateful to God for giving me success, health, happiness and well-being.

Part 5

Four Guptas and a Mehra

'As one looks up to the palm tree, I looked up to my mother in awe of her integrity, her rootedness and her strength of character. She inspired me to be the straightest, tallest and best version of myself.'

1

Shakuntala Gupta

The lota has fallen on the floor. Water has spilled everywhere. A thin, quivering hand reaches for it, hoping to get the last few sips that might still be at the bottom. But it's too far away.

When I think of my mother, I often picture this lota. In the last stage of cancer, bedridden, one night she tried to reach for some water and accidentally spilled it on the floor. Too weak to get out of bed, too frail to call for help, all alone and in pain, she stayed thirsty all night.

My father wasn't there that night. My brother wasn't there either. I was in Bombay, shooting for *Khandaan*. She was alone. All alone. And lonely . . .

Shakuntala Devi, née Kinra, was the oldest of ten children. Her mother, my Nani, did her best to raise them well after my grandfather, a freedom fighter, was arrested and sent to jail by the British.

But other than the little details here and there, I don't know a lot about my mother's upbringing. It pains me to admit that while she was still alive, I took her for granted as children often do. But I do know that as the oldest child, she helped out a lot with her younger siblings while growing up.

We didn't share a very open, friendly relationship like I do with my daughter. Masaba and I discuss everything. We speak to each other as equals and even if we fight, we make up just as quickly.

243

My mother and I had a very different relationship. She was strict and orthodox. She watched over us very intently and disapproved vehemently when we did anything she didn't deem appropriate. She wanted me to become an IAS officer which is why she refused to let me go to NSD immediately after my graduation. It took many years, only after I completed MPhil, and the unavailability of a suitable guide for my PhD, to convince her to let me attend NSD.

So many times I started writing this book but stopped because I didn't want people to know about the things my mother went through. I didn't want to lay bare her secrets, shame and the pain it caused her.

Moreover, I realized over the years that I didn't know my mother well at all. There were many things about her life and character to which I never received any answers. Not because she didn't give them to me. But because I never had the courage to ask.

While my mother was alive, I never asked her about her childhood or how she met and fell in love with my father.

Growing up, I never really questioned our circumstances nor was I curious about why I never got to meet my father's side of the family.

To be honest though, we didn't visit my mother's siblings either. They were scattered around the country—many were in Kanpur and Calcutta. But we barely visited even the ones in Delhi. I met my nani, who lived in Rohtak, only once.

I was too afraid to ask my mother why this was, but I gathered she didn't want us to get too close to our cousins because it would mean that we would spend weekends at their houses and then we in turn would have to invite them over to ours. You can learn a lot about a family when you spend the night at their house.

My mother, I know now, didn't keep us away from our aunts and uncles because she was a bad person who didn't love her family. She did this because she had a secret that she guarded ferociously.

In fact, she often pretended that this secret didn't exist at all. That if she closed her eyes and pretended it wasn't there, it would cease to exist.

That was just the way she was, my mother. She did the same thing when she was diagnosed with multiple myeloma many years later, once I had grown up.

'I was sitting next to this doctor on the bus while going to visit your nani in Rohtak,' she told me. 'I was telling him that I have multiple myeloma and he said, "Oh, you have bone marrow cancer?" I just laughed and said of course not. It's just multiple myeloma. Not cancer.'

Before we were born, my mother was a schoolteacher. But she gave that up to be a full-time parent once we came along.

I would not call her a housewife or a homemaker because, quite honestly, she was a lot more than that. She didn't enjoy being in the kitchen and wasn't much of a cook. Instead, she preferred to spend as much time as she could outside the house. She'd go to the bank, pay bills and spend days and months campaigning for the Congress party.

She even took us along to voting booths on election days where she volunteered. My brother and I never complained because we loved to be in the midst of all the action. Also, the tiffin boxes they gave all the volunteers and their children were delicious.

She was an idealist, a Gandhian who for a long time only wore khadi—both cotton and silk. Always natural fabrics. I don't think I ever saw her wearing anything synthetic.

But her idealism, as noble as it was, also worked against her because she suffered a lot because of it. In turn, we suffered too.

Her principles kept her from attending her own sister's wedding because her mother had taken a loan for dowry.

'How can you even think of giving dowry?' she shouted at my grandmother. 'And that too by taking a loan? This is wrong. I'm boycotting this wedding.'

I felt sorry for my nani then because she was only doing what was, at that time, still a very common practice in society. It had its evils, but it was a practical thing given the times.

During our summer vacations, my mother would bundle us up and we would take a train or sometimes a bus to Nainital for two whole months. We absolutely loved this because it meant escaping the worst of Delhi's heat. During our winter vacations, she took us to different parts of India. We visited many beautiful places thanks to her—Ooty, Trivandrum, Mount Abu, Chennai. She just loved to travel and she never left us behind.

It never occurred to me to ask her why my father didn't join us on these holidays. When we went to Nainital, my father would join us for a week or so, but it was understood that he would have to return at the earliest because he couldn't afford to leave work for too long.

I never wondered until much later how difficult it must have been for my mother to lug two children all over India on trains that sometimes put us on waitlists or took us off altogether. I remember once when we got to Nainital, we realized that the room we had booked wasn't vacant. The landlords instead gave us a tiny room, the size of a bathroom, to spend the night. It was disgusting but my mother made us as comfortable as she could. She was a strong and hardy woman. As a child, I never once doubted her ability to protect us and keep us safe. But even her strength and confidence had their limit.

'You have to start spending more time with us,' she told my father once in Nainital. I had just turned fourteen, a teenager, and starting to show signs of puberty. 'I can't handle a teenage girl all by myself. She gets stared at everywhere she goes. She needs her father's protection . . .'

But, of course, my father could not be with us any more than he already was. And deep down, even though she pretended otherwise, my mother knew this too. So, she went about her life, playing the role of both parents and refusing to address the elephant in the room.

She paid extra attention to our education and ensured that we always did our homework properly. I was very weak in maths and she took it upon herself to pull me through the subject.

I was good at many other subjects, but maths, for some reason, turned me into a complete fool. I'd look at the numbers and symbols and just multiply everything.

'Multiply, multiply multiply,' my mother once yelled in exasperation. 'One day I am going to get you married to "multiply".'

I laugh when I think about this statement. More so when I ended up marrying a CA who is excellent at maths.

Even though she had strong ideals and principles and was a noble human being, there was always something about her that really bothered me. It was and still is a mystery to me and I only wish I had had the courage to ask her . . .

Why did she stay committed to my father?

Don't misunderstand me here for asking this question because as wonderful as my father was, he had also been weak-willed for doing what he did.

You see, my mother and father were from different communities. My mother was a Punjabi whereas my father was a baniya—a Gupta.

He came from a very conservative background where one only gets married to whoever the patriarch—his father in this case—chooses for you.

My father was brave enough to marry my mother for love. But he was also a dutiful son who couldn't refuse when his father forced him to marry another woman from his community.

This betrayal from my father shattered my mother to the extent that she actually tried (and thankfully failed) to end her life.

It took me a while to realize that it wasn't normal for fathers to leave after dinner every evening. That fathers didn't come home in the morning for breakfast and a change of clothes before leaving for office. That fathers didn't spend the night with some variation of 'Seema Aunty' (that's what we called his other wife; name changed) and returned the next morning.

My mother was left alone to manage the two of us—our studies, our homework, our tantrums and rebellions—and looking back I can see how difficult it had been for her.

My mother, the idealist, the Gandhian, was also a very proud woman and she could not deal with the fact that her husband had another wife, another family, two sons.

She didn't want society to know—although, quite honestly, everybody knew. How could they not? Everyone loves a juicy situation and the unconventionality of ours gave the neighbouring gossip mills enough fodder to feed on.

My mother shut her eyes and pretended that things weren't the way they were. Much like her cancer many years later, she believed that if she pretended the situation didn't exist, it would simply vanish.

But despite her attempts to lock up this 'secret', she suffered greatly. In fact, if there is one word I associate with my mother, it's 'pain'.

When I think of my mother, I can only think about all the pain she suffered. How she took my father's other marriage as such a personal failure that even her idealism and double MA couldn't soothe her. Sometimes I wonder if this invisible pain is what metastasized into a very real cancer that finally took her from us . . .

I wish I could ask her about these things. When I was younger, it didn't occur to me to wonder why my mother stayed with my father despite his weakness. This one act he committed to please his father ruined many lives, including those of his children.

My mother may not have been practical, but she was very highly qualified. She was very politically active and had great connections. I don't understand why she never cut off from this situation. Why didn't she leave my father and find a job?

Was it because of societal pressure because divorce was still very much looked down upon back then? Or was it because deep down she truly loved him? I won't ever know because I cannot ask her now. But it makes me wonder if she stayed behind because she too, despite appearances and her inner strength and bravado, suffered from low self-esteem. Like me.

There are so many things that haunt me about my mother. About how when she was in the last stage of cancer, my father would still leave her at night and return to Seema Aunty. My brother lived in another house with his family and did as much as he could. I was living and working in Bombay.

My father would spend most of the day with her. He would then tuck her into bed, leave a jug of water (we called it a lota) next to her, lock the door from the outside and leave.

My mother had no strength to move. She could barely make it to the toilet. So, my father tried to keep everything she might need by her bedside, so she didn't have to move.

I'm haunted by the nights when my mother, weak, alone and uncoordinated, would drop the lota of water and have no strength to pick it up. On those nights, she would stay thirsty until my father came back to her the next morning.

Pain, a spilled lota of water and a million unanswered questions that will forever stay unanswered because now even my father and brother have passed away.

I didn't want to write this book, I realize, not because I wanted my mother's pain and embarrassment at having to share her husband stay hidden. I didn't want to write this book because on some level, I didn't want to face the fact that the woman who raised me, scolded me, moulded and comforted me, was someone I know very little. Someone I will now never fully know.

'My father's love was like the shade of a tree on a hot summer's day, unwavering in its protection, never obtrusive and yet always there . . . A shade I knew I could return to whenever I wanted to find my strength again.'

2

Roop Narain Gupta

'I made one mistake in my life and I ended up ruining six lives,' my father confessed to me once, many many years later. This was after he had lost both my mother and Seema Aunty and had moved to Bombay to live with me.

I know that many of my readers might not think very highly of Roop Narain Gupta based on what they have read in the chapter about my mother. That he was weak for marrying another woman when he already had a wife. That he was not strong enough to stand up to his father.

That he stole my childhood and my mother's peace of mind.

But that's what makes it even more important for me to dedicate an entire chapter to his story because you need to know the man I knew; the man I resented as a child for his absence and the constant pain and humiliation his actions brought to my mother.

My father, Roop, was the son of a very traditional man. My grandfather was a manglik—born under the star that's infamous for killing spouses unless they too are born under it. He married three times and all three of his wives, non-mangliks, passed away.

My father's mother passed away when he was very small and was brought up mainly by servants in his Bazaar Sitaram house. His ancestral house that still stands in Takhat Wali Galli, Mohalla Imli, Bazaar Sitaram, New Delhi, had a large courtyard, rooms surrounding it, a common kitchen on each floor and common bathrooms.

I don't know much about his childhood, but he did tell me that he owed his independence to the fact that he was a motherless child. He learnt early on that he had to fend for himself even if he lived in a joint family. He knew how to cook for himself, washed and ironed his clothes and, in general, wasn't heavily reliant on the women in his life.

He had an LLB, but he didn't pursue law and worked as an officer in the State Trading Corporation of India till he retired. Over the years he made good investments in up-and-coming properties and eventually sold them all at good profits which he distributed fairly among his four children from both marriages.

Growing up, I didn't share much of a relationship with my father because he had to divide himself between two households and two sets of families.

It was something that shamed my mother, and my brother and I always had this dark cloud looming over our heads.

But looking back on my childhood today, I realize there wasn't a single thing that my brother and I lacked. We both went to good schools and colleges. We both wore extremely stylish clothes and ate well. And thanks to my mother, we were well travelled and eloquent.

Likewise, Seema Aunty and her sons were also well provided for. My father confessed to me years later that he didn't come along with us on holidays or came only for a few days because he always had to apply for enough leave for two holidays—one with us and another with his other family. He had to compromise a lot because he couldn't take that much time off work.

Over the years, I also realized that my father, juggling two families and trying to do right by both of them, had to work really hard to provide for us.

It makes me appreciate this man who, all through his life until his children settled down, had to balance not one but two sets of households. How difficult it must have been for him. How much pressure he must have endured. How much time, effort and energy it must have taken for him to keep us comfortable.

'Did you ever eat food at Seema Aunty's house?' I asked him once. I had been wondering about this because he always ate every meal—barring lunch, which he ate at office—at home with us. He would arrive before we woke up and eat breakfast with us. He would return home from work in the evening, eat dinner with us and then set off for Bazaar Sitaram.

Even during the cold, winter months of Delhi, he would finish dinner, bundle up in a winter jacket, a scarf and a muffler, get on his Bajaj Vespa and scoot off to Bazaar Sitaram.

'I would eat very little at our house,' he laughed and said, 'I had to eat a second dinner at the other house too.'

When I was younger, I didn't think much about how Seema Aunty must have felt having had an arranged marriage to a man who was involved with another woman. Did she also cry when my father left her first thing in the morning and returned only after dinner at night? What kind of life did she lead, living like we did, only in another part of the city? Did she too resent our existence the way we resented hers?

But we never met her, and my mother forbade us from even thinking about her. We met her two sons, our half-brothers, a few times but we were never allowed to get too close or friendly. That is just the way my mother wanted it to be.

She never wanted us to get to know them or that part of the family because she was so ashamed of the situation. She was well educated, highly respected in society and well regarded among her friends. The fact that someone like her—strong, confident, well rounded and worldly—had to share a husband was something she could never accept. But leaving my father wasn't an option for her either because at the end of the day, she loved him deeply.

My parents were compatible as a couple. They stimulated each other mentally and intellectually. My earliest memories are of them sitting at the breakfast table holding newspapers in their hands. They would discuss the news, politics, culture and religion. They went for plays and cultural events. My mother resented Bollywood, so she refused to watch Hindi films. Instead, she and my dad would go attend international film festivals and gorge on world cinema.

Seema Aunty, from what I gathered, also had plus points. She wasn't worldly and street smart like my mother, who didn't rely on anybody to get her bank work done, pay the bills or chase the gas company. But she was a good, kind woman who loved being a housewife and taking care of people. As far as I know, she had no other interests, but her simplicity was something my father appreciated.

My mother wanted my father to be with us exclusively so much that she would often cry at night after he left. I didn't know how to comfort her because she would never tell me what was bothering her.

When I was older, I suggested to her that perhaps Papa could divide his time fully between the two homes. That maybe he could live with Seema Aunty for one month and with us the next.

But my mother would hear of no such thing. My father had to come to us every single day, and even though she lost him at night, it was better than not seeing him at all.

But in all of this, caught between two women, two sets of children and families, I didn't consider gauging how my father felt. Was he happy with this arrangement? How did he cope? What and whom did he truly want?

I didn't realize this double life was taking a toll on my father until the day he didn't come home. My mother became frantic and started thinking the worst. Had something happened to him? Had he left us for good? Did he not want to be with us any more?

She got my brother to call his other house to find out if he had come home yet. But when they told us that they hadn't seen him either, my mother's mental state took a hit. We lived in fear for days. Where had my father gone? When would he come home? Would he ever come home?

Then one day we received a postcard in the mail. It was from my father and it had just a few lines written on it. I don't remember the exact words but he told us he was tired of living this double life. He wanted mental peace. He was leaving all of us and that we shouldn't try and look for him.

My mother broke down completely as I read and reread the postcard. I noticed then that the stamp on the card said it had been mailed from Mount Abu.

My brother, who was still young then, was sent to live with my aunt while my mother and I caught the next train from New Delhi to Mount Abu.

What would we say to him if he found him, we kept wondering on the long journey there. Would we even find him? The postcard had no return address.

When we reached Mount Abu, we didn't know where to start but something told my mother that he might be taking refuge in an ashram. So, we started asking around for ashrams and checking them one by one. I don't remember how many places we visited but my father was nowhere to be found.

Finally, one day we found out about a Brahma Kumari ashram and decided to look it up. That's where we found my father, and I will never forget that first glimpse of him after searching for him for so many days.

He looked weak, thin and, for the first time in my life, I thought he looked old and exhausted.

After a lot of cursing (on my mother's part) and crying (on all our parts) we finally managed to get him on a train and brought him back to Delhi.

'You have to let him divide his time equally between the two houses,' I begged my mother. 'Look at the toll this life is taking on him. What kind of life is this? This time he ran away. Next time what if he commits suicide?'

But even the threat of losing my father did not move my mother to agree. She refused to budge from her stance.

'If he wants to spend time in only one house, then let him go and live with them,' she shouted. 'I will not have any of it.'

But my father could not spend his time in only one house. He could not let my mother suffer alone. So, eventually, we went back to the same arrangement and, luckily, exhausted as he was, he never ran away again.

He spent most of his life trying hard to be there equally and fairly for his two families. It was difficult to say the least and also traumatizing.

Eventually, this trauma took the form of prostate cancer but by some miracle he was able to beat it.

My mother's misery and pain also metastasized as multiple myeloma. My father loved her and never left her side—except at night. He took care of her throughout her illness. He fed her, washed and changed her and at the same time, he also went to work and stayed with his other family.

The cancer treatment was not cheap but his property investments came in handy. He sold a house and paid for my mother's treatment.

He also bought me not one, but two houses in Bombay. He bought my brother a house in South Extension and gave property to his other sons as well.

When my mother died in 1985, I wondered if he felt relief.

I know he was sad. My mother's death shattered me. But I wondered if my father would now be able to lead a normal life, not having to split himself between two women and families.

My brother and I were settled by then. My brother was married, and I had a career in Bombay. So, on some level, as much as I loved my mom, I do hope that her death brought him some relief and allowed him to deal better with his own pain, struggles and guilt.

'You shouldn't feel guilty,' I told him years later when I didn't want him to feel bad any more. 'Whatever the situation, you did right by all of us.'

* * *

My father didn't want me to have a child without getting married. He didn't like the idea of me being a single mother. He didn't want people to say the things they did about me back then.

But once I made the decision to bring my child into this world, he supported me throughout.

In fact, when I delivered the baby, he came to Bombay to help me out. But in a very strange move, he also brought Seema Aunty with him.

That was the first time I met Seema Aunty and she was everything I didn't want her to be.

She was kind, considerate and extremely warm. She took care of me post-partum because I had had a major surgery. She doted on Masaba. And often, when I suffered from sleepless nights, she took Masaba to her room so I could get a good night's rest.

Out of loyalty to my own mother, I wanted to hate Seema Aunty. But when she left three months later, I was truly sad to see her go and missed her. It was even more painful because fifteen days after returning to Delhi, she suffered a massive heart attack and passed away.

My father was now alone. His children, two of whom he lived with in Bazaar Sitaram, were grown up, married and settled. My brother had his own life.

He continued to stay with his sons for many years, but in the 1990s, he finally decided to move to Bombay to live with me; this came as a blessing and relief.

The father who had spread himself too thin when I was a child, now had nothing but time and energy to focus on me.

All the things he couldn't do for me earlier, he did now. He doted on me. He took care of me. He took on all the household chores, so that I could live my life and focus on my career.

He took over the menu planning with the staff. He was present when the electrician or plumber arrived. He decided how much bonus to give everyone working in our house and building. Basically, he did everything that I didn't have the time or the mind space to do while juggling a career and a small child.

I still recall him standing in my Juhu house, wearing a white kurta pyjama with his pockets full of money. All day long, he had to keep paying someone or the other— for the gas cylinder, the watchman, groceries and staff. The first thing he did every morning was put money in his pocket.

In fact, as I write this in Mukteshwar, walking around handling staff, paying gardeners and buying things, I am reminded of him because I too haven't gone one day without putting cash in the pockets of my pants.

My father was my rock.

Of course, it wasn't easy in the beginning because he and Masaba would fight for my attention.

I would leave for work at 8.30 a.m. and return at 10.30 p.m. . . . The minute I would return, they would both appear in front of me, bursting with stories about their day and asking questions about mine.

Masaba didn't like it if my father got to speak to me first.

'Why are you always after my Mummy?' she would shout at him. 'She's mine. Not yours.'

I had to reprimand her for speaking to him this way, but I also understood that it was very confusing for her. She was so used to being the centre of attention, the one whom I took care of on priority and was always available to that it didn't occur to her that I too was someone's child. That my parent wanted to take care of me and wanted some attention after having missed me all day.

The Juhu flat had three bedrooms. One for me, one for Masaba and one for my father. The flat was originally two smaller apartments that had been merged into one. My father's room had his own front door which gave him a great sense of privacy and ownership.

He never drank or smoked. In fact, he didn't even eat meat, raw onions and garlic. But he did enjoy a good cup of tea and snacks, so he often invited his friends over and entertained them there.

He was really popular and had lots of friends. Some lived right in our society and others he met at a park on the beach where they organized laughter club meets and senior citizen exercise groups.

I won't say that our coexistence was always peaceful. There were little things on which we disagreed.

My father loved tube lights in the house. He thought my preference for lamps—not even wall lamps, just floor lamps—was depressing. So, he campaigned to have them all changed. But I wasn't having any of it because tube lights, though energy-efficient, are also very bright and I found it hard to relax under them.

'You can instal a tube light in your room. But nowhere else in the house,' I relented.

'And in the kitchen as well. It's not like you spend any time in there,' he retorted. So, we compromised, and he got tube lights wherever I didn't spend much time in.

My father also made it very clear what he thought of Vivian visiting us.

'Do you really think this is a good idea?' he would ask. 'You know he isn't ever going to be able to marry you. Why do this to yourself?'

It would irritate me when he said these things because I knew they were true. But like so many children who don't value their parents' words until they're much older, I would just shrug and say I didn't mind. I was very happy with the way things were.

My father never once showed his displeasure to Vivian though. He was always perfectly courteous and polite. The fact that we'd cook up a non-vegetarian feast when he was down was something he didn't appreciate. But he didn't mention it. When we'd sit down to dinner, he would just move his plate and glass over to a table in the living area away from us because he couldn't take the smell of meat.

When he first moved in, he was quite shocked that we cooked non-vegetarian food at home. Especially since I too don't eat meat except eggs. But Masaba was a growing girl, who really loved meat so I didn't want to deprive her of that.

'At least use separate utensils to cook and eat non-veg then,' he requested.

We tried, but honestly, it didn't last long and eventually he stopped complaining and just went with it.

That was the thing about my father. He was the king of adjustment.

One year, I wanted to host a Diwali party in my house, but my father wasn't too happy about it.

'You can't cook non-veg in the house on Diwali,' he said.

'But all my friends love non-veg. We have to have some meat dishes,' I said.

'No, no. Not on Diwali.'

That evening he heard me talking to a friend about moving the party to someone else's house. He could hear how disappointed I was. So, he came to me and said, 'You know, why don't you make the non-veg dishes the day before? Then you can still have the party here.'

It was a funny solution, but I took it. I know it makes no sense. What difference does it make when the meat is cooked? But to my father, who was from a different generation, adjusting to these things seemed nearly impossible. That he was trying to adapt and adjust to so many new things spoke volumes of him as a human being and his love for me.

I don't think I can stress enough on what a boon it was to have my father live with me until he breathed his last. I was truly privileged to have got to spend so much time with him to make up for all the time we lost when I was a child.

He was the man of the house. Growing up without a mother had made him very independent and unlike so many of his generation, he actually enjoyed housework. He was a natural nurturer and he often acted as my protector.

Once I came home in tears because I had had an altercation with the chairman of our building. They were planning to set up a big hoarding for advertisements on top of our building and were going ahead without getting every resident's permission. I wasn't opposed to it because I knew the money made from that hoarding would benefit us all, but I was trying to explain to him that it was equally important to get every resident's permission before going ahead with it. In fact, I had even approached the press to cover the story and that is exactly what had angered this man so much.

Things got ugly and the chairman became irate. I won't go into the details of exactly what he said but his last words to me, before I fled, were, 'People like you are a stain on this community and should not be allowed to live in any respectable society.'

I cried to my father as I recalled what the man said. My father got so angry that he went to seek him out. They had a huge altercation in public, which ended with my father vowing to overthrow him as chairman and taking over the society's responsibilities himself.

And that's exactly what he did. He began campaigning, bringing people over to his side at the next election and he actually bagged enough votes to win. It was amazing and he did all of that only because someone had been rude to me.

My father was also very protective, and he constantly worried about me. When I first introduced him to Vivek, he knew of our situation.

'You're still married and cannot get a divorce. Yet you say you love my daughter,' my father told him. 'Tell me one thing, when you go out in public, how will you introduce her to people?'

He was a very logical and practical man. He understood the magnitude of the many things I did even before I took a moment to pause and reflect. In time, and perhaps much much too late, I realized that my father was always right. But regardless of the choices I made, he always had my back.

I think my biggest regret when it comes to our relationship is not being there for him more. Not sitting down and talking to him more and listening to what he had to say.

As the sole breadwinner of the family and with my hectic schedule, it was difficult for me to be there for him all the time. But I honestly wish that I had consciously made more time for him.

I also took him for granted while he was around because I didn't think he could want or need more from life. He was active and walked with a straight back well into his eighties and only started to deteriorate after he contracted a lung infection which ultimately took his life at the age of eighty-six.

I often teased him that I should probably buy him a cane but he sternly refused. He didn't need any help from anybody, let alone a walking stick, until he was at the end of his life.

I still feel guilty about how I once dismissed him and walked away when he said he didn't feel good and wanted to return to the hospital.

'You just got back from the hospital a few days ago,' I said, thinking he was being overly cautious and paranoid. 'Wait a few days for your medication to take effect.'

But as I turned away to walk away, he collapsed behind me, and that's one more thing I regret because it makes me wish that I had listened to him more.

I have only one request to you, my readers. Please always be there for your elders. They don't want much from you except to talk and for you to listen. It isn't too much to ask for because once they're gone, this is the one thing you will regret for the rest of your life.

My family dynamics are not what you might call normal. But that isn't to say that I don't love them. My mother ensured that I got a good education and always wanted me to have a high-flying career—not as an actor, but still. My father may have spread himself too thin and was absent from my life a lot but he more than made up for it in the end.

When I think of love, I don't think of grand gestures or boxes wrapped in bows. I think of the little things in life.

My mother, I know, loved me because she educated me well and always took me in no matter how badly I had behaved.

My father loved me, I know, because he always peeled two oranges, tasted them both and then let me have the sweeter one.

That, to me, is the greatest expression of love, and I feel so lucky to have received it.

'Much like the weeping willow, my brother to me symbolized tragic beauty.'

3

Pankaj Gupta

I like to remember my brother, Pankaj Gupta, born two and a half years after me, as a sweet, gentle soul who was kind, intelligent and very good looking, even as a child.

Despite our family dynamics, the two of us always managed to have a good time. We played together a lot. Sometimes we'd play games of our own invention or run together outside to play with our friends in the area.

Together, we managed to build a wonderful relationship through our childhood but as is the case with many sibling, we drifted apart once we grew up.

A lot of our distance came after I moved Bombay to try my luck in films. Looking back, I feel like I might have been selfish and thought of nobody but myself at that time.

But I also cannot deny that a lot of it happened because of Pankaj's personality and the choices he made in life which were his and his alone.

You see, when it came to our genes and personalities, I got the best of both my parents.

I got some of my mother's strength and idealism. But it was my father's practicality that ultimately turned me into who I am today.

Pankaj got all of my mother's intellect and extreme idealism and none of my father's practicality.

During those times, girls were always overprotected, sheltered and controlled to ensure they didn't go astray. But when it came to my mother, she didn't discriminate between her daughter and son because she was strict with both of us. If anything, I feel like she was stricter with my brother.

At the back of her mind, she wanted to prevent me from the fate she had suffered—marrying for love and suffering for the rest of my life—but more than that she wanted to prevent my brother from following in his father's footsteps, putting a woman through that kind of turmoil.

She believed the best way to do this was to ensure we didn't socialize too much. Didn't have close friends of the opposite sex and gave our studies and future careers more thought than anything else.

Following my mother's orders and getting an MA and then an MPhil in Sanskrit was my way of appeasing her. But eventually I somehow, in a logical and practical manner, managed to get out by applying to NSD and moving into a hostel.

My brother, however, didn't do the same. He let his idealism get in the way of practical decisions, leading him to rebel in many ways. He studied in St Stephen's College for two years and then dropped out. Throughout his teenage years, he and my mother were constantly disagreeing on various things and he fell into the wrong company.

My brother and my mother were very similar, and this was why they refused to bow down and compromise no matter how petty their issues were.

Being the child of an absentee father and a depressed, lonely and strict mother affected Pankaj way more than it affected me. I got out at the first opportunity I got. My brother on the other hand didn't. It started to grate on him and affected his mental health too.

Things were a little good for him when he was in a relationship with a girl while he was in Stephen's. But for reasons still unknown to me, she called off their courtship. This broke my brother's heart, and he went off the deep end for a while.

Eventually my brother did get his career on track. He passed the CA exam at the first attempt. This was something we were all proud of because we all knew clearing the exam was one of the most difficult things.

We finally had hope for him and thought this would change his life and personality. He even agreed to have an arranged marriage to a wonderful woman named Madhu.

But when I came to Delhi to meet her before the wedding, I was honestly unsure about the match. The two of them were vastly different people and I didn't know if they would be compatible in the long run.

But my brother brushed off my concerns. 'I just want to get this over with,' he told me and went ahead and got married.

My mother, the mother of idealism in fact, impressed everyone by refusing to take a single penny in dowry even though everyone said, 'Pankaj is a CA! He's worth at least a few crores.'

But my mother was insistent that not one rupee would be transferred to the Guptas. 'Give your daughter whatever you would like. We don't want anything.'

It was impressive and extremely progressive. It made both my brother and me very proud.

Unfortunately, her principles didn't extend to their personal life behind closed doors. She had a certain way of living and my bhabhi, who came from a different home with different rules, seemed to have habits that grated on my mother.

Pankaj and Madhu moved in with my mother for the first few years, and I remember my mother would complain about her daughter-in-law.

'She has eaten all the malai again,' she'd tell me over the phone. My mother, who had been making ghee and butter at home for decades, always kept the cream from the milk aside in the fridge. My brother and I were never allowed to eat this while growing up so I never developed a taste for it. But my bhabhi loved to eat malai and my mother, instead of stocking up on more milk and keeping some malai aside for her, always complained about it.

It was quite frustrating for me to listen to these things because I found them petty. I tried to explain to her that my bhabhi was brought up differently and expecting her to abide by her rules, like Pankaj and I did as kids, was unreasonable. I also knew that my mother was extremely possessive of Pankaj and accepting a new woman in his life was tough for her.

But my mother, being the person she was, refused to budge or adjust in any way. So eventually my father, who had a property in South Extension, let my brother and his wife move out of my mother's house and into their own flat.

My brother was doing very well by then. He was taking CA classes for young boys and girls in a flat right below the house.

He had two daughters, Vasudha and Aastha, both lovely girls, with whom I didn't get to spend too much time being in a different city, but tried, in my own way, to spoil with gifts and clothes.

But their period of peace didn't last very long because my brother, once again, got caught up in something that ruined their finances and eventually, their family.

My brother, I found out later, invested in a chit fund and convinced his friends to do the same. The whole debacle ended very badly, and my brother lost all of his money. He went through a very hard time for a few years because he had to earn money not only for himself but also to pay back his friends whom he had roped in.

His family life started to crumble. He started drinking and neglected them. He sold his house, moved into a rental and reopened his CA coaching classes in Trans Yamuna.

I heard about all of these things through my parents and then eventually from his daughters when they grew up. My bhabhi really struggled during this time because my brother left home.

I feel bad when I hear about all of these things because I should have been there for him more. I should have reached out before it was too late and knocked some sense into him.

But I had my own struggles to contend with so I, very selfishly, focused on myself instead of lending a helping hand.

Through this whole ordeal, my bhabhi suffered the most because my brother didn't look after their financial interests. He would send some money, but it was never enough to cover their needs.

Years later, my nieces told me that their mother managed as best she could, but they were still wanting. Having food on their table and a roof over their heads felt like a luxury. Being able to afford a box of mangoes during mango season seemed like a huge privilege that they rarely experienced.

My father, however, who had moved to Bombay with me by then, did his best to take care of them. Whenever he visited Delhi, he made it a point to look in on them and ensure their well-being. My bhabhi was a wonderful woman who took really good care of my father. She always ensured that all the food she cooked was to his liking and he had the hottest rotis on the table.

But my father still came away distressed and unhappy with what he saw and tried his level best to help them financially.

'I don't like how insecure their lives and futures are,' he told me once. 'Would it be possible for you to help with some money so that I can at least buy them a house? I want them to have a stable roof over their heads, if nothing else.'

'Of course,' I said without hesitation. I was earning a decent living by then. 'My money is your money, Papa. Do what you feel is right.'

So, my father, using my money, bought them a house in Delhi and tried his level best to help out in other ways too.

One day, we found out that my brother had cancer. He never told us what kind of cancer. He refused to let us accompany him to appointments and didn't show us the reports. He did visit Singapore often 'for blood transfusions', he told us.

The cancer started to spread all over and eventually spread to his mouth. My once handsome brother had to get one of his lips removed and it was painful to watch.

'Come to Bombay like Papa and stay with me,' I told him. 'Bring your whole family. I will take care of all of you. You can start your classes here and make a lot more money.'

My brother did give it a try but left in a few days. Bombay, as wonderful a city as it is, isn't for everyone. It's a big adjustment in terms of living and working. You have to be very, very strong to survive here because success is a slow and steady process. We all have to fall at least a hundred times before we find our feet.

Pankaj couldn't take this. He was too used to living on his own, answerable to nobody. By this time, he had also stopped eating. He lived only on gin day in, day out.

My father was ashamed of what his son had become. It pained him to see my brother like this and sometimes he felt guilty, wondering if it was because of something he had done . . .

At times like these, I had to embrace my father and assure him that I was his child too. That despite his absences in our childhood and the decisions he made, if I could turn out okay, Pankaj's downfall couldn't be his fault.

A few months after my father passed away, my bhabhi suffered from a brain haemorrhage and passed away too. This came as a big shock to me because I honestly didn't expect my brother, who had been in ill health for years now, to outlive her.

My brother, who attended the funeral and showed solidarity with his daughters, looked sincerely sorry for this loss. But Madhu's family was having none of it. They blamed him for all the pain he had inflicted on her.

After Madhu's death, my brother finally moved in with his daughters to mend their relationship and be a real father to them.

But his bad habits and temper, not to mention the girls' resentment at his past behaviour, couldn't be brushed under the carpet. So, my brother eventually fought with them and moved back into his little room in Trans Yamuna.

I heard different versions of their fights from both ends. My nieces didn't like their father's behaviour, whereas Pankaj didn't like that they disrespected him.

At the best of times in their relationship, Vasudha would help my brother at his coaching classes because she too had studied CA and was really good even though she hadn't completed the course.

But at the worst of times, the girls refused to speak to my brother. They were very close to Madhu's brother and sister-in-law, their mama and mami who doted on them and looked after them as best as they could.

Eventually, my brother and his daughters became completely estranged.

Pankaj's health, by now, had started to deteriorate. He was losing weight and looked truly haggard.

He may not have been able to commit to his family or do right by his daughters, but he was truly passionate about teaching. He continued taking classes almost until the end. He would wake up at 4 a.m. to go over the day's notes and worked relentlessly throughout the day.

Finally, one day, he went into a coma and passed away.

When I went for his funeral, I was shocked to see the number of people who had come to pay their respects.

'You're Pankaj Gupta's sister, aren't you?' they asked. 'Your brother was a wonderful human being. It's because of his tutelage that my daughter/son is so successful today.'

Throughout the hawan, people came over and touched my feet, held my hands and told me what a wonderful human being my brother was. I was shocked to learn about how many lives he had touched because of his CA classes. Many of them told me they weren't able to afford the fee, but Pankaj still took them in. He had taught a number of boys and girls for free, and they had gone on to do wonderful things in their careers.

Listening to these beautiful things being said about my brother brought tears to my eyes and made me long for the brother I had grown up with—the sweet, gentle, idealistic little boy who somehow lost his way.

Looking back on my relationship with my brother, it still pains me that I wasn't there for him when he needed me. That I wasn't able to guide him when he needed it the most. That I somehow, through some twist of fate, escaped the pain and turmoil that turned him into the person he was.

It also makes me think extensively about marriage and divorce.

People often say that marriage is a compromise. That we all need to make adjustments to our lives and our attitudes. We have to try really hard to make our marriage work under any circumstances.

But what are the acceptable circumstances in such a situation? I know my brother's marriage and his subsequent downfall isn't unique. One hears a lot of stories, cautionary tales, of men and women who get married first because they think they have to and then stay married for the sake of their children.

But what happens when this leads to so much bitterness that every member in the unit suffers? My bhabhi and nieces suffered immensely. My brother also suffered a lot because of his choices.

It takes courage to end a marriage, no doubt about it. But it's also a big trauma because once two people unite, their whole existence, their families are held together by a thread. When this thread starts to weaken, everyone suffers. But is it worth staying in this mess, refusing to let the thread snap, just to appease society? To keep up appearances?

I don't know. I hope my readers will have more insight into this because I honestly feel that in some cases, it's best to let the thread break and move forward rather than bind so many lives into eternal misery.

My mother is dead. My father is dead. My brother is also no more. When I think about this, a sense of loneliness envelops me because it feels like there is no one who has known me my entire life; who knows my entire history.

I find some solace in knowing though that they did exist and they enriched my life in whatever way they could while they were around, even my brother.

I try not to remember Pankaj for what he had become. I try to keep him alive in my memories as the sweet, innocent boy I grew up with. And when I want to think about him as an adult, I only bring to mind all the people I met at his funeral and even at airports in India and abroad who still come to me and say, 'You're Pankaj Gupta's sister, right? He was a wonderful teacher and a great human being.'

'Masaba is happiness. The colourful laugh and loving blossom in my garden of life.'

4

Masaba Gupta

'Your son is your son until he gets a wife. Your daughter is your daughter for all her life.' My father used to love saying this to me while he was still alive, and I never realized how very true it was until I started reminiscing my own journey as a parent.

When I found out that I was going to be a mother in early 1989, I experienced a plethora of emotions. I was confused about how this had happened. I was scared about what it meant. I was nervous about how I would manage. But mostly, I felt happiness and elation because I realized I was ready. That I wanted a child. Most importantly, I wanted *this* child.

There was no doubt in my mind that this child was half Vivian Richards's, because we had been seeing each other for a while and he was the only man I had been with.

But this complicated things immensely because he was known internationally, and I too was known nationally in my own right. Our affair had been fuelling the gossip mills for a while, and I just had to brace myself for what would happen once they found out about my pregnancy.

However, before we could even get to that stage of drama, I had to get Vivian's go-ahead. I knew I really wanted to be a mother. I loved Vivian and I was thrilled to be having his child. But as the father, I had to give him a choice in the matter because if he wasn't on board . . . I honestly don't know what I would have done.

Luckily, it didn't come to that because Vivian, when I told him about my pregnancy and asked if he was okay with me having his child, said he was happy and that I could go ahead.

This was a huge relief, but it didn't last long. Everyone else in my life was strongly against me bringing a child into this world without being married to the father.

'Think about the kind of life your child will have, not being able to live with their father or know his side of the family,' they said.

'Think about how this decision will affect your own life, Neena. How will you do this alone? Do you even know how hard it is to be a single parent?'

'What will society say? Your reputation will be ruined.'

I listened to what everyone had to say, and I instantly put their words aside. This was my child. I wanted him or her. I didn't know if it would be a boy or a girl, but I did know that no matter what, this child was wanted and would be loved immensely.

I had it in me to do this, I told myself. I was strong enough to face all adversity for this child.

My father was dead against it. He was worried not only about what society would say but how I would fare. He also didn't think this would help my career in anyway.

But I was adamant. Call it youth, folly or basic motherly instinct, I wanted this and so I went ahead and did it.

My family members, may they rest in peace, came around quickly enough. That's just the way they were. They would caution against my choices. They would oppose many of my decisions. But once the deed was done, they supported me with all their heart. Especially my father, and I loved him for that.

That summer, a few months before Masaba was born, my family and I took a trip to Mussoorie. My friend Tom Alter, an actor and poet, had helped us find a beautiful colonial bungalow nestled in the hills which was owned by a British couple who had returned to England for the summer. The house was very quaint, comfortable and from another era. My father, bhabhi, nieces and I absolutely loved it. My brother couldn't join us for the whole trip, but he did make an appearance and spend a few days with us.

My father was a spectacular cook and prepared all our meals. We'd often have Tom and his family over for dinner. On other days, he would invite us to play tennis on his ancestral property, and while I couldn't play because of my pregnancy, we spent a lot of quality time just talking and relaxing.

It was also exhilarating for me to be in the hills where there was nobody around for miles. I got to go on walks without having to cover up my growing belly. I could stay out as long as I wanted. And my dad, who was just recovering from surgery for his prostate cancer, and I really benefitted from all the fresh air.

In retrospect, it was a bit bold of me to go live in such a serene yet secluded place because the closest road to the city was at least a few kilometres away. We didn't even come in our own car and were reliant on public transport. The closest doctor was 10-15 km away in a mall in the city centre. I shudder to think what would have happened if something had suddenly gone wrong with my pregnancy or if I'd had a fall.

But luckily, everything was absolutely fine, and I finally returned to Delhi and then back home to Bombay to find work—I was running low on money.

Very few people in Bombay knew about my pregnancy. My friend Soni Razdan was one of them and eventually, Om Puri found out.

I didn't mean to tell Om but it was inevitable. We were working on a set together and he was asking me to do some really risky steps that involved climbing a ladder or jumping. I can't remember. I was really thin back then, so I wasn't showing very prominently just yet. But Om was insisting I do something rigorous for the part and I was scared.

So, I finally told him to stop asking me to do it because I was pregnant.

He started laughing heartily. 'What are you saying? That's the fake excuse you're going with?'

I told him I was serious and confessed the whole thing to him. He was really sweet and supportive after that.

He too had a house in Juhu, so he often let me go over to eat, sit and talk. It was really nice because in Om's house I didn't have to pretend for or worry about the keen eyes of the media.

Om often dropped me back home in his car. He would drive very slowly so that I wouldn't get hurt because of the bumps.

The pregnancy was still very lonely for me because I could not tell anyone about it. Everywhere I went, I had to take great pains to hide my big stomach and not draw too much attention to myself.

My doctor had instructed me to walk for one hour every day so that I was strong and healthy for delivery. But I couldn't walk in the evening when everyone was around, so I used to walk at night. It helped that my house in Juhu was on the third floor without a lift, so I definitely got enough exercise climbing the stairs.

As my due date approached, I started to worry because I had very little money in my account. I could afford a natural birth because it would cost only Rs 2000. But I knew if I had to have a C-section, I would be in trouble because the surgery cost almost Rs 10,000.

Luckily, a tax reimbursement of Rs 9000 came through a few days before my delivery and I finally ended up with Rs 12,000 in my bank account.

Good thing this money came through, because my doctor informed me that I would need a C-section. My father who had come down at the time to help me through the birth was livid. He said this was a ploy to just charge us more money.

But I assured him that it was okay and that we should trust the doctor. So we went ahead with the C-section and on 2 November 1988, my beautiful baby girl Masaba came into my life.

I sent word to Vivian via Soni who called him and told him the news. He was thrilled to hear about it.

The name Masaba, of Swahili origin and meaning 'princess' in his culture, was given by him.

'Masaba,' I said, looking at her, and it was such a perfect fit that I didn't even think of naming her anything else.

We left the hospital a few days later and started a new phase of our lives.

* * *

The first few days of being a mother were challenging because I felt lost and out of my depth. Born just a few days before Diwali, the crackers, noise and pollution had Masaba wailing and shaking from fright. I had to hold her against me every time a cracker went off and bundle her in as many blankets as I could to make her feel safe and secure.

My father, aunt and Seema Aunty were there to help me but I still found myself second-guessing every decision I had to make as a parent. Was I nursing enough? Was she warm enough? Was she too warm? Was it my fault that she was waking up so many times during the night?

It was during those first few weeks of parenthood when I started to question this decision. I realized how difficult it was to care for a baby as a single parent, with nobody to help except my elders, whose knowledge of babies by then was dated given all their children were well into adulthood. I regretted doing this without a partner.

I also started to feel the first few tremors of post-partum blues (I don't think I can call it depression, because I was completely in love with her). What I felt was a sense of dread. That my life was over. My career was over. That there was no end in sight, and I would be spending my entire life just feeding and caring for my infant. I also couldn't go outside because everyone told me I could bring back an infection and make my child sick.

It was horrible and I felt like I was stuck in a rut.

But then one day Soni called me and invited me to her daughter's birthday party.

'I can't come,' I told her. It was the norm for new mothers to stay home for forty days to reduce the risk of infection. I had already completed those forty days, but I was still very, very scared. 'I don't want to risk leaving her. What if I fall sick and then make her sick too?'

'You're being silly,' Soni said. 'You cannot lock yourself up forever. Your child will fall sick when she has to anyway. That's how all children grow and develop immunity. You need to look after your own mental well-being too. You need to get out and get some fresh air. If you aren't happy, neither is she.'

Her words really gave me an insight into how I would need to be if I were to take care of myself, physically and mentally, along with my daughter. So I left the house for the first time after giving birth and had a wonderful time with Soni.

When I returned that night, I realized that everything was perfect. Masaba had been fed, changed and was fast asleep. So, I lay down next to her to catch a few hours of sleep before she woke up demanding her next feed.

Her birth obviously caused quite a stir among the media and speculation ran rife about who the father was. I didn't want to reveal anything at that time because there was much at stake for Vivian as well as for me.

The media wrote what they wanted to, but I refused to speak to journalists. Let them say what they like, I thought. They will tire of me soon and move on to the next sensational story.

But then one day Soni called me and said that a very reputed journalist wanted to interview me. He was the editor of a weekly magazine under one of the biggest media conglomerates in India. She said that her husband, Mahesh Bhatt, had personally spoken to him and made him promise that he won't twist my words and stories. That whatever I said would be printed as is with no sensational spin to it.

I trusted Soni and Mahesh, so I agreed to the interview. The journalist arrived at my house and we spoke for a long time. I kept mum about who the father was and requested that he respect my wishes in this regard.

But when the article came out, it was a disaster. The journalist hadn't kept his word and had gone ahead and put his own sensational spin to things. Worse still, and this is what made me feel very, very betrayed, Masaba's birth certificate was printed with the article.

I was in absolute shock because as her parent, even I hadn't got Masaba's birth certificate yet. We had applied for it at the BMC office and were waiting for the date given in the receipt to go collect it. How had this man managed to get this important piece of documentation then?

Worst of all, now everyone knew who the father of my baby was because it was printed on the birth certificate. It was a complete disaster.

Soni and Mahesh felt awful about this situation and blamed themselves for being so naive. But I wasn't angry with them at all. I knew they were only trying to help.

What I wanted, more than anything, was to solve the mystery of the birth certificate. I sent my aunt to the office immediately to see what had happened.

'Your birth certificate was collected by your relative,' they told her.

'What relative? How can you give the certificate to anybody else? I have the receipt as proof. You're telling me you just gave the certificate to anyone without a receipt?'

The person at the counter had little to say to this. He issued another birth certificate for Masaba and my aunt came home with it.

Eventually, after a whole lot of hounding and threatening legal action, I got back Masaba's birth certificate from the publication.

To this day, I cannot believe how a man of such repute, an editor and a very important person in the media, could stoop so low and infringe on our privacy like this.

It's one thing to write what you must about me, or say what you like, everyone else was at that time anyway, but to actually steal my child's birth certificate just to satiate your own (and the nation's) curiosity is a different level of sliminess.

The identity of my daughter's father wasn't a matter of national interest, it was just something the nation was interested in. They would have eventually found out anyway once I was ready to reveal it. But this man gave me no choice in the matter and violated my faith and privacy—my newborn's privacy—so unethically that it still makes my blood boil. And for what? To sell a few extra copies of his now-defunct weekly?

* * *

Masaba has always been a wonderful child. She never once complained about the long hours I had to work. She never once demanded that I stop working and stay with her full time.

She was kind, considerate and extremely accommodating. She was also very hard working in school; she is very hardworking as an adult too. I think watching me struggle all those years to put food on the table and a stable roof over our heads gave her a great sense of what a woman must do when she doesn't have a partner beside her.

As an only child, Masaba wasn't used to sharing me with anybody, and she and my dad were often at loggerheads because of this. But, eventually, they made their peace with having to share my attention and we all learnt to live amicably.

Masaba went to Jamnabai Narsee School in Juhu and did well in her studies. But she also had to learn early that she needed to fight her own battles. I found out much later that she would get bullied because girls considered her bum too big and her hair too curly. But never once did she come home crying or ask me to step in. She faced all her adversaries bravely and evolved into a beautiful, independent little girl.

When I look back on her childhood, I feel bad about how much of her life I missed. How many times she probably needed me, but I was too busy with my 8 a.m.–10 p.m. schedule to be there for her.

It makes me feel very guilty because she went through a lot, especially in her teenage years when girls are unsure of their bodies. If I had been around more, I could have told her that she was and still is beautiful just as she was. I would have probably caught and tackled the acne that covered her face, making her so self-conscious that she sometimes refused to leave the house.

When she felt like she would never be loved by a man because of her skin, body or whatever else plagues girls at that age, I wish I had been there to tell her how any man would be lucky to have her.

I think of my journey as a parent and feel that yes, I provided her with everything she wanted. But emotionally, I didn't give her what she needed.

I also regret that I couldn't give her a sibling. After me, she would have had someone, who was her own flesh and blood, to lean on and be her family. But because of my circumstances, it was impossible to go through that again.

Masaba never holds this against me. Even now, when she's all grown up with a life, home and career of her own, she doesn't resent me for the choices I had to make back then.

She also doesn't make me feel rotten about uprooting her and moving her to Delhi when Vivek and I started getting serious. Her life was in Bombay. Her school, college and friends were in Bombay.

But she didn't once complain when I told her she would have to finish college in Delhi because I had met a man and was in love.

Of course, our stint in Delhi lasted less than one month because Vivek, who was still not divorced, bought us a home away from his own.

'You shouldn't have moved here without getting married,' his mother told me once when I was lamenting my situation. 'You have made a mistake by coming to be with him with no commitment from his end.'

It's true. If I were his wife, I would at least have the right to be there in that home, be considered part of his family. But without marriage, I was a nobody. I was the mistress.

So, a month after we shifted, I packed up again and returned to Bombay with Masaba, my father and Sindhu, my helper who has been with us since Masaba was born.

It was a disaster and I felt like a fool. More so when I realized that admissions for colleges had already been closed and Masaba had nowhere to go. I tried really, really hard to get her into a good college—and then any college—but it was futile. Masaba had to eventually complete her undergraduate degree privately and it was all my fault.

But again, this girl is such a gem that she never once made me feel like the fool I was or ridicule the choices I had made.

Destiny, however, leads us exactly where we need to be and I truly believe this because once Masaba earned her bachelor's degree, she enrolled in a course in fashion design. She had always been artistic and loved working with her hands. She joined the course because another friend of hers was going to attend too, but it changed her life and career.

Her first independent show as a designer was part of the Lakmé Fashion Week, in a category called Gen Next. She was invited to participate in it, and she won a prize and gained a lot of recognition. From there on, it felt like the sky was the limit. She didn't complete the internship that was a mandatory part of her course. Instead, we rented a space in Juhu, hired a few tailors and started the base for what has now become House of Masaba.

I cannot even express how proud I am of my daughter, for who she is and what she has become. She has her own fashion house and collaborates with some of the biggest brands in the country. And her talent isn't just limited to clothes because she has designed a lipstick for Nykaa and a watch for Titan. She has made a big name for herself because of her unique designs. She also learnt to adapt to the changing times, especially after independent businesses were hit hard due to the pandemic.

For all those months in lockdown, she spent her time in Goa dreaming of her next big venture—designing homes—and it fills my heart with pride to know that she is my daughter.

She also made her debut as an actor in August 2020 with *Masaba Masaba*. The producer of the show, Ashvini Yardi, was very inspired by Masaba's Instagram posts and her social media persona. Masaba has a very good sense of humour and doesn't mind poking fun at herself. It makes her very real to her followers and much liked too. It was this side of Masaba that Ashvini wanted to bring out in *Masaba Masaba*.

When Masaba told me they wanted her to star in a TV series that was part reality, part fiction, I was a bit concerned about what they would put in it. But they were really nice about it. They sat with us and went over every incident that they would use and ensured that it wasn't something we weren't comfortable sharing with the world.

When Masaba was fourteen years old, she wanted to become an actor. A lot of her friends were also making their forays into the entertainment industry and she was inspired. But I, her mother and biggest critic, had to tell her the truth.

As an industry insider, I knew better than anyone, what the industry looked for in a heroine. And Masaba's face and body were very different from that. I didn't want her to be told that her unique beauty was not appreciated in this country.

'You may get roles as a supporting actress,' I told her. 'But will you be happy with that?'

It was years before Masaba finally saw my side of things and decided to pursue fashion instead. And what a big name she's made for herself. I was glad at the time that she had finally listened to me because mothers know best, don't they?

I don't think I have ever been happier to be proven wrong because with *Masaba Masaba*, my daughter showcased her natural talent as an actor. She was also an inspiration to all young women who are told they don't have what it takes.

I also love that she doesn't hold it against me for discouraging her from acting when she was younger.

'What mom said made sense,' she tells people in interviews when they ask her why she didn't pursue acting to begin with.

I'm glad things have started to change in the industry now and that there is enough room for women with all types of faces, bodies and, yes, of all ages.

Beautiful, hard-working, talented, Masaba is my best friend and confidante, in addition to being my only daughter. She has made all my struggles, suffering and hard times worth it just by being herself. I really can't wait to see the wonderful places she will go.

'With his heart as enduring as an evergreen tree, Vivek is my calm, my constant, my anchor, my smile, my friend.'

5

Vivek Mehra

Vivek Mehra, a CA who retired as a senior partner with PwC and now has his own practice in Delhi, makes the best Bloody Marys in the world! And I'm not being biased here because I love him or because he plied me with booze while writing this. He seriously knows the secret to getting Bloody Marys perfectly right and balanced.

It's strange to think that he wasn't actually supposed to be seated next to me on the Air India flight in 2000 when I was flying back to Bombay from London. But the lady who was assigned that seat had a baby and felt like she would be more comfortable elsewhere. So, she approached Vivek and requested him to switch seats with her.

I wonder where this woman is all these years later and whether she will read my book and realize she unknowingly played matchmaker.

On that nine-hour flight, Vivek and I chatted up a storm over Bloody Marys—he made them for us personally because he was proud of his recipe. We spoke about our lives, careers and children. He confided in me, somewhere over an unknown country's airspace after the alcohol had kicked in and loosened us up, that he didn't get along too well with his wife.

I told him how sorry I was to hear that, but, in reality, I didn't quite believe him because I felt like married men often used that line to flirt with women they were interested in. But over time, as we kept in touch and got to know each other better, I realized it was the truth. He told me they had not been getting along since a few years.

The marriage made neither of them happy but they were together because there was just too much between them—children, family and many other things.

Over the years, our relationship has had to weather many storms. There were times when we didn't know if we would pull through. Some days we were hopeful and on other days we were talking about why it would be best if we walked away.

Relationships, even the good, stable ones, can be tricky at best. Here we were, two individuals who had met at such a mature stage of our lives, but had too much to lose if we chose to stay together. Had we been younger and our circumstances not so complicated, I don't think we would have faced so many problems. But life can play cruel jokes on us sometimes.

I had been living independently for way too long. I was used to being the head of the family, taking care of my father and daughter, earning my own living. Now, suddenly, I felt like I was twenty-something again, having to impress her boyfriend's family and be accepted into their fold.

Vivek's problems were, of course, different from mine. Divorce isn't just something that takes place between two individuals. It's something that can even sever the ties between two families. I can't imagine it would have been very pleasant for his daughters to witness this.

But eleven years ago, Vivek's divorce finally came through and we got married in a small ceremony in Lima, Ohio. It was at his sister Nutan Behal's home, and it was sweet and perfect. Masaba was there too, and it made the day even more special for me.

Vivek has a big family and once married, they became my family too. His mother was my biggest advocate, and his sisters and I get along very well. We visit each other, take holidays together and have a wonderful time.

The most important person in my life, Masaba, also took to Vivek because he's a very nice man. He's kind, considerate and has a very good heart. He is also brilliant at his work and his business advice to Masaba is invaluable to her.

In fact, Vivek isn't just helpful to Masaba. Anybody who calls, maybe an old colleague or a distant relative, finds him to be the most generous and helpful person around.

'You want to make the whole world happy but me,' I shout at him when I think he's getting too involved in helping others.

But alas, we cannot have everything. Our marriage is a long distance one because his work is in Delhi and mine is in Bombay. When he was still at PwC, he used to come to Bombay very often, sometimes for fifteen days at a time. But now his visits here and mine there are for short periods. This can create issues and loneliness. But who's to say two people living in the same home 24/7 don't feel lonely either. Our relationship is stronger, sometimes, because we still get to miss each other and then make the most of the few days we get together.

We're happy, the two of us, regardless of our arrangement.

We're compatible, we like the same kind of food, the same places and have a lot of the same values. We have the same aesthetics in the way we choose colours for curtains and sofas. We were also great companions while living together 24/7 for almost five months during the lockdown in Mukteshwar, Uttarakhand. This period assured me that we had made the right choice in picking each other.

Vivek brought a sense of balance and stability to my life. For years I had been working without a break. I was just running and running with no finish line in sight. I had no personal life. I rarely even took a day off to go spend the money I was earning on clothes or pamper myself at a beauty parlour. But once we got together, I allowed myself little luxuries like a whole day at a spa or a weekend getaway just because I didn't have to worry about chasing work and more work.

More importantly, thanks to Vivek, I got what I had always wanted—a family. I have Vivek and Masaba, and I have wonderful friends—the Bhatts, Nayaks, the Pradhans and many more whom I consider my own. With my career being better than ever before, I feel like I have very little to complain about. Life is good, but . . .

Sometimes, there is still a *keeda* (a worm) niggling at my mind, reminding me of all the slights I had to face, the brush offs, the backbiting, the outright rejection. This keeda can be really mean because it keeps reminding me of the times when I was chasing acceptance from people but never got it.

On good days, I politely ask this keeda to quieten down and let me be. 'I'm very happy and content. Please go away.'

On bad days, when my emotions are running high and the smallest thing can set me off, I tell this keeda, 'Go to sleep, you fucker!!'

'I don't care about anyone else's damn acceptance any more,' I shout at it. 'I love myself. I accept myself.'

And I think you, dear reader, should too.

Epilogue

When I first started writing this book, I didn't know what I would call it. Or if I would even finish it, to be honest. But once I got halfway through, there was absolutely no doubt in my mind that I would not stop, and somewhere along the way, I realized that this book would be my truth. That's when I thought of the name *Sach Kahun Toh*', to tell you the truth . . .

All my life I have tried, sometimes successfully and sometimes unsuccessfully, to tell the truth. Some of you heard me and some of you didn't. If you have picked up this book and got this far, I want you to know that everything I have written is the truth. But also forgive me because in many places I have had to conceal identities. You must be wondering why I have done this.

'If she's telling the truth, then why hide names, incidents and identities? What has she got to fear when she has the truth on her side?'

There are two reasons for changing names and concealing identities. Three reasons, actually.

Firstly, I changed names out of respect for the families of these people. I didn't want to be the reason they saw someone they loved in a different light all of a sudden.

Second: The lawyers at Penguin Random House advised me to do so just to be on the safe side, so I said, okay. Why not?

Third: Please pardon me but in a lot of places I actually forgot the names of some of the people because so much of it happened a long time ago.

While reading this book again before sending it out, I started laughing because even though I have called it *Sach Kahun Toh*, so much of the *sach*, the truth, has been concealed for these reasons. But what can I say? I have tried my best to be as truthful as I possibly could. I'm sure you understand.

This being said, you must think that I'm some *doodh ki dhuli* saint of a woman. Protecting people who probably don't deserve to be protected . . .

Please don't think that of me. I am in no sense doodh ki dhuli. I have my reasons for doing this. Moreover, I too have made mistakes and done things I am not proud of. All of us have . . . And again, sach kahun toh, I have withheld a few of those incidents because I realized my mistakes but did not want them immortalized in ink and paper. I'm sorry about that.

I hope you enjoyed reading my book. My life as I remember it. My truth. It means a lot to me that you picked it up and took to walk down memory lane with me. I hope you see yourself or someone you know in my journey because that has been one of the greatest drivers to pen this book in record time.

Acknowledgements

I would like to thank all the wonderful people who have contributed to my life's journey.

Thank you, Gopa Kumar, for the beautiful sketches of the five trees you made.

Thank you, Sagari Nayak, for the poetic captions you wrote for the trees.

Thank you, Joseph Radhik, for the cover picture.

And finally, a very special thank you to Afsha Khan Jayapal, for helping me on the journey of this book.